W9-CDT-754

IN SEARCH OF THE
GOLDEN FROG

IN
SEARCH
OF THE
GOLDEN
FROG

Marty Crump

The University of Chicago Press

CHICAGO AND LONDON

BOWLING GREEN STATE
UNIVERSITY LIBRARY

MARTY CRUMP is Adjunct Professor in the Department of Biological Sciences at Northern Arizona University and a Conservation Fellow with the Wildlife Conservation Society. She is a coauthor of *Herpetology* (1998).

The University of Chicago Press, Chicago 60637
The University of Chicago Press, Ltd., London
© 2000 by The University of Chicago
All rights reserved. Published 2000
Printed in the United States of America

09 08 07 06 05 04 03 02 01 00   1 2 3 4 5
ISBN: 0-226-12198-4 (cloth)

All photographs, unless otherwise indicated, are by the author.

Library of Congress Cataloging-in-Publication Data

Crump, Marty.
    In search of the golden frog / Marty Crump.
        p.   cm.
    Includes bibliographical references and index.
    ISBN 0-226-12198-4 (alk. paper)
    1. Amphibians—Central America. 2. Amphibians—South America. I. Title.
    QL656.C35 C78   2000
    597.8'098—dc21   99-048238

∞ The paper used in this publication meets the minimum requirements of the American National Standard for Information Sciences—Permanence of Paper for Printed Library Materials, ANSI Z39.48–1992.

For my family:

Bob, Judy, Jan, Cathy, Alan, Peter, Karen, and Rob

Contents

	Acknowledgments	ix
	Preface	xi
1	From Kansas to the Emerald Forest	1
2	Amazonian Brazil	29
3	Field Course in Costa Rica	56
4	The Many Ways to Beget a Frog	71
5	Want Some Respect? Wave a Viper.	101
6	Expressing in the Rain	119
7	Lost Gold of the Elfin Forest	144
8	Mama Llamas and Toothy Escuerzos	166
9	The Maxus Experience	195
10	Remembering Ayahuasca	219
11	Tadpole Toters	236
12	Reflections	261
	Epilogue	269
	Maps	271
	Appendix A: Common and Scientific Names of Amphibians and Reptiles	279
	Appendix B: Declining Amphibian Populations	282
	Bibliography and Suggested Reading	287
	Index	291

Acknowledgments

I ORIGINALLY HAD intended to record my stories from the field for my children, but after encouragement from family and friends to share them with a wider audience, I contacted the University of Chicago Press. There I found Christie Henry, who surely must be the world's most supportive, helpful, and capable editor. She began by reading all the first drafts of chapters and toned down my exuberance in trying to describe every detail of frog biology. Later she read revisions and offered insightful suggestions. Erin DeWitt did a meticulous job as copy editor and cheerfully incorporated my last-minute additions and deletions. Thank you, Christie and Erin!

I owe a huge debt of gratitude to my mentors from the University of Kansas, Drs. William (Bill) E. Duellman and Linda Trueb. They nourished my curiosity, supported and encouraged my goals, and provided unconditional friendship. Nearly three decades ago, Bill gave me a copy of his two-volume opus, *Hylid Frogs of Middle America*. In it he inscribed the message "May all your frogs be beauties." They have been, and for your roles in making them so, I thank you, Bill and Linda.

Over the years my work in the tropics has been supported by the National Science Foundation, the National Geographic Society, Wildlife Conservation Society, World Wildlife Fund, the University of Kansas, and the University of Florida. Without their financial support, my stories would not exist.

Thanks to the many people who have provided warm hospitality away from home, especially the following: Tom and Mopsy Lovejoy in Belém, Brazil; John and Doris Campbell and Paul Smith in Monteverde, Costa Rica; Ildefonso and Blanca Muñoz in Santa Cecilia, Ecuador; Monique Halloy in Tucumán, Argentina; Alberto and Cecilia Veloso in Santiago, Chile; Jaime and Gloria Carcamo in Nahuelbuta National Park, Chile.

My field companions in Central and South America, with whom I have shared these stories, have been special. From North America these include Ronn Altig, Joe Anderson, Joe Collins, Alan Crump, Bill Duellman, Steve Edwards, Louise Emmons, Peter Feinsinger, Robin Foster, Art Freed, Jim Gaw, Frank Hensley, Bob Kaplan, Blaise Kovaz, Julian Lee, Tom Lovejoy, Dave Pearson, Alan Pounds, John Simmons, Dan Townsend, Linda Trueb, and Jim Waddick. From Latin America my colleagues include Rocío Alarcón, Marco Altamirano, Verónica Benítez, Werner Bokermann, María Burbano, Gloria Correa, Rubén Cueva, Cesar Cuevas, Abraham Gold-gewicht, Liddy Guindon, Wolf Guindon, Antonieta Labra, Mario Larrea, Alfredo López, Patricio Mena, Marco Mendez, Alexandra Quiguango, Armando Ruíz, Eduardo Soto, Estéban Suárez, Eduardo Toral, Marcos Vaira, Ana María Velasco, Alberto Veloso, and Eliseo Vergara.

I am especially grateful to my family. My parents, Bob and Judy Crump, have always encouraged me to pursue my love of biology and natural history—from filling my pockets with tent caterpillars at age four, through grade school attempts to raise tadpoles and orphaned baby birds, to my frog research in the tropics. My children, Karen and Rob, provide help and companionship in the field and tolerate my sometimes long absences from home. My husband, Peter Feinsinger, supports and encourages my frog studies and willingly shares child-rearing duties. Without his understanding and participation, I could not combine field biology and motherhood successfully.

Several people provided helpful comments on the manuscript, particularly Peter and Karen Feinsinger, Bob and Judy Crump, and Alan and Irma Crump. I thank Karen for permission to include several of her journal entries from Argentina.

Preface

WOLF GUINDON and I trudge uphill along a slippery path through constant drizzle and deep boot-devouring mud, first through cloud forest, then through gnarled elfin forest. We plunge through the thick and drifting mist and stumble over tangled tree roots. Shivering beneath long underwear, a wool sweater, down vest, and a waterproof jacket, I walk as fast as I can, trying to keep pace with Wolf. "This is miserable!" I think to myself. "Why am I doing this?"

At the next bend I see one of the most incredible sights I've ever seen. There, congregated around several small pools at the bases of dwarfed, windswept trees, are over one hundred Day-Glo golden orange toads poised like statues, dazzling jewels against the dark brown mud. At that moment I recall the Central American legend of searching for the golden frog—actually quite a different animal from the golden toads in front of me*—and I remember why I'm here.

---

* The toads I witnessed in the elfin forest are not the animal to which the legend refers, despite the similarity in names. Golden toads (*Bufo periglenes*) are found only in one isolated mountain range in northwestern Costa Rica. The Indian legend is based on a different but equally real animal, the golden frog (*Atelopus zetecki*), which is only found farther south in Central America in a different isolated mountain range.

Those who have viewed at first hand the steep, dark-green, forest-covered slopes of the Cordillera de Talamanca-Chiriquí of Costa Rica and Panamá, with their ever changing aspect of sun and cloud, moon and mist, bright blue sky and bright green mantle, driving rain and boiling fog, come away with a feeling of overpowering awe and mystery at the variety of nature and the magic of the human soul. It is not surprising that the primitive peoples in this region also regarded the mountains and their forests with mystical reverence, so near and yet towering abruptly upwards to 4,000 meters from their lowland valley habitations.

Among the Bribri, Cabécar, Boruca, Changina, and Chiriquí, when the chicha has been drunk, the night grows late and dark, and the fires die down to burning embers, the wisest old man of the tribe tells his engrossed listeners of a beautiful miraculous golden frog that dwells in the forests of these mystical mountains. According to the legends, this frog is ever so shy and retiring and can only be found after arduous trials and patient search in the dark woods on fog shrouded slopes and frigid peaks. However, the reward for the finder of this marvelous creature is sublime. Anyone who spies the glittering brilliance of the frog is at first astounded by its beauty and overwhelmed with the excitement and joy of discovery; almost simultaneously he may experience great fear. The story continues that any man who finds the legendary frog finds happiness, and as long as he holds the frog happiness will follow him everywhere. The story tellers record many men who have scaled the highest peaks and searched the darkest forests for even a glimpse of the golden frog, but only a few ever see it. Fewer still capture the cherished creature and hold him for a few moments, and a very few are able to carry him with them for a longer period of time. One story tells of the man who found the frog, captured it, but then let it go because he did not recognize happiness when he had it; another released the frog because he found happiness too painful.

Like the Indians of Talamanca and Chiriquí, each human being is also on a mission searching for the golden frog. Field biologists in particular seem always to be searching for mystical truth and beauty in nature, and frequently at some unperceived level, for that happiness promised by the Indian seers. (Savage 1970, 273, 275)

I'm in the cold mist of this Costa Rican elfin forest because as a field biologist I'm searching for exciting new discoveries. It's part of my personal search for the golden frog, or as Jay Savage so eloquently phrased it, the search for "mystical truth and beauty in nature." This search—in more prosaic terms my development as a frog-chaser—has often involved chance and serendipity more than it has reflected careful long-range planning.

MY FASCINATION with nature goes back to my early childhood in the Adirondack Mountains of upstate New York. There my father, a mining geologist, taught me about trillium and pink lady's slippers, cardinal and blue jay feathers, and chickadees, leopard frogs, and chipmunks. He encouraged me to observe and to ask questions, not simply learn the names of the objects of my interest.

At twelve years old I was raising tadpoles, salamanders, and orphaned baby birds, not all with equal success. I went through my share of exotic pets, including sea horses and flying squirrels. I loved animals, but the thought of making them the focus of a career didn't occur to me until I took a ninth-grade biology class taught by the enthusiastic Ms. Hutchison. We watched amoebas ooze about in drops of water, tadpoles burst free from their egg capsules, and planaria regenerate into two individuals after we cut them in half. We dissected lilies and learned about plant sex. And we took nature walks and experienced firsthand the beauty and mystery of the living world. Thanks to her class, science became my passion and I vowed to become a biologist.

The first day of my sophomore year in college, I wandered into the Museum of Natural History at the University of Kansas looking for a job. The receptionist first called the mammalogy department. The curator had an opening for a student typist. I said, "No thank you. I really had something more exciting in mind." Next she rang up the ornithology department. Again, the curator wanted a student typist. Then she contacted the ichthyology (fish) department, with the same result. Last on her list was the herpetology department. A short conversation later, the receptionist happily told me that the curator needed someone to catalog and tie tags onto specimens. That sounded more interesting, and an hour later I found myself working with amphibians and reptiles.

The succeeding undergraduate years in the herpetology department provided me with a strong sense of belonging. As I listened to tales of field adventures from remote jungles in Panama, I daydreamed that perhaps someday I too could explore exotic tropical rain forests. Although the graduate students reveled in telling dirty jokes in my presence just to watch me blush, they accepted me as a potentially worthwhile biologist and they nurtured my interest. The graduate students were my big brothers, and Bill Duellman, Professor and Curator of the herpetology collection and the second party in that fateful telephone call, was my supportive mentor. His wife, Linda Trueb, a freshly graduated Ph.D., was my female academic role model during those years. At that time the biology faculty at KU included no women.

One day early in my senior year, Bill invited me to join a summer expedition he would be leading to the upper Amazon Basin in eastern Ecuador. The object of the trip was to compile a list of the species of amphibians and reptiles in the area. Not only did I seize the opportunity, I decided to stay on at the University of Kansas for graduate work. I had barely begun to scratch the surface of the fascinating field of herpetology. From what I had seen during the many hours of tying tags onto specimens, the animals were intriguing: frogs whose tadpoles are three times the length of the adult frogs; two-legged salamanders and legless lizards; frogs that look like scorched pancakes and others that look like inflated balloons with tiny legs attached. Even more intriguing to me was their ecology and behavior: lizards that eat marine algae, sea turtles that eat jellyfish with stinging spines, and snakes that eat bird eggs three times the width of their heads; lizards, snakes, and frogs that glide through the trees; frogs that brood their eggs in pouches on their backs; turtles that lure their prey by wiggling a wormlike appendage on their tongues; snakes that spit venom and lizards that squirt blood. I had found my niche.

Thus began my symbolic quest for the golden frog. For three decades my quest has led me back to Ecuador many times as well as to Brazil, Costa Rica, Colombia, Argentina, and Chile. I've learned that fieldwork encompasses the wondrous thrill of discovery and the painful realization that a species may have gone extinct; the satisfaction that comes from a successful experiment and the disappointment of a wasted field season; the awe of watching animal behavior in nature and the sorrow of losing a field site. Field biology enables you to visit exotic places and to observe the equally exotic plants and animals that inhabit them. Fieldwork invites you to participate in vastly different cultures. Most importantly, fieldwork forces you to become better acquainted with yourself through unique, and often challenging, experiences. Life in the field demands that you let go of personal comforts. Daily changes of underwear and socks are a luxury. Forget about privacy. Get used to bedding on floors and bathing in glacier-fed lakes. The satisfaction of being thousands of kilometers away from the looming deadlines and endless chores and responsibilities of fast-paced day-to-day life in the States plus the joy of being in the field, though, are worth any amount of discomfort. Fieldwork is the glue that holds my being together. Each field biologist has his or her own stories. These are some of mine.

IN SEARCH OF THE
GOLDEN FROG

FROM KANSAS TO THE
EMERALD FOREST

"**Y**ES! Take me with you!"

I was a twenty-one-year-old senior biology major at the University of Kansas and would be starting graduate school in the fall, working with Dr. Bill Duellman, the world's expert on tropical treefrogs. He had just invited me on an expedition to survey amphibians and reptiles at a remote field site in the tropical forest of Amazonian Ecuador. A year earlier he had made a preliminary scouting trip and had found much of the rain forest to be fairly intact. The animals were incredibly abundant and diverse, and he speculated that the site could prove to be one of the richest in the world for biodiversity of amphibians.

I knew little about Ecuador other than the fact that the equator passes through it, hence the name. In preparation for my first visit to the tropics, I read extensively. I learned that the highland areas of what is now Ecuador used to be part of the vast, though short-lived, Inca Empire. In 1534 Spanish conquistadors overthrew the empire, and the Spanish ruled the area for almost three hundred years before Ecuador gained its independence in 1830.

The Andes, from the Colombian border in the north to the Peruvian border in the south, provide a mountainous backbone to the country. Two main ranges, the Eastern and Western Cordilleras, are separated by a central valley. Both rims of the central valley are scattered with majestic volcanoes, some of which are still active. Between the Western Cordillera and the Pacific Ocean lies the Costa, or coastal lowlands. The Andean highlands, called the Sierra, form the middle part of the country and include the central valley. East of the Eastern Cordillera is the Oriente, a vast expanse of lowland tropical forest extending from the eastern foothills of the Andes to the upper reaches of several Amazon River tributaries. The Oriente comprises almost half of the country in land area but is sparsely populated with only about 5 percent of the population. We would be going to the Oriente.

The "we" of the expedition included Bill Duellman and his wife, Linda Trueb, also a herpetologist; Steve, a graduate student in parasitology; William, a graduate student in ichthyology, and his wife, Janice; Jim, a graduate student in herpetology, and his wife, Laura; Dr. Frank Cross, an ichthyologist at the University of Kansas; Werner Bokermann, a Brazilian herpetologist; and myself. Bill, Linda, and Werner had many years of experience working in tropical lowlands. Their love and enthusiasm for fieldwork quickly infected the rest of us. Steve began the trip excited to discover unusual parasites embedded in or living off tropical amphibians and reptiles. He ended the trip eager to transfer over to the Herpetology Division for graduate work. William and Frank raved nonstop about the abundance and diversity of fish they encountered each day, some of them previously undescribed species. Jim began the trip enthralled with Surinam toads and ended the trip enthralled with Surinam toads. And I, youngest and most naive of the group, became permanently hooked on tropical fieldwork.

5 June 1968

As I gaze out the plane window at the cottony white clouds, I can scarcely believe that I graduated from KU three days ago and that I'm on a plane bound for Ecuador. The past week has been hectic, with finals, graduation, farewells to four years' worth of friends, boxing up my belongings for storage, and packing for Ecuador. My mind and body alternate between states of catatonic stupor and adrenaline highs. What adventures lie ahead? What living conditions will I experience? Food? People? Forests? Animals?

As we descend into the valley that nestles Quito, I gasp at the rugged beauty of the Andes and the surrounding snow-covered volcanic cones. Quito sits at 2,850 meters above sea level, on a plateau at the foot of the Pichincha Volcano. The glare from the equatorial sun on the snow-capped volcanoes of Chimborazo and Cotopaxi is blinding. Green and brown cultivated plots inch up the mountainsides like strips of patchwork quilts, alternating with small towns scattered in the valleys. The magnificent setting of this capital city, the second highest in Latin America, seems perfect.

Once in the city, however, I realize that Quito itself is no fairyland. From the taxi window I see widespread poverty and despair. Drunkards sleep in gutters. Barefoot Indian women dressed in ragged clothing beg on street corners with their infants and toddlers. Aggressive street urchins pester every passerby to buy cigarettes, Chiclets, or cheap trinkets. Indian *cargadores,* people who carry anything anywhere on their backs, pad up and down the streets in bare feet, staggering under their mammoth loads. Suddenly, though, we drive through posh neighborhoods of stunning mansions. The tranquillity of their well-manicured lawns and gardens of bougainvilleas, fuchsias, roses, and geraniums seems incongruous after the teeming street life. Behind the doors live wealthy non-Indian Ecuadorians. The stark contrasts bombard my senses, and I become uncomfortably aware of being a privileged North American.

Miraculously the taxi arrives at the hotel without running over pedestrians or colliding with other vehicles. Several hours later Señor Ildefonso (Ilde) Muñoz and his wife, Blanca, our hosts for the summer, usher us by taxi to the Tally Ho Club for a private party, complete with filet mignon, drinks, and dancing. Live bands play the Mexican Hat dance, polkas, Colombian *cumbias,* and Ecuadorian *pasillos.* A group plays traditional Andean Indian music on wooden flutes, panpipes, and guitars—plaintive and haunting music, simple phrases repeated over and over.

Ilde is a character: stocky, of average height, an impressive beer belly, and an exuberant personality. His dark, ruddy complexion complements his flashing, expressive black eyes. His booming voice and laugh seem to emanate from the depths of his diaphragm, especially as he bellows out orders to everyone within earshot. In her quiet way, Blanca warmly welcomes us. The wrinkle lines in her narrow fifty-year-old face suggest that her life has not been easy. Ilde and Blanca are Colombians but have lived in Ecuador for over a decade. Bill says they have an interesting tale concerning their immigration. He encourages me to ask Ilde about it once I know him better.

6 June 1968

This morning, after changing American dollars into sucres, we buy a few necessities for the field: batteries, plastic bags, Life Savers, chocolate, and raisins. We then begin to explore our surroundings. Most of the city is impersonal and dirty, but the colonial center, Old Quito, is charming with its steep and narrow cobblestone streets and its ancient plazas and buildings constructed by the Spaniards when they ruled Ecuador. Although the Spaniards took considerable wealth from the country, they also left behind a priceless heritage of sculpture, painting, and architecture, much of which is housed in the ancient churches and monasteries. We visit the Church of San Francisco, the first religious building constructed by the Spanish in South America. Inside, the glittering gold is nearly blinding. To my eye, it overpowers the exquisite wood carvings adorning the choir stalls and the lovely paintings on the walls.

We next explore a sprawling market that offers a bit of everything: handwoven baskets of every possible shape and size; fresh and dried herbs, from mundane teas to peculiar medicinal folk remedies; plastic bowls, cups, plates, and buckets in every primary color. Stomach-churning odors drifting out from the meat section originate from huge quarters of beef and entire pigs dangling from hooks on the wall. In one section, body parts of chickens are arranged separately in a series of bins—necks, heads, and feet. I can understand why one might buy chicken necks, but why heads and feet? Still musing about the chicken parts, I wander into the fruit and vegetable stalls. Imagine the largest farmers market you've ever seen and then multiply it by ten. I count twelve types of potatoes—ranging in size from cherries to grapefruits, round to oval to irregular, white to purple to red to brown—and six kinds of dried beans of assorted sizes, shapes, and colors. Women sit on three-legged stools selling freshly cut flowers of red, yellow, orange, purple, lavender, blue, white, pink, and all possible color combinations. Perfumes from the flowers thicken the air and overwhelm the less savory odors emanating from the meat market.

7 June 1968

At 5:30 A.M. we load our suitcases and equipment into a run-down bus that should have retired decades ago, and we head south through the Andes. The scenery is striking, dominated by jagged snowcapped peaks set against a brilliant blue sky. Winding tortuously through narrow mountain passes, the road is alternately cobblestone, dirt, or pavement. Eventually we descend the eastern slope of the Andes. The vegetation changes dramatically from bare rocks and scrubby grass on the steep hillsides of the dry highlands to fingers of evergreen cloud forest. Tree ferns, orchids, and bromeliads compete for space. Spectacular waterfalls plunge into deep canyons. We ride through the undulating lushness of tropical landscape at the base of the Andes and finally arrive at the town of Pastaza.

From Pastaza we fly for fifty minutes on a small chartered plane. After a bumpy ride we land on the tiny Santa Cecilia air strip at about 2:00 in the afternoon. Oppressive heat and humidity hit us in the face as we deplane. The air is heavy and suffocatingly still. Within seconds our skin is sticky.

9 June 1968

The general area of our survey, Santa Cecilia, consists of about three square kilometers on the north bank of the Río Aguarico (Rich Water River), about twenty-five kilometers south of the Colombia-Ecuador border. The Río Aguarico flows into the Río Napo, which eventually empties into the mighty Amazon. Until three years ago, Santa Cecilia was a Quechua Indian village. In 1965 Texaco opened up an area of rain forest nearby, established a camp for oil exploration, and built a small airstrip. Last year Texaco discovered oil. Exploration and drilling continue. Soon a road will be constructed to transport the oil from the forest, over the Andes, and to the coast. Once a road is built, the whole region will be vulnerable to colonization and habitat destruction. Currently, however, travel in and out of the area is restricted to boat, helicopter, or small plane.

Our base camp—a two-hectare compound affectionately called "Muñoz-landia," belonging to Ilde and Blanca Muñoz—is located between the Texaco camp and the Río Aguarico. Muñozlandia originally consisted of a house, kitchen and dining area, outhouse, and outdoor shower stall, but over the years Ilde has expanded his empire. Last year he built a laboratory and several small houses to be used by our research team this summer. All the buildings in Muñozlandia are constructed in the typical Quechua style of bamboo frame, split bamboo walls and floors, and palm thatch roofs. The buildings are perched on stilts because occasionally the Río Aguarico floods its banks and creeps into camp. I'm living in one of the two rooms attached to the side of the laboratory. There's just enough space for a narrow bed, bamboo chair, and a dresser constructed from wooden crates. Bright orange curtains cheer up the otherwise dreary room and offer a little privacy. When the old generator works, we have electricity from about 6:00 P.M. to 10:00 P.M.

There are still some Quechua families living nearby. Their homes are surrounded by cultivated plots. Each family owns a few chickens, perhaps a pig, and at least one scrawny mutt. Many families keep parrots and monkeys as pets. The forest is riddled with hunting trails, but the Quechuas' main form of transportation is the piragua, a roughly carved dugout for river travel. A small village of Cofán Indians is located on the south bank of the Río Aguarico. The Quechua are a widespread Indian tribe of about

Quechua home near Santa Cecilia, Ecuador.

sixty thousand individuals living in the Oriente. The Cofán nation, in contrast, consists of about six hundred individuals who live in a few communities along the Río Aguarico and a few other rivers.

I eventually ask Ilde about his immigration to Ecuador. He boasts that he and Blanca fled Colombia with their two young daughters in the mid-1950s toward the end of La Violencia, the bloody civil war between the Conservatives and Liberals. The family crossed the border illegally by boat, Ilde with a ten-inch-long bayonet wound across his belly. I flinch as he proudly shows me his massive scar. They stopped when they could go no farther, at the village of Santa Cecilia, where the Quechuas helped nurse a weak and frail Ildefonso back to his robust, commanding self.

10 June 1968

Our main goal at Santa Cecilia is to compile a list of all the amphibians and reptiles in the area and to record relative abundances so that we can compare this assemblage with others in the tropics. We search for animals morning, afternoon, and evening, exploring swamps, temporary ponds, a lake, a stream, primary forest, secondary forest, and disturbed areas around human habitation. Whenever we look for animals along a path, one person searches along the left side, the other along the right. Bill insists that for safety reasons no one works alone. Going out in pairs or in small groups adds to a sense of camaraderie, and we've all become quite competitive in a friendly way. We each hope to find the most unusual, the rarest, or the most animals. Individual pride is at stake.

Many of the common forest plants are familiar to me because they are sold as houseplants in the States: ferns, bromeliads, orchids, begonias, and philodendrons. Not confined to pots, here they grow into giants. Huge dominating lianas, or woody vines, dangle from the canopy and twist around tree trunks. I feel dwarfed by all this plant life. And exhilarated.

Tonight we find twelve species of frogs at one swamp: little yellow frogs on broad leaves around the edges of the water; large green frogs on tree branches; tiny brown, white, and black frogs on leaves emerging from the water; and medium-size brown frogs on the ground. The cacophony is amazing. Males of each species belt out their characteristic calls to attract females. A few females sit by the sidelines, waiting patiently for just the right males.

Bill is most excited about a little brown mushroom-tongue salamander* that I find sitting fully exposed on a leaf. (Bill swears he will find one soon also.) The slender salamander is about the length of my little finger. By far the greatest abundance and diversity of salamanders occurs in the temperate zone, but two genera have expanded into South America. These genera belong to the family Plethodontidae, a large group of salamanders that do not have lungs. Instead, they breathe through their skin. The genus of our salamander, *Bolitoglossa*, has diversified into many species that live in a variety of wet habitats. Only six salamander species have been found in Ecuador.

By the edge of the trail, I spy the pencil-thin body of a snake coiled around a branch at my eye level. The snout at the tip of its black head has a white line running across it, and a wide white band encircles the neck. The rest of the body is rich reddish brown, with large chocolate brown blotches outlined in white. Nervously I tell Bill I've found a snake. He spins around, looks at it, and as his serious expression changes to a grin, casually replies, "Well, catch it." My heart races. The only live snakes I've ever held were garter snakes. Should I admit that I'm scared? No way. Sensing my fear, Bill assures me that it won't bite and says I should just gently pick it up

---

* For those interested, scientific names corresponding to common names of amphibians and reptiles throughout the text are found in appendix A.

Snail-eating snake. The snake grabs a snail with its jaws and pulls it off the substrate, then sucks the prey out of its shell.

about one-third of the way down the body. Trembling, I reach out and cautiously wrap my thumb and fingers around its slender body and lift it off the branch. Sure enough, it doesn't try to bite, and it appears more calm than I. Bill identifies it as a snail-eating snake.

Snail-eating snakes find their prey by following mucous trails. They touch their forked tongues to the ground, and when the tongue is inserted back into the mouth, the smells are picked up by their chemosensory system. Once the snail at the end of the mucous trail is found, the snake grabs the shell in its jaws and jerks its head quickly to lift the snail from the substrate. Then it twists its neck and coils around the shell. Bracing the shell against the roof of its mouth, the snake sucks out the snail's body within a few minutes. These snakes also feed on slugs, which are easier to eat than snails since no extraction is required.

For me, the most exciting discovery on this first field night isn't an amphibian or reptile, but rather a seven-centimeter-long, cinnamon brown, soft-bodied animal with lots of stumpy legs and large antennae. I gently touch it to see if it feels as velvety as it looks. It does. There's no doubt in my mind what it is—an onychophoran. I'd learned about these animals in introductory biology four years ago and I'd seen pictures of them, but I'd never dreamed of seeing, let alone touching, a live one. Here, resting on a rotting log in front of me, is what my professor had called "a biological jewel."

The onychophorans make up a small invertebrate phylum consisting of about eighty species that resemble both annelids and arthropods. Annelids are segmented worms such as earthworms, polychaetes, and leeches. Arthropods are invertebrates with hardened exoskeletons and jointed appendages, such as centipedes and insects. Like annelids, onychophorans have unjointed appendages, but like arthropods they molt their external skeleton. Their excretory system is annelid-like, but the circulatory and respiratory systems are arthropod-like. Many researchers consider onychophorans to be "living fossils" or "missing links" between annelids and arthropods. Onychophoran-like creatures lived as far back as 500 million years ago.

Today's onychophorans are predatory, feeding on small invertebrates such as termites and other insects, snails, and small worms. They're nocturnal and are particularly active seeking prey on humid nights such as tonight. A small eye resides at the base of each antenna. Once a prey has been spotted, an onychophoran discharges two powerful streams of adhesive from its slime glands up to distances of thirty centimeters. The adhesive slime hardens quickly, entangling the prey in a weblike net. The tiny beast grasps and cuts up the prey with its jaws. After its salivary secretions pass into the prey and begin to digest the tissues, the onycophoran sucks the semi-liquid tissues into its mouth.

Onychophoran, a "missing link" between annelids and arthropods.

15 June 1968

While shining my headlamp into the dense canopy looking for snakes, I spot another tropical animal I had hoped to see. My first glimpse is a gray, dull green heap of coarse fur slumped in the crotch of a tree about two meters above the ground. "Where's the head?" I ask myself out loud. As I maneuver through the thick undergrowth to get a closer look, the crackling sound of a branch startles the fur ball. It very slowly turns its head toward me. A sleepy, comical-looking sloth peers at me through beady eyes as if to say, "Well, what do you want?" I watch awhile, thinking how appropriate the Spanish name is: *perezoso,* meaning "lazy."

Sloths sleep, eat, and reproduce in the trees. They eat almost exclusively leaves, which, though energy-rich, are high in indigestible fiber. To cope with this diet, sloths have a large multichambered stomach, a long intestinal tract, and a very slow rate of metabolism. They move from tree to tree every couple of days by "walking" while hanging upside down from branches. Sloths climb down to the ground to urinate and defecate every week or so. Once down, they dig a shallow depression in the ground with their short, stubby tails, defecate, and then urinate over their feces. They cover their wastes with leaves and then climb back into the canopy. Considering how slothful sloths are, it's amazing that the entire process of climbing down to the ground, voiding and covering their wastes, and returning to the canopy takes only about thirty minutes. Sloths spend much of their time hanging upside down, with their hooklike claws wrapped around a branch. They even sleep and give birth in this position.

I slowly reach up to stroke the coarse fur. The sloth looks at me but doesn't move. Its greenish hair, the color acquired from algae that live in the microscopic grooves and notches in the hairs, helps to camouflage the animal in its leafy surroundings.

THIS AFTERNOON Bill gives me the job of collecting and raising tadpoles. There are staggering numbers of tadpoles here, and since no identification keys for tadpoles exist for the Amazon Basin, we have to start from scratch. Once the tadpoles metamorphose, we should be able to identify the species, assuming the tiny froglets resemble the adult frogs. Then, by working backward, we'll be able to make our own identification key for the tadpoles of Santa Cecilia. Each species of tadpole is unique in shape, size, and color. Some are extravagant in their colors and patterns: dark brown with a cream bar on the snout, light brown with two yellow bars on the snout, silvery white belly with three longitudinal black stripes, and metallic gold throat and belly with black-spotted gray tail.

19 June 1968

We've been here ten days and already we've found seventy-six species of amphibians and reptiles: toads, treefrogs, poison dart frogs, boa constrictors, vine snakes, and anole lizards. The most common are several species of yellow and brown treefrogs that congregate by the hundreds in water-filled ditches and ponds in open, disturbed areas. The ecological and behavioral interactions at these ponds are fascinating: frogs foraging for insects, male frogs calling for females, mated pairs of frogs laying eggs, and snakes sneaking around searching for a frog supper.

Lizards are abundant, active during the day and asleep at night. Most conspicuous in the forest are three species of anoles. Males of each species have a distinctively colored fan-shaped throat flap, or dewlap, an area that's expanded and displayed during courtship, territorial defense, and aggressive encounters. The dewlap of one species is blue with tiny white flecks and a red margin; another is rose pink with white flecks, bordered with white; and the third is orange-red with black flecks.

Where a tree has fallen in the forest, the small clearing created attracts sun-loving lizards and thus makes an ideal spot for watching lizards feed, defend territories, and bask. The largest sun-loving lizard is the black tegu, which can reach over two-thirds of a meter in length. Ilde tells me that Quechuas consider tegu meat a delicacy. He agrees. Local Quechuas trap the lizards in wooden crates baited with chicken eggs.

We find more snakes at night than during the day. I've overcome my fear of snakes—at least those that don't bite—and I especially like the graceful and charming arboreal snakes that resemble forest vines. When moving through the branches, a vine snake can extend one third to one half of its total length into space without support before resting its chin on the next branch and proceeding on. The other night I held one balanced with the midpoint of its body on my index finger. Some species have skinny necks and large heads with huge eyes. Two species eat snails, but most of the other vine snakes eat small frogs and anole lizards. One species, the cat-eyed snake, also eats frog eggs.

Ilde's workers helped us dig a meter-deep trench. We check the trench several times each day and night to retrieve any animals that fall in. Our most exciting find from the trench so far is a large, dark bluish gray caecilian, known by the common name of Linnaeus' caecilian, after the famous Swedish naturalist who named the species in 1749 (although at that time it was believed to be a snake). To me, it looks like a giant earthworm— a little over two-thirds of a meter long and about two centimeters in diameter. It's impossible to hold because of the slime it exudes, but I finally maneuver it into a damp cloth bag so that Bill can identify it back in the laboratory.

Caecilians, a group of amphibians found only in the tropics, lack limbs. Most are highly specialized for burrowing, although some species are aquatic. Caecilians' small eyes are covered with skin or bone. A pair of sensory tentacles located on each side of the head between the eye and the nostril helps in locating and identifying prey. Very little is known about the ecology or behavior of these secretive animals.

WE RECENTLY added the ruby poison dart frog to our species list. These miniature frogs, about half the length of my little finger, hop wildly in random directions in the thick forest undergrowth. They are nearly impossible to catch and are spectacularly colored. The top part of the body is ruby red, and at the base of each arm and leg is a bright yellow spot. The flanks, throat, belly, and undersides of the limbs are turquoise blue with black spots. The common name reflects the fact that some species in the family are used for poisoning darts.

Many Indians in the lowlands of northern South America use poisoned darts in blowguns for hunting game. The most commonly used substances for poisoning darts are the plant alkaloids strychnine and curare. In the Chocó region of Colombia, however, an even stronger alkaloid is used to poison darts: batrachotoxin, obtained from the skin of three different species of poison dart frogs. Batrachotoxins are among the most potent naturally occurring nonprotein toxins known. They are cardiotoxins, meaning they cause heart failure in their victims. Because batrachotoxin is destroyed by heat, once the poisoned animal is cooked the meat is safe for human consumption.

Indians in the northern Chocó poison their darts with skin secretions of the black-legged poison dart frog and the Kokoe poison dart frog. They impale a frog on a stick, and the stress of this torture causes the frog to release secretions from its skin glands. In contrast, Indians in the southern Chocó poison their darts with skin secretions of the golden poison dart frog, a frog that contains about twenty times more poison than does either species used in the north. Darts are poisoned simply by rubbing them several times across the back of a frog. The difference in techniques used by Indians in these two areas reflects the difference in toxicity of the frogs.

The golden poison dart frog is one of the largest species in the family, at nearly five centimeters. These bright yellow, yellow-orange, or pale metallic green frogs are so toxic that the Chocó Indians protect their hands with leaves while handling them. A single frog may contain up to 1,900 micrograms of toxin. An indirect estimate of a human lethal dose is 200 micrograms or less. Thus a single frog has enough poison to kill about ten people. A person could die from handling one of these frogs if even a small amount of poison entered the bloodstream through an open wound. Biologists have estimated that one golden poison dart frog contains sufficient toxin to kill twenty thousand mice. There is no effective antidote known for batrachotoxin poisoning.

Many, though not all, poison dart frogs are brightly colored as a way of advertising their toxicity: often black and a contrasting bright yellow, orange, red, blue, or green. We're careful when handling these frogs. We don't lick our fingers or rub our eyes afterward, and we don't handle the frogs if we have fresh scratches on our hands. Although the species at Santa Cecilia are not toxic enough to be useful for poisoning darts, they are potent enough to cause extreme discomfort if any secretion gets into one's mucous membranes or bloodstream.

22 June 1968

Day-to-day living is comfortable for the most part, except for the notable lack of privacy. Everyone knows how everyone else is feeling physically and mentally, what everyone is thinking. To compensate, each of us occasionally wanders off from the group. The others understand the need.

I'm still trying to define for myself how I want to be treated in the field. I want to be independent and treated like one of the guys, but at the same time I'm flattered when one of them offers me a hand while I'm crossing treefalls, negotiating log bridges over streams, or sliding down muddy embankments. It's not that I can't manage on my own, but I do appreciate the attention. Not having yet resolved the dilemma, sometimes I graciously accept help and other times I snap back, "Thanks, I can manage." Feeling a need to prove my worth, I push myself harder than I might otherwise. For example, last night after dinner I felt totally exhausted from chasing lizards all day in the hot sun. But when Bill said, "Who would like to hike up to the swamp with me tonight?" I eagerly said I'd go. The others stayed back in camp and played hearts, obviously not feeling a need to prove their worth. They're not women in a field dominated by men.

The food so far has been tasty and abundant. One of the main staples is the cooking banana, called *plátano,* or plantain. *Plátanos* are hard and starchy, lower in sugar content than regular bananas. I learned firsthand that one does not eat them raw unless one enjoys the taste of raw turnip followed by a puckered mouth. Boiled *plátanos* are rather tasteless, but all the other variations are delicious. *Chifles* are thinly sliced sections of *plátanos* fried in hot oil, sprinkled with salt. *Patacones* are two-centimeter sections of *plátanos* smashed with a fork and then fried and salted. For a special dessert treat, we have baked *plátanos* smothered in brown sugar and evaporated milk.

Ecuadorians, or at least displaced Colombians, eat a lot of starch. In addition to the *plátanos*, we've had rice at least twice each day and *yuca*, also known as cassava or manioc, at least once daily. *Yuca* is a small shrub, native to South America, whose thick, starchy roots are eaten fried or boiled. Fried *yuca* is delicious, but hunks of boiled, stringy *yuca* are about as appetizing as a boiled *plátano*. Andean peoples have a great way of fixing potatoes, called *llapingachos:* fried mashed potatoes filled with meat, cheese, or finely diced salad. Blanca's specialty *llapingachos* are filled with tuna and canned peas.

Our main source of protein is beans—a mound of beans merging into the ever-present pile of rice on the plate. Sometimes the beans are mixed with slices of pork skin sprouting course black hairs and chunks of pork fat. If I allow myself to think about it, I nearly gag. It's better just to abandon them on my plate than to force myself to eat these foreign objects that must require a culturally acquired taste. Our Quechua and Cofán neighbors occasionally sell game to Ilde, so we've tried some unusual meats: armadillo, parrot, monkey, and snake. The monkey meat, a bit stringy and tangy, was served in a stew with potatoes, *yuca*, and onions. Roasted armadillo is delicious, a cross between tender pork and chicken.

Last week I finally discovered the mysterious destiny of all those chicken feet I saw in the market in Quito: *caldo de gallina*, apparently one of the most ubiquitous dishes in Ecuador. Blanca proudly served us each a bowl of greasy broth with a submerged scaly chicken foot, tendons dangling. We all ate the broth of our "chicken foot soup" but studiously avoided the feet. At meal's end each bowl enshrined a glistening appendage. I'm still wondering about the fate of all those chicken heads but am afraid to ask.

Papaya is the most common fresh fruit here, readily available and delicious. I was warned about the lack of fresh raw vegetables. Indeed that is the one thing I miss. How I long for a huge tossed salad—lettuce, spinach, carrots, green peppers, tomatoes, broccoli, and mushrooms. It's not worth the risk of contracting parasites, however, so the few vegetables served are always overcooked and limp.

SEVERAL RECENT events have earned me a nickname. Today Linda made a wooden sign with "CALAMITY CRUMP" painted in black. She ceremoniously nailed it above my door. A few days ago, in full view of all, I slipped and fell into the creek while washing my underwear. Yesterday at lunch I cracked a molar on a *plátano* chip. The final (and nickname-generating) blow happened this afternoon in the shower. The outdoor shower employs water flowing from a spring through a split-bamboo flume system to the top of the fungus-covered wooden shower stall. The shower water is quite diverse, often delivering tadpoles, gobs of slimy green algae, or pigeon droppings onto one's unsuspecting head and shoulders. This afternoon, precariously balanced on the aging boards of the shower stall floor, I bend down to pick up the bar of soap when suddenly one of the floorboards disintegrates. My leg falls through. I find myself sprawled on the surviving fungus-covered boards, one leg thigh-deep in odorous mud. Steve hears the crash and my anguished yelp, and I have to confess to him through the wall what has happened. He roars with laughter. After considerable effort I manage to extract my leg from the mud. It's only bruised a little, but my pride is badly wounded.

Tonight Werner teaches me an important lesson: Stay in sight of your buddy. He and I are working in primary forest well away from trails. I'm busy turning over logs when I look up and realize he's gone. Every direction looks the same: a dense understory of ferns and broad-leafed herbs blanketing the ground, topped by huge trees that tower above the beam of my headlamp to form a canopy thirty meters above the ground. I have no idea which way Werner has gone or how to return to Muñozlandia. I strike out in one direction for a few minutes, then another. No sign of Werner. I start to panic. After ten more minutes of aimless but increasingly desperate wandering, I decide to stay put. Surely Werner will miss me, eventually return, and see my light. It begins to drizzle. Wet and cold, I shuffle about in a ten-meter-square area halfheartedly looking for frogs, my mind conjuring up all sorts of terrible consequences of having to spend the night alone in the forest. Finally, forty-five minutes later I see a light approaching me. I crouch down and roll over a log, not wanting to confess that I was terrified. I'm sure Werner knows that I got lost and panicked, and I'm sure he feels relieved to find me. All he says, though, is "Did you find anything?" Werner heads off and for the rest of the night I stick to him closer than a tick to a lizard's ear.

26 June 1968

We've found thirteen additional species of amphibians and reptiles in the past eleven days, bringing our total to eighty-nine. Every day is filled with the thrill of discovery because every walk through the forest and every visit to a swamp is unique. You know there are fascinating animals within reach, but you don't know which ones you'll see. Tonight you might see a monkey peering at you from the safety of a branch or a baby boa constrictor searching for its first meal. You might see a glittering hummingbird sleeping on its tiny nest or two frogs battling over a calling site. Even my tadpole husbandry work turns up unexpected surprises. This afternoon one of my ugly duckling tadpoles metamorphosed into a radiant lime-green froglet.

To me the most exciting aspect of the biology of the frogs and toads at Santa Cecilia is the amazing diversity in the ways they reproduce. In the United States we are taught that frogs and toads lay eggs in water. The eggs hatch into tadpoles, which develop in the water until they sprout legs, absorb their tails, and climb out onto land. This scenario is indeed true for almost all species in the United States. But the greatest numbers of frogs and toads are found in the tropics, where they have experimented with unique ways of reproducing that allow greater independence from standing or running water.

At Santa Cecilia less than half the species lay eggs in water. These species, which include a couple of toads and most of the treefrogs, breed in small water-filled ditches, ponds, swamps, and lakes. The most unusual of these is the gladiator frog, so named because males fight each other with large spines protruding from their thumbs. Males construct shallow depressions in the mud or sand near the river. After water seeps into the depression and fills the nest, the male calls to attract a female. If he's lucky a female responds, and the pair lays and fertilizes a clutch of small black-and-white eggs in the nest. The eggs float on the water surface, where oxygen concentration is highest. Although reproductive behavior of this species hasn't been studied, we know quite a bit about a closely related species of gladiator frog from Panama. In that species for the first couple of days after fertilization, males guard their offspring from other males that try to enter the nest. If an intruder manages to disturb the nest, the surface tension of the water is broken, the eggs sink to the bottom of the nest, and most embryos die for lack of oxygen. In the Panamanian species, fights between males for access to females and for nest defense can result in physical harm, as males direct their spines toward each other's eyes and ears.

Leaf frogs lay their eggs on leaves above water. Upon hatching, the tadpoles flick themselves out of the egg capsules and fall into the water below, where they continue to develop. The untested assumption is that this mode of reproduction reduces egg mortality, since ponds and swamps are often swarming with insects and fish that feed on frog eggs. Leaf frog eggs aren't home free in their leafy abode above the water, however. Recently I saw a cat-eyed snake draped over a large leaf at the edge of a swamp with a clutch of leaf frog eggs hanging from its mouth. Totally engrossed in its meal, the snake seemed unaware of my presence as I watched it work the eggs farther into its gullet and then engulf a few more. I was imagining how difficult it must be for a snake to eat sticky frog eggs and not be able to wipe its mouth afterward, when suddenly the little snake cocked its head to one side and slid its lower jaw along the leaf. Mission accomplished, without hands or napkins.

Poison dart frogs also lay their eggs out of water and have a tadpole stage, but they accomplish this feat in a radically different way. Eggs are usually laid and fertilized on the damp leaf litter of the forest floor. From then on, either the male or female (depending on the species) guards the eggs. The guardian may even moisten the eggs by emptying fluid from its bladder onto them. After the tadpoles hatch, the guardian parent squats down, the tadpoles climb aboard, and the parent carries them to water. In some species all the tadpoles, whether just a few or thirty, are carried at once to slow-moving streams. In other species the parent makes many trips each to a different spot, carrying one tadpole at a time to a water-filled basin in a plant.

Gladiator frog. The male constructs a shallow depression in the mud near a river. When the depression fills with water, the male calls to attract a female.

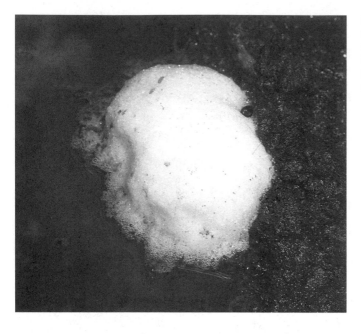

Foam nest produced by white-lipped frogs. The eggs are suspended in the froth and thus receive some protection from desiccation and predators.

White-lipped frogs and their relatives do things quite differently. During mating the male kicks his hind legs vigorously, churning up air, water, his own mucus and sperm, and eggs and mucus from the female into a froth that resembles whipped egg whites. This results in the eggs being suspended in a frothy nest of foam. Most species in this group fabricate the foam nest either at the edge or on the surface of water. After the tadpoles hatch, they flip out of the foam and swim into the water, where they continue development. One species at Santa Cecilia, however, deposits the foam nest under logs on land. After hatching, the tadpoles remain within the foam, develop, and eventually metamorphose into froglets without ever having eaten an outside source of food. They rely solely on their large amounts of yolk. For all these species, the foam provides the eggs with protection against desiccation and predators. Since clasping pairs of kicking frogs are quite active during nest construction, males of two species have spines on their thumbs for maintaining a secure grip on the females, and another has a cluster of spines on the chest and greatly enlarged forearm muscles.

Dink frogs, so called because of their *dink-dink-dink* calls, breed entirely out of water. As the female lays her eggs under a log, inside a clump of moss, or under leaf litter, the clasping male fertilizes the eggs. In some species either the female or male guards the eggs, but in most species the eggs are abandoned. Development is slow. The embryos require several weeks or months to develop before they hatch as miniature frogs. Because there is no tadpole stage, this type of development is called direct. Direct development of terrestrial eggs appears to be a successful way of reproducing, with over 550 species of dink frogs spread over the New World tropics. Biologists have speculated that these frogs originated in mountainous areas where pools of water are scarce. Although species later spread out into lowland areas, the regions of highest diversity are still at higher elevations.

Females of two species at Santa Cecilia brood their offspring by carrying direct-developing eggs on their backs. We found one of these recently, while netting for tadpoles in a forest pond: a Surinam toad, the treasure Jim had longed to find. This is the first record for the genus in Ecuador! Unlike most frogs (I use the word *frog* here because a toad is simply one type of frog, just as a terrier is a type of dog), this one is completely aquatic. It has drab brown, bumpy skin and looks as if someone had stepped on it, squashing its body and deforming its head into a broad triangular mass. In her book *Living Amphibians of the World* (1961), Doris Cochran described a Surinam toad as being "shaped like a squarish pancake—a somewhat

Surinam toad. The female carries her eggs embedded in the skin on her back. Eventually the young emerge from their incubation chambers as miniature frogs.

19

scorched pancake at that." Tiny beadlike eyes perch on the top of the head, and flaps of skin dangle from the corners of the mouth. Each long, slender finger ends in a star-shaped cluster of filaments that allow for enhanced touching sensation in the muddy sediments where these odd creatures live. They use their fingers to sift though the mud and then to sweep small fish and invertebrate prey into their gaping tongueless mouths.

Mating in Surinam toads consists of a series of elaborate acrobatics as the pair somersaults through the water, with the fertilized eggs miraculously falling onto the skin of the female's back. After about sixty to a hundred eggs have been released and fertilized, the female's skin slowly swells and thickens to enclose the eggs, each in a private incubation chamber. After a few months, tiny black froglets push their way out of these chambers and swim away.

The other frog that carries its young is the egg-brooding horned tree-frog. My jaw fell when I saw one perched on a branch, looking just like pictures I had seen. It was about the length of my index finger, light golden brown in color, with a somewhat flattened body, huge triangular head, and large toe pads. Wicked-looking bony projections extended from the side of the head, a fleshy proboscis sprouted from its snout, and "spines" of skin jutted from the eyelids. As I gently picked her up, she opened her cavernous mouth and displayed a bright yellow-orange tongue and mouth lining. I chuckled and commented, "I wonder what would happen if I put my finger inside her mouth."

In response to Bill's teasing, "Try it and find out," I stuck in my little finger and the frog snapped her jaws shut in a viselike grip. What I didn't know (and what Bill didn't bother telling me) was that the teeth on the upper jaw are modified into miniature fangs. The margin of part of the lower jaw is modified into toothlike serrations, with a single large fanglike structure called an odontoid in the center. After considerable effort I finally pried her mouth open and gently extracted my throbbing finger. I thought about the dumb thing I had just done. It makes sense that these frogs would have modified teeth for restraining prey, since they feed on other frogs and insects that are nearly as long as they are.

Females of these treefrogs brood up to thirty eggs on their backs. Mucous glands from the skin secrete a substance that forms a sticky layer to which the eggs adhere. All development takes place within the egg capsule, so that eventually little froglets pop out. The reproductive particulars of this species have not been observed, but they are assumed to be similar to those of a closely related species from Panama. In that species, at hatching each froglet is attached to the back of Mother by a pair of "gill stalks" still connected to the egg capsule. After an unknown period of time, the stalks break, the froglets are freed, and the gill stalks are sloughed from the female's back, thus completing the early life cycle of one of nature's most bizarre amphibians.

7 July 1968

This morning several of us putter by motorized dugout to Dureno, a small Cofán village on the south bank of the Río Aguarico about one and a half hours from Santa Cecilia. Ildefonso told us that the Cofáns often have necklaces and other handmade items that they're willing to sell. Traffic on the Río Aguarico consists of only a couple of Quechuas in their piraguas. One piragua, filled with *yuca* and *plátanos,* is paddled by a boy about five years old. He seems in no hurry to get anywhere in particular. We see and hear quite a few parrots and macaws flying and squawking overhead, and several alligator relatives, called caimans, sunning on sandbars.

Once we scramble up the steep mud bank to the village, we're greeted by several little boys. We ask to speak with someone who might have necklaces to sell, and we're directed to a woman who shows us several handsome ones. I buy two. One consists of quartets of brown seeds alternating with a gray seed. In the center of each brown quartet is a large iridescent green beetle wing or a pearly-white freshwater clam shell. The other necklace is made of small black seeds alternating with gray ones. At regular intervals red and black seeds, rough brown nuts, and large iridescent green scarab beetles alternate with each other. The effect is striking.

A bit later we're pelted with large raindrops. The chief of Dureno offers us shelter in his home. We climb up the split bamboo ladder, and once inside enter another world. His house is sparsely furnished with hammocks and wooden crates. Handwoven baskets brimming with *yuca* and *plátanos* line the floor. Blackened aluminum pots with bubbling concoctions hang over the fire. Our host seems pleased to entertain us throughout the hour-long storm, beginning with a demonstration of his blowgun. Seemingly without effort, he blows several darts into a patch of *yuca* about thirty meters away, then hands the blowgun and a dart to Jim. Jim inserts the dart, holds the blowgun to his mouth, and exhales strongly. Lethargically, the dart exits the blowgun and fizzles to the ground. I ask if I can try. The chief looks at me dubiously, but he inserts a dart and hands me his weapon. I blow with all my strength. Nothing happens, except that I gain newfound respect for the skill and strength required to kill one's dinner with a blowgun. Next he shows us his spears, hammocks, and fishing nets, all made by village members.

Once the show-and-tell ends, Steve passes out bubble gum to everyone. Ten of us sit on the rough bamboo floor in a big circle, chewing as crudely and loudly as a herd of cows masticating their cuds. Every few minutes a Cofán spits his wad of gum into his hands, molds the wad between his fingers while giggling in delight, then pops the gum back into his mouth.

14 July 1968

Today several of us fly by helicopter to Puerto Libre to survey the fauna. Puerto Libre is an intermittent gold-mining camp in a narrow valley at the base of the Andean foothills. Our chopper lifts straight up off the ground, seemingly without effort, and within seconds we're above the emerald forest. We traverse vast expanses of lush rain forest broken only by winding rivers, sometimes flying so low we almost brush the treetops.

Housing at Puerto Libre is primitive, but the beds are comfortable. The outhouses are less than comfortable but functional. Our bathtub is the cold river. We were told to help ourselves from the well-stocked pantry, so we're feasting. For breakfast we make scrambled eggs, oatmeal smothered with brown sugar, and pancakes drenched in real Log Cabin syrup. No rice! For supper we prepare tuna-noodle casserole, spaghetti, and canned chili. No rice! One night we treat ourselves to canned Danish ham and instant mashed potatoes. Laura bakes oatmeal-raisin cookies, two chocolate cakes, and a fruitcake. No rice pudding!

Trees have been logged in the immediate vicinity of camp. The pristine forest farther from camp, however, is magnificent: trees huge both in girth and height, widely separated from other mature trees by saplings competing for limited sunlight and nutrients. Undergrowth is sparse, so we can easily walk through the forest without a trail.

This afternoon I sit on a log and watch an anole lizard defend his territory. He faces the intruder, raises up high on all four legs, extends his dewlap, and bobs up and down. The intruder responds with extended dewlap and equally forceful bobbing. At one point a dazzling metallic green hummingbird hovers twenty-five centimeters from my head, checks out the red bandanna it had thought was a rich patch of nectar-filled flowers, and retreats in disgust.

Tonight while searching for salamanders, I'm crouched on the ground poking in the leaf litter when Bill comes up behind me. In a strained voice, he says, "Marty, step back slowly without raising up." I comply without questioning. Then I see a large brown-and-gray fer-de-lance viper staring at me from a branch at eye level. One of the largest and most deadly of all venomous snakes in South America, fer-de-lance (French for "lance blade") are more inclined to bite than are most other large vipers, which tend to retreat when threatened. Bill and I give the snake a wide berth as we continue on our way.

Fer-de-lance are very successful snakes in many parts of the New World tropics. They live in both wet and dry forests and often are one of the most abundant snakes in a given area. Instead of laying eggs, females give birth to twenty-five to sixty-five little snakes—each with fully developed fangs and poison glands. Fer-de-lance are pit vipers. They use heat-sensitive "pits" or depressions located between the eyes and nostrils to sense heat radiated from prey such as birds and mammals. When a prey is detected, the snake strikes and sinks its hollow fangs into the animal, injecting poison. After the prey dies, the fer-de-lance then swallows its victim whole. Enzymes present in the venom help to speed up digestion of the prey's tissues. Although the fangs and venom glands are thought to have evolved primarily as a method for subduing prey, they can be important in defense as well.

18 July 1968

Most of the species we've found at Puerto Libre are the same as those at Santa Cecilia, but the relative abundances are different. Most notably, salamanders are very common here. On each of two nights, we saw twenty to twenty-five individuals. Even Bill has found salamanders here.

The return helicopter ride is thrilling in a different way from the trip a few days ago. This time it's the thrill of danger. We can't see much through the thick fog, and we're all keenly aware that the pilot can see no more than we can. It's amazing that the chopper can pierce through the thick clouds. I think about the possibility of crashing into the dense tangle of vegetation below and quickly refocus my mind on the happy anticipation of returning to Santa Cecilia.

25 July 1968

Santa Cecilia is an entomologist's heaven. There must be thousands of undescribed insects crawling, flying, and walking in these woods, species with unique behaviors that haven't even been imagined yet. Giant grasshoppers strut through the vegetation on legs outfitted with long, sharp spines. When disturbed, female walkingsticks, a third of a meter long, slowly sway back and forth mimicking twigs in the breeze. Tiny males, less than a quarter of the females' length, ride piggyback in copula and passively sway in concert. Katydids, closely resembling leaves, come in every shade of green imaginable. Veins in their wings mimic the veins of leaves, jagged wing edges mimic leaves that have been munched by herbivores, and brown spots mimic blotches on diseased leaves. Although the bodies of most of the katydids are less than the length of my little finger, many have threadlike antennae twice as long.

I stop to watch the reddish brown leaf-cutter, or parasol, ants neatly snip leaves and flowers into smaller pieces. Some carry the pieces over their heads like umbrellas, down toward the ground. Others, empty-jawed, march back up into the tree to snip another leaf. A close look at the columns of leaf fragments marching along the ground reveals that each is being carried by an ant. Leaf-cutter ants are basically farmers. They grow fungus in damp underground nest cavities, and they use pieces of leaves and flowers as fertilizer for the fungus. The ants live in colonies, composed of three main castes. The largest individuals, called maximas, have large jaws and are the soldiers that protect the colony. Medium-sized ants, or medias, are most commonly seen. They're the ones who cut and transport leaf and flower fragments back to the nest. The tiny ants, minimas, have two main functions: they tend the baby ants inside the underground nest, and they hitch rides on the leaf fragments to protect the hardworking medias from the parasitic flies that attempt to lay eggs on them. The minimas wave their legs about to scare off the flies. When the flies ignore the threat and continue to approach, the minimas snap at them.

At the other size extreme of insects are the huge Hercules beetles that swarm around the outdoor lights at the Texaco camp. The beetles, and especially their weapons, are impressive. Males are nearly the length of my hand, and more than half their length is a curved horn that extends downward from the top of the body. This horn meets with a smaller one that curves upward from the lower part of the body, creating a pair of pincers that can inflict considerable damage, especially on other males. Males fight among themselves for dominance and for access to females in battles that compare favorably with the best Hollywood action scenes of flashing sabers or lively fistfights. They lock all four horns in an apparent attempt to crush each other's head and bang the other against the ground. Females lack the long horns, but even at half the length of males they are massive beetles.

1 August 1968

Jim and I are visiting Campana Cocha, a small placer mining camp on the bank of the Río Aguarico, where we'll do a quick two-day survey of amphibians and reptiles. The trip by motorized dugout this morning was uneventful save for the whitewater rapids that threatened to dump us into the raging section of river. Our Quechua boatman skillfully guided us through, carefully avoiding a rock bank and several floating logs, but he couldn't prevent the Río Aguarico from entering our piragua and thoroughly soaking us.

Late this afternoon, after crashing through the thick tangle of undergrowth in secondary forest and clambering over logs in a clearing looking for animals, we return to camp ravenously hungry. Our Quechua hosts have laid out dinner on a wooden crate: two bowls of watery broth with bow-tie noodles and potatoes, a bowl of cold rice, a bowl of boiled stringy *yuca,* and a bottle of ketchup—to add the only spot of color to this all-white array of starch. Jim graciously shares a pack of Life Savers with me, he says to stimulate our taste buds.

2 August 1968

Restless sleep from being cramped in awkward positions in my jungle hammock afforded me many hours to listen to the night sounds of the forest: insects, frogs, birds, and mammals. Most soothing were the soporific low trills of marine toads, reminiscent of the monotonous hum of an outdated refrigerator.

This morning one of the local Quechua kids tells us he uses Surinam toads as fishing bait. He offers to guide us to his special collecting swamp. We spend the entire day hiking through nearly impenetrable forest to reach the swamp but find no Surinam toads there. Apparently the boy simply wanted the prestige of guiding us but had no intention of revealing his prime spot. As we turn to leave, I sink in soft swamp mud up to my belly button and cannot extract myself. My frantic shrieks bring Jim and the kid running. They grab my arms and try to haul me out. Jim begins to sink. The Quechua kid first pulls Jim out, and then lays a log onto the muck and motions for me to hang on. After considerable effort, Jim and the kid finally drag me and the log from the quagmire. All the way back, I think about what would have happened had I been alone. Now I understand Bill's insistence that we work at least in pairs.

Once back in camp, I haul my filthy self into the river and wash the mud out of my clothes, hair, and body. We're served the identical combination of starch and ketchup for supper. Although a smoked stingray hangs in the kitchen, we're not offered any. And Jim has no more Life Savers.

10 August 1968

Today is Ilde's birthday. We decorate the dining area with hand-colored cards and signs we make from notebook paper and felt-tip markers. After lunch Linda takes on the somewhat onerous task of making me presentable. "No more pigtails," she declares. In the privacy of her cabin, she teases, cajoles, and finally forces my hair into a beehive coiffeur. Next she tackles my eyes, giving them more makeup than they've ever seen or will ever see again. I wear the one dress I have here, although it's musty smelling. My green mold-covered leather flats add a festive touch.

We feast on salty roast pork, baked potatoes, and chocolate birthday cake. The pork is especially delicious because we know whom we are eating—the bully that had run free in Muñozlandia, rooted in the garden, and terrorized us with unexpected charges. As the high point of the evening, Ilde and his sixteen-year-old daughter, Tierza, dance the traditional Colombian *cumbia* together. They dance counterclockwise, revolving in a circle with Tierza on the outside and Ilde inside. With a lit candle held high in her left hand, Tierza rapidly shuffles with a series of short steps. She usually moves to one side or the other, but occasionally forward. Ilde holds his machete in his right hand and dances around Tierza in a zigzag pattern, leaning on his left foot and propelling himself with the other. Occasionally Ilde bends down, flamboyantly sweeping the floor with his machete. The two often pass back to back. Periodically Ilde reaches up and touches Tierza's arm, after which they both turn completely around in a sensuous show of emotion before returning to their normal positions. The dance is lovely, and the two move in perfect synchrony.

12 August 1968

Waist-deep, I navigate a swamp using my long-handled dip net to search for tadpoles. Through the muck and vegetation in the net, I see a large wriggling body. Thinking it to be a Surinam toad, I reach in and grab hold. The shock is so strong that I lose my balance and fall backward into the water. I've grabbed an electric eel.

Of the five hundred or so species of fish that generate electrical discharges, the electric eel gives the most powerful shock. Although these fish can reach over two meters in length, fortunately the one that got me was less than a meter. Electric eels live in murky, muddy rivers and swamps in northern South America, using electric discharges to detect underwater objects, stun prey, defend themselves, and signal each other. These fish have three pairs of electric organs, composed of thousands of modified muscle cells called electroplaques, on each side of the body. When stimulated by a nerve, each electroplaque gives off a small charge of electricity. The combined charges of all the electroplaques can produce 350 to 650 volts—enough to make a 115-pound biologist drop her dip net and fall backward into the water.

I experienced another defensive behavior recently. Bill and I were surveying a forest trail when my headlamp picked up the red glowing eye shine of a South American bullfrog, a handsome, large reddish brown frog with dark brown blotches. Bill whispered, "I'll keep my light on it, you go around behind and grab." Without hesitating, I circled around, lunged, and grabbed the frog with both hands. The frog emitted a loud shrill yowl reminiscent of a cat whose tail has been stepped on. Startled, I dropped it, but not before it had coated my hands with slime. Rapidly it leaped out of sight. Bill snickered and confessed that he'd just played his favorite field joke on me.

17 August 1968

Last day in Muñozlandia. As I packed up all the tadpole-rearing trays, I reflected on how much I'd learned about fieldwork in general over the past ten weeks and about tropical amphibians and reptiles in particular. We have a species list of somewhere between 130 to 145 amphibians and reptiles. With another month here perhaps we could add another twenty-five species. Even now, Santa Cecilia holds the record for housing the greatest diversity of amphibians of anywhere in the world. And the abundance is amazing—frogs are everywhere.

After the first few weeks, I settled comfortably into how I wanted to be treated by my male field companions. Through an unspoken series of compromises, the issue of "independence" versus "helpless female" became a non-issue. The guys gave me more credit, but offered a hand when they sensed it would be appreciated. Although life at Santa Cecilia has been special, I confess I'm looking forward to returning to hot showers, flush toilets, twenty-four-hour electricity, classical music, washing machine and dryer, telephones, libraries, pizza, and friends.

We fly to Quito on a Texaco DC-3 plane, gasping for oxygen as we reach 5,200 meters. Eventually we drop to 2,850 meters at the Quito airport. I shiver as I descend the steps from our little plane and wrap my musty sweater securely around my shoulders.

Playing tourists in Quito for two days, we visit Plaza de la Independencia with its monument to Ecuador's independence, beautiful gardens and palm trees, cathedral, and Presidential Palace; Casa de Cultura with its art and natural history museums; and the church of La Merced with its beautiful stained-glass windows and poignant paintings depicting glowing volcanoes erupting over the church roofs of colonial Old Quito. We intersperse sightseeing with a heavy dose of souvenir shopping for wood carvings, horsehair paintings, woven wall hangings, ponchos, and jewelry. And we devour pizza, hamburgers, and banana splits.

20 August 1968

I sleep most of the flight home. Mom and Dad meet me at the Pittsburgh airport at 3:45 in the morning. For the next seventeen hours, I regale them with tales of jungle adventures. They are fascinated by my vivid descriptions of Surinam toads, poison dart frogs, and egg-brooding horned treefrogs. "Wait till you see my pictures," I promise. The glow on my face gives me away. They know I'll return to the tropics at the first opportunity.

2

AMAZONIAN BRAZIL

ND RETURN to the tropics I did, less than five months later. It all
began one afternoon when Dr. Philip Humphrey, Director of
the Museum of Natural History at the University of Kansas,
called the Herpetology Division and said he wanted to see me.
"What did I do now?" I worried. The flight of stairs to his office seemed
endless.

Dr. Humphrey motioned me to a seat. With a twinkle in his eyes and a
grin on his face, he began. "Marty, rumor tells me that you enjoyed your
fieldwork in Ecuador last summer."

I nodded emphatically, breathing a great sigh of relief.

"How would you like to go to Belém, Brazil, and work as a field assistant on an ecological study of birds?"

Before hearing any details and without asking any questions, I blurted,
"I'd love to!"

Over the next hour, Dr. Humphrey outlined the job. I would be working for Tom Lovejoy, a graduate student from Yale University. Tom's
study focused on the distribution of about three hundred species of birds
among different habitats in the Guamá Ecological Research Area near
Belém. My job would be twofold. I would spend two and a half days each
week in the field, working with the birds and supervising the field crew. The
other days, except for Sunday, I would summarize the data. In return for
my assistance, my travel and room and board would be covered and I'd

receive $10 per week spending money. I would also have ample opportunity to do fieldwork for my master's thesis.

AGAIN I DID my homework and learned some facts. In 1500 Pedro Alvares Cabral, a Portuguese fleet commander, sailed from Lisbon bound for India. He and his fleet wandered off course just a bit during a storm, headed west across the Atlantic, and landed on the shore of what is now Brazil. Naturally, Cabral claimed his unexpected discovery for Portugal. Subsequent Portuguese explorers called a tree they found in this new land "brazilwood" because, when cut, the bright orange wood is the color of glowing embers (*brasa* in Portuguese). They named the land after the trees—Terra do Brasil, or Land of Brazil. Brazil was a Portuguese colony from 1500 to 1822, and it has the distinction of being the only South American country to have achieved independence through peaceful means. Brazil declared independence from Portugal in 1822, and three years later Portugal granted independence to its former colony in return for 2 million pounds sterling.

Today's result of Cabral's nautical mistake is a great nation that borders all other South American countries except Ecuador and Chile and whose population size exceeds that of the rest of South America combined. The region to which I was going, the state of Pará at the mouth of the Amazon River on Brazil's north coast, is a tiny tile in the colorful mosaic of this vast expanse.

Belém, Portuguese for Bethlehem, is Pará's capital city and Brazil's main port for the steady stream of products extracted from the Amazon region: rubber, cacao, timber, Brazil nuts, and wildlife. The city sits just south of Marajó Island on the Guamá River, about 150 kilometers from the Atlantic Ocean and about the same distance south of the equator. Situated at only about twelve meters elevation, Belém is hot and humid.

WINTER–SUMMER 1969

19 January 1969

The long-awaited day has finally come. Not only am I thrilled to be getting back to the tropics, I'm looking forward to learning about birds. My body is full of vaccines: smallpox, polio, tetanus, typhus, typhoid-paratyphoid, gamma globulin, and yellow fever. And I've started my malaria prophylactic, Aralen. My field gear consists of a fishing vest, several dip nets, three field notebooks, a millimeter ruler, and a raincoat.

I'm on the last leg of a twelve-hour milk-run flight to Belém. So far we've stopped in Barbados, Port-of-Spain (Trinidad), Georgetown (Guyana), and Paramaribo (Suriname). My head is spinning with phrases from my Portuguese grammar book. *Não falo português.* (I don't speak Portuguese.) *Não entendo.* (I don't understand.) *Como vai você?* (How are you?) *Bem, obrigado.* (I'm fine, thank you.) *Bom dia.* (Good morning.) *Onde fica o toalete?* (Where is the bathroom?)

After clearing immigration, I join the mass of frantic arrivals scrambling for luggage on the conveyor belt. I throw my suitcases onto a cart and head for the customs area, where I'm intercepted by a young guy who grins engagingly and asks if I am Marty. Tom Lovejoy holds out his hand, we shake, and then he assumes control. Speaking in fluent Portuguese to the customs agent, Tom explains who he is, who I am, and produces official-looking papers complete with impressive gold seals and red ribbons. While other passengers open their luggage and customs officers paw through the contents to the last sock, I am waved through without having to unlock a suitcase.

Tom and I chatter all the way to his house, where I'll be staying with him, his wife, Mopsy, and their twin thirteen-month-old daughters. I like Tom already. He has a charming, charismatic personality and an impish sense of humor.

21 January 1969

Screeching as I throw off my heavy backpack, I unbuckle my belt and yank down my jeans. Without realizing it, I've been standing in the path of an army ant swarm. Army ants have climbed up my shoes. Dozens are now biting my legs. As I frantically hop up and down on the boardwalk, I hear voices. Valfir, Nelson, and Crizolindo, my Brazilian assistants, appear. Their jaws drop at my half-naked, gyrating, ant-covered body. Without a word, they turn and flee back down the boardwalk. After brushing the ants off my welt-covered legs, I hike up my jeans and continue on my way.

I'm walking in varzea forest on my first day in the field. The varzea, located along the edge of the Guamá River, is flooded by tides twice daily. For ease in getting around, Tom has had a network of boardwalks built over the swampy areas. Palms dominate this forest, and thick, fluffy mosses cover the trees.

The routine of fieldwork is well orchestrated and efficient. Tom has set up a line of mist nets, looking a bit like flimsy volleyball nets, along trails in the forest. When the nets are open, the fine nylon mesh is almost invisible, so unsuspecting birds fly in and get tangled up. Here in the varzea, forty-five nets capture birds that fly between fifteen centimeters and two meters above the ground. Several high nets, raised through an ingenious rigging of nylon lines and pulleys, capture birds flying at heights from ten to twenty meters. My three Brazilian assistants and I gently extract the birds from the nets. We pop them into individual cloth bags and take them to a thatched hut, where Tom and his assistants attach a small metal band to one leg of each bird not yet banded. Any bird already banded has its unique identification number read and entered onto the field card. Each bird is identified by species, sex, and age (adult or juvenile), and weighed. In addition, a small amount of blood is drawn, to be analyzed at the Belém Virus Laboratory. After the data are recorded, we release the birds at their sites of capture.

Tom says it's been a fairly slow day. We've captured fifty birds. Often the total is around a hundred birds in a day. It's 4:30 P.M., time to begin closing the nets. I get to my last net and find the ground swarming with more army ants.

Army ants march through the forest in swarms or narrow columns, flushing up insects, spiders, and small vertebrates, which they sting for later consumption. Instead of building permanent nests, army ants bivouac in sheltered spots beneath tree buttresses and fallen tree trunks. In his book *Sociobiology* (1975), E. O. Wilson dramatically describes the bivouac and hunting behavior of a large species of reddish brown army ant, found from southern Mexico to Brazil, including our study sites.

> As they gather to form the bivouac, they link their legs and bodies together with their strong tarsal claws, forming chains and nets of their own bodies that accumulate layer upon interlocking layer until finally the entire worker force constitutes a solid cylindrical or ellipsoidal mass up to a meter across. . . . Between 150,000 and 700,000 workers are present. Toward the center of the mass are found thousands of immature forms, a single mother queen, and, for a brief interval in the dry season, a thousand or so males and several virgin queens. The dark-brown conglomerate exudes a musky, somewhat fetid odor.
>
> At the height of their raids the *Eciton burchelli* workers spread out into a fan-shaped swarm with a broad front. Dendritic columns, splitting up and recombining again like braided ropes, extend from the swarm back to the bivouac site where the queen and immature forms remain sequestered in safety. The moving front of workers flushes a great harvest of prey: tarantulas, scorpions, beetles, roaches, grasshoppers, wasps, ants, and many others. Most are pulled down, stung to death, cut into pieces, and quickly transported to the rear. Even some snakes, lizards, and nestling birds fall victim. (425, 426)

I'm already learning that if I plan to work in this forest, I've got to respect the army ants. They certainly won't move aside for me.

30 January 1969

This morning Tom introduces me to his gemstone contact, an entrepreneur named Jake. Jake proudly shows me around his store filled with stuffed iguanas, turtles, toucans, and sloths. He also shows me boa skins, trays decorated with colorful butterflies, and paperweights containing scorpions and tarantulas. Jake senses my disapproval of the dead animals for sale and quickly ushers me into a small room at the back of the store. He offers me a seat at a wooden table. From a suitcase he extracts wads of newspaper, which he spreads on the table. He then returns to the front of the store. I carefully unwrap the newspaper wads and find handfuls of glistening topaz, tourmaline, amethyst, and aquamarine. An hour later I've chosen a luscious reddish brown topaz and a clear blue aquamarine.

Tom and I visit the local natural history museum, the Museu Goeldi. While Tom talks birds with the resident ornithologist, another scientist, Ricardo, gives me a guided tour of the museum. The museum houses and displays the richness of the flora, fauna, minerals, and indigenous cultures found in the Amazon Basin. In addition to the indoor museum, the complex includes a zoo with local animals and a large outdoor garden resembling an Amazonian jungle. In one section of the garden, a lake supports a nearly continuous blanket of giant water lilies. Their flat, round emerald-green leaves with narrow vertical rims reach two meters in diameter, and their showy white flowers are thirty centimeters across.

Ricardo offers me a *cafezinho*, sugar-laced coffee served in a tiny demitasse cup. Tom had warned me that it's impolite to refuse a *cafezinho*, so I accept, though I'm not wild about sweet coffee. Since Brazil is the world's largest coffee producer, it's no surprise that nearly everyone in the country is addicted. Most Brazilians don't ask if you take sugar in your coffee. It's assumed that you want a little strong coffee in your sugar.

At a local restaurant, Ricardo and I have a national dish of Brazil— *feijoada completa,* a delicious stew made of numerous kinds of fresh, smoked, and cured meat, black beans, onions, and tomatoes, stewed in a hot chili sauce with spices and herbs. Traditional *feijoada* uses fifteen kinds of meat, including tongue of pig, lamb, and calf, spicy pork sausage, salted and dried bacon, smoked pork loin, dried beef, salted pork, fresh pork (including ears, feet, snout, and tails), and fresh beef. *Feijoada* was concocted by slaves from Africa as a way of combining the leftovers from their masters' tables. *Farinha,* a toasted version of manioc meal that bears a remarkable resemblance to sawdust, is sprinkled over the top. After eating a bit, one sprinkles on more *farinha*. And more.

Dinner conversation drifts to bizarre topics. Ricardo warns me not to bathe in rivers in the Amazon Basin because of candiru—tiny freshwater parasitic catfish with spines. These fish normally live on blood within the gill cavities of other fish, but they are also attracted by chemical compounds in urine and enter the urinary bladder of larger fish, where they feed on mucus. This explains their nasty habit of taking a wrong turn and traveling up the human urethra, where they get stuck. Their backward-pointing spines prevent them from retreating, so there they stay, spines lodged in the human host's urethra, creating a painful state of affairs.

8 February 1969

On field days we leave home at 3:45 A.M. so that we can open the mist nets before sunrise at our study sites outside Belém. Our first stop is the Virus Laboratory, where we pick up our Brazilian field assistants. Second stop is a nondescript bakery in a back alley, where we buy four loaves of warm freshly baked bread. We usually share two of these as we drive to the field site and save the other two for lunch, to be eaten with our canned sardines or tuna.

In addition to nets in the varzea forest, we have mist nets set up in igapó and terra firme forests. Igapó is a permanent swamp forest in low-lying areas, continuously flooded with "black water," loaded with tannins and other compounds from decaying vegetation. An extensive network of boardwalks allows easy access to the mist nets. Although some trees are rooted in the deep mud, much of the igapó vegetation is supported on small islands of tangled root masses that emerge from stagnant interconnected pools. In contrast, terra firme is a fairly dense forest on well-drained high ground that never floods.

Today I find an old friend that also occurs at Santa Cecilia—a crested toad. She very much resembles her background of dead brown leaves, and I don't see her until she hops out from underfoot. A spectacular toad, she is brown with chocolate splotches. She's covered with prominent tubercles, and her iris is bronze with a narrow border of greenish gold that glistens in the sunlight. Her most striking characteristic is her head, adorned with greatly enlarged bony ridges and expanded crests, not unlike those of the crested duckbilled dinosaurs.

I take a few pictures of the toad before continuing along the path to my next mist net. There, a woodpecker is struggling to escape the net, which is laced with dozens of biting army ants. I don my bat gloves, shake the net, and brush the frenzied ants off the bird. The bird is a recapture from this morning, so I release it. It flies off, traumatized but alive.

One of the ants is now crawling under my T-shirt. As I lift my shirt to remove the ant, I hear a leering "wolf call" from nearby. I whip around, expecting to see Valfir, Nelson, and Crizolindo, but there's no one in sight.

18 February 1969

Today as I deliver my cloth bags of birds to Tom at the hut, another loud wolf call erupts nearby. Grinning at my offended expression, Tom explains, "That's not your field assistants. It's a bird—the squirrel cuckoo."

I've designed a research project for my masters degree that builds on the ongoing cooperative program at the Guamá Ecological Research Area. One of the goals of the program is to understand how animals and plants are distributed within the habitat. For this reason, the study areas have been divided into a network of squares, each corner marked with a numbered stake. From other investigators' studies, we have data on distribution of standing water, temperature, humidity, and vegetation structure and density. Tom will add his bird data to that extensive pool of knowledge. I'll follow suit and take advantage of the elaborate grid system to map the ecological distribution of the frogs, salamanders, and lizards within the three main types of forest: terra firme, varzea, and igapó. I'll map the occurrence of every amphibian and lizard I find in between making rounds of my mist nets and will also hire Cabeça, our driver from the Belém Virus Laboratory, to take me out to the forests for nighttime fieldwork. I'm anxious to begin collecting my own data, as it's been frustrating spending all my time working on Tom's project. Being a field assistant is an ideal way to learn how to do research, but I'm also ready to jump in and learn by making my own mistakes.

My favorite place to visit on Sundays is the Ver-O-Peso market facing the pier. The market dates back to 1688, when it was established as a checkpoint by the Portuguese. All merchandise that passed through the port of Belém was weighed so that a tax could be charged—thus the name Ver-O-Peso (Watch the Weight). Here, in one of the most active markets in Brazil, an endless variety of fresh fruits, vegetables, and flowers is sold, along with huge quantities of Brazil nuts.

Exotic smells emanating from a large food bazaar tempt me to investigate. Recently I tried *tacacá,* one of the traditional street dishes consisting of shrimp tails in a rich, spicy *tucupi* sauce made from the juice of manioc root and lots of *jambu. Jambu* is a green leafy herb that has the peculiar

Ver-O-Peso (Watch the Weight) market in Belém, Brazil.

quality of numbing your mouth. After eating *tacacá* my lips tingled for the next hour. *Tacacá* is served in a *cuia,* the dried shell of the calabash fruit.

A never-ending series of herb stalls winds through the market—herbs to cure ulcers, impotence, warts, and cancer. Animal parts are sold for remedies, prophylactics, and magic. A tea made from dried sea horses, ground into a powder and boiled with an herb, cures asthma. An armadillo's tail heated then rubbed between the toes cures athlete's foot. Necklaces made from water buffalo teeth, if worn regularly, guard women against venereal disease. Dried powdered lizards, sprinkled on a husband, cool his sexual appetite. Dried eyes of the freshwater Amazon River dolphin, locally called *boto,* are prized as aphrodisiacs. One elderly woman explained to me that *botos* transform themselves at night into handsome young men who lure virgins from their homes, seduce and impregnate them, and then leave them. No doubt the legend provides a handy explanation for unexpected pregnancies.

And then there's the macumba paraphernalia: black candles, incense, fetishes, and idols. Particularly common are statues of the devil and of the mermaid god Yemanjá, the most venerated woman from Yoruba theology of Africa. Small, shiny beads of every color are for sale. A vendor explains to me that because each spirit prefers a certain color, you should wear the color beads of the patron saint under which you were born. Macumba is a highly developed mixture of African cults and Roman Catholicism, half pagan, half Christian. Resembling the voodoo religion of the Caribbean, macumba has its roots in the African slave trade but has since evolved to satisfy the spiritual needs of poor Brazilians. During macumba rituals, roosters, sheep, and other animals are sacrificed to the saints and gods. Beating drums and chanting induce hypnotic states, which are followed by intense emotional releases. Participants become possessed by a particular god and then take on his attributes. Mediums in trancelike states are consulted to answer questions concerning love, money, and health. Macumba incorporates superstitions, hexes, fetishes, idols, and offerings to summon and consult supernatural spirits. Both black and white magic are practiced. I buy a few *figas* (carved wooden charms of clenched fists used in spirit rituals) to take home as souvenirs.

Vendors line the market sidewalks. Men wearing blood-smeared aprons sell beef, chicken, pork, and fish. A teenage boy deals in padded bras and garish nylon bikini briefs. Several others sell rainforest animals for pets: baby sloths, monkeys, boa constrictors, parrots, and songbirds. A woman sells coconuts, opened at the top, with a straw for drinking the coconut milk. Children hawk plastic plates, bowls, and trinkets ranging from cigarette lighters to mirrors to shower caps. Near the wharf, a grizzled old man sells crude clay pots.

19 March 1969

A few days ago we banded our 185th species and our ten thousandth individual bird. I'm getting much better at extracting birds from the nets and have come to appreciate their unique personalities. Puffbirds seem calm (and almost appreciative) as I untangle them. Parrots and toucans fight like cornered rats and put their impressive talons and beaks to good use. Manakins nearly always defecate berry juice and pulp all over my hands. Woodpeckers sink their sharp claws into my palms.

Many of the birds are spectacularly colored. The fork-tailed woodnymph hummingbird is dressed in brilliant iridescent green body feathers that contrast with its violet-blue cap and belly. The bright red iris of the blue-crowned motmot peers out from behind a black mask, bordered by turquoise and violet. The aptly named opal-crowned manakin sports a cap of feathers whose play of colors resembles an opal. In addition to its long yellow bill, the yellow-billed jacamar has a metallic green upper body, a shimmering purple-brown crown, and a cinnamon underside.

Male red-headed manakins, glossy black birds with stunning brilliant red heads, engage in lively courtship behavior that involves tail and wing shaking, flying back and forth between branches, foot stomping, tap dancing, and rapid wing fanning. Because the bird is associated with a variety of legends and superstitions, manakins are commonly sold in the Ver-O-Peso market—as living, frightened creatures hopping about in tiny bamboo cages; stuffed or flattened dried skins; preserved carcasses in alcohol; or bits of red head feathers stuffed into small glass vials. Purportedly, this bird, or its parts, will bring love, happiness, and wealth to its possessor.

My all-time favorite bird is the royal flycatcher. As I reach out to untangle one from the net, it suddenly twists its head toward me, spreads its crest into a bright red fan, swings its head back and forth, and gapes silently, its open mouth exposing a vivid orange lining. This defensive spectacle makes the bird appear larger than it really is. To add to the threat, the brilliant blue spots in the middle of the fan resemble large eyes.

Because army ants are abundant in our study sites, three species of ant-following birds are also common: plain brown woodcreeper, white-shouldered fire-eye, and black-spotted bare-eye. These birds, and other less common species, follow swarms of army ants and prey on the grasshoppers, crickets, roaches, and other conspicuous insects that jump or scuttle frantically to escape from the relentless ants. This unusual foraging behavior is critical to the birds, as they obtain at least half of their food by following ants. It's efficient, as a bird can nab a new prey almost as fast as it can gulp down the previous one.

14 April 1969

A few days ago I received a letter from one of my favorite professors at the University of Kansas, Gerry Smith. He emphasized what a unique opportunity I have. In a professorial sort of way, he suggested that I observe all aspects of nature, not just birds, amphibians, and reptiles, and take notes on everything I see.

I've taken his advice to heart. Last year in Ecuador everything was so new that I needed time to digest. Slightly less naive, I can now reflect better on my surroundings, and I'm able to think more deeply about what I'm seeing. I wonder more about the functions of structures and the consequences of behaviors, and I'm more cognizant of interactions.

More than ever I'm fascinated by the leaf-cutter ants marching determinedly past me, one by one, hundreds of them, thousands of them. Each is carrying a piece of leaf or flower. They work hard to provide for their extended family, without sick or personal days, maternity leave, health insurance, company cars, or retirement pensions. How pampered we humans are, and how foreign leaf-cutter ant society is to us. Which society is more advanced, ours or theirs?

I'm more aware of flowers than before. Not just their shapes and colors, but also what they're "saying." A teacup-sized bluish purple passion flower with concentric circles of yellow, blue, violet, white, and pink flamboyantly displays its yellow sex organs for all the world to admire and broadcasts its sweet aroma to attract large bee pollinators. Nearby, miniature white blossoms cling to a fragile herb in the coffee family. I peer closely and see a tiny pollen-covered fly on one of the delicate flowers. This strategy works too.

A tamandua, or anteater, no more than two meters from me takes what he wants by brute force as he tears open a termite nest and slurps up the frantic occupants. Unconcerned by my presence, he stops and watches me, but then returns to his meal. His long, sticky tongue whips out of his toothless mouth, gloms on to some termites, and disappears back into the tiny opening at the end of his narrow tubelike snout. Suddenly he wraps his prehensile tail around a branch, grabs on with his hind feet, raises his body into the air, and stretches out his forelimbs to either side, as if to say, "I'm king of this tree!"

3 May 1969

"Cabeça!" I shout until my throat is dry and my voice is raspy. No answer. I'm really in trouble now. I've spent the past thirty minutes standing in one spot, calling for Cabeça. I'm totally lost, and the bulb in my headlamp has burned out.

It's my own fault, I tell myself as I replay the evening's events in my mind: I hear treefrogs *bonking* from a distance and, without telling Cabeça, I follow the sounds to a swamp. It's a call I don't recognize. Maybe I can add another species to my list for this forest. The frogs stop calling, so I turn off my headlamp and wait a few minutes. One calls from behind me. I turn and try to track it down. The *bonks* lead me to a hollow tree. The frog must be inside. Another calls to my left, so I force my way through a tangle of vines. The *bonks* are coming from at least three meters above the ground. I follow two more calls to tall trees. After forty-five minutes I realize I've been roaming in random directions, oblivious to my surroundings. I have no idea where I am or where Cabeça is. I begin shouting, but no one answers. The treefrogs stop calling in response to the noise. I'm alone.

Then it happens. The bulb in my headlamp flickers and burns out. I have no food or water or extra clothing with me. How cold will the forest get tonight? Are there any wild animals that might be interested in me as a meal? I mustn't panic. I'll just sit here and wait for daylight.

Soon the frogs resume calling, but their *bonks* no longer tempt me. All around me I hear the chirping and peeping of insects, mournful hooting of owls, and rustling of vegetation by unknown creatures. Truncated thoughts flit through my brain. I think about my warm, dry bed. I picture the slice of chocolate cake that is waiting for me at Tom's house. What if daylight comes and I still can't find my way out? I've got to do something. Now. My eyes have accommodated somewhat to the darkness so that I can barely make out individual trees. I stumble a few meters in one direction, then another. My face plunges into something that gives and stretches— one of our mist nets! I grope for the pole. My hand brushes against a ribbon of plastic flagging tape. I know where I am. This is the farthest one of Crizolindo's nets. The path is just the other side of a tangle of vegetation.

I stumble along the path and finally reach the bird-banding hut. Inside, I slump into a chair and begin to plan my next strategy. Suddenly I hear a frantic voice calling my name. "Martinha!"

After sheepishly explaining what happened, I promise Cabeça and myself that we will never again forget to take spare bulbs. Cabeça and I share his dimming headlamp and return to the truck. The traumatic experience of being lost for more than three hours without light has so exhausted me that I sleep all the way back to Tom's house.

25 May 1969

Today is the sort of day that earned me my sobriquet of Calamity Crump back in Santa Cecilia. The day in the varzea forest begins with two feisty bats in the first net. They rip the net, leaving big gaps in the mesh. Midmorning a flock of parrots flies into the high net. I spend thirty minutes untangling and bagging nineteen screaming, clawing, pecking bodies. Just before lunch the water level rises and covers the boardwalk. I walk cautiously, but my footing is off by a few centimeters and I fall into the murky water. During lunch, as I sit on a log in the sun trying to dry out, a large caterpillar falls from a branch above me, onto my bare arm. It is lavishly decked out with green and yellow spines projecting from a lime-green body. Each spine has numerous branch spines projecting at right angles, like tiny Christmas trees. Almost as soon as this ostentatious creature lands on my arm, my skin begins to tingle. I knock the caterpillar off with a twig, but already my arm itches like crazy. Within minutes it's on fire, covered with huge welts. Late afternoon I step off another submerged boardwalk. As I fall, I grab on to a spiny palm tree and a large black spine lodges in my thumb.

On days like this I envy Tom working on birds in the shelter of the hut. He only has to contend with irritating mosquitoes. He doesn't even get wet when it rains. But I quickly remind myself how special it is to be out in the forest all day. In high school my dream was to become a biologist and travel to exotic places. And here I am.

TONIGHT CABEÇA has a surprise for me—a visit to a swamp where lung-fish live. There are six species of lungfish in the world: four in Africa, one in Australia, and one in South America. South American lungfish have poorly developed gills. Most of their breathing is done through a pair of primitive but functional lungs. These eel-shaped fish often find themselves living in temporary swamps that dry out. When this happens, the lungfish dig burrows in the mud and remain under the surface until rains refill their swamps.

As we reach the swamp, Cabeça confidently states that conditions are just right. The water level is low, but the lungfish probably have not bur-rowed underground yet. Sensing movement in the shallow water, I bend down and see my first live lungfish. The prehistoric-looking creature gracefully glides through the water, fluttering its threadlike fins until it dis-appears in the muck.

Cabeça has another odd fish to show me. We drive to a stream and shine our headlamps into the water. After a few minutes Cabeça's light reflects off the eyeballs belonging to a fish cruising just under the water's surface—a four-eyed fish. These fish swim with the upper half of their eyes protruding above the water and the lower half in the water. The cor-neas are divided and the retinas are separate in the back, hence the name. An object in the water is seen through the lower part of the eye and is brought into focus on the upper retina. In contrast, an object out of water is seen through the upper part of the eye and is brought into focus on the lower retina. The result of this odd arrangement is that the upper eyes watch out for predators while the lower eyes search for food.

4 June 1969

The eminent ornithologist Roger Tory Peterson and his wife, Barbara, are visiting for a week. Early this morning, Tom and I take Roger up the thirty-five-meter-high observation tower to bird-watch and to experience sunrise above the forest canopy. We are intensely aware of the sounds, first the chirps of insects and peeps of treefrogs, and later the chattering of monkeys and the dawn chorus of birds, including toucans, parrots, and flycatchers. The air is cool and humid from last night's rain. The company is superb. Roger is thrilled to be above the rain forest, watching birds. I'm thrilled to be watching Roger Peterson watch birds.

Later, in the terra firme forest, I comment to Tom that the numerous spiders jumping out from under our feet like popping popcorn seem to be an ecological replacement for the small frogs that were so abundant in the leaf litter at Santa Cecilia. We discuss my observation, and then Tom records my thoughts in his field notebook. Suddenly I feel like a real biologist. Tom, at least, is taking me seriously as a scientific colleague.

20 July 1969

At the American consulate we listen to the broadcast. A Brazilian shouts in Portuguese, "Twenty-one seconds to go!" and then, "They've landed!" We all burst into shouts and hug each other seconds after U.S. astronauts Neil A. Armstrong and Edwin E. Aldrin Jr. land *Apollo 11* on the moon.

The governor of Pará is here, along with other Brazilian dignitaries and about twenty-five Americans. We go outside, raise the American flag, then pose next to it while newspaper photographers take our picture. Afterward we troop back inside for several rounds of champagne to celebrate.

On the way home from the consulate, we stop at a stream to watch fishing bats skim the water surface. These bats have long legs, enormous feet, and strongly hooked claws at the tips of their toes. They use echolocation to detect disturbances in the water. Once they detect fish, the bats drop their feet slightly below the surface of the water with claws facing forward and impale their victims. Behind the skimming bats, the moon's reflection in the water is lovely and peaceful.

21 July 1969

Today my Brazilian assistants ask me about the moon landing. They're afraid that North Americans will claim the moon for themselves. Valfir says he heard that the astronauts had taken samples of rocks and soil. "How much of the moon will they take back to the United States?" he asks. I explain that two years ago more than ninety nations, including the United States, signed a space exploration treaty stating that no natural body in outer space, including the moon, can be owned by any country or used for military purposes. The moon belongs to everyone. The moon belongs to no one. My assistants seem to accept this explanation but are still a bit suspicious.

1 August 1969

We finish last-minute packing after breakfast, then Cabeça drives Tom, Mopsy, the twins, and me to the airport. Over the past six and a half months, I've participated in many airport farewells. Now it's our turn to travel and for others to send us off. About twenty friends are here to say good-bye. We all are weepy amidst the hugs and kisses.

Once on the plane, my thoughts turn to my notebooks full of data. Although amphibians are abundant in the forest surrounding Belém, the diversity is low compared to Santa Cecilia. There are thirty-seven species of frogs here, eighty-one at Santa Cecilia; half of the species here also occur at Santa Cecilia. That's a wide distribution, from one end of the Amazon Basin to the other! The lizards are comparable, with twenty-four species here and twenty-seven at Santa Cecilia. Ten occur at both sites. The one salamander around Belém is a different species from the two that occur at Santa Cecilia. Curiously, no salamanders have been reported from the central portion of the Amazon Basin. I wonder why

Nauta mushroom-tongue salamander, common around Belém.

The time in Brazil has been so terrific that I'm already daydreaming about the next trip. Maybe to search for salamanders along the Amazon? My full data notebooks are immensely satisfying, but more importantly I feel like a real biologist now. The bachelor of science degree just didn't give me that sense of accomplishment.

SUMMER 1970

After returning to Lawrence, I questioned my adviser why salamanders had never been recorded from the forests along the middle section of the Amazon River. Had no one looked? In typical Duellmanesque fashion, he responded, "Well, why don't you find out?" So, I wrote a proposal and received funding from the KU museum to spend part of the following summer searching for salamanders along the Amazon. Included in my request was partial funding for an assistant, my fourteen-year-old brother Alan.

THE AMAZON RIVER system is the largest body of fresh water on earth. Although the Nile River is longer, the Amazon carries more water than the Nile, Mississippi, and Yangtze Rivers combined. Amazonia refers to the vast basin of forests and wetlands encompassed by the Amazon drainage— the world's largest rain forest, covering nearly 6.5 million square kilometers in Brazil, Venezuela, Colombia, Suriname, Guyana, French Guiana, Ecuador, Peru, and Bolivia. The earliest people to live in the Amazon rain forest are thought to have migrated from the north, across the isthmus of Panama, and into Amazonia about ten thousand years ago. Since the early 1500s, population sizes of indigenous peoples have steadily dwindled due to enslavement, social and cultural disruption, and European diseases such as smallpox, influenza, and the common cold.

What originally lured European explorers into the mosquito-ridden, oppressively hot and humid rain forest? Lust for gold and other riches. A popular myth in the 1500s held that the wealthy kingdom of El Dorado (Spanish for "the gilded") lay hidden deep in the forest. The king of El Dorado regularly coated his body with gold dust and floated on a raft in the middle of a lake while his subjects tossed jewels into the water around him.

In 1541 Gonzalo Pizarro and Francisco de Orellana led an expedition from Peru to explore a mighty river they'd found and to conquer El Dorado. After many of the men began to starve and sicken with disease, Orellana and about fifty men separated off to hunt food for the group. Instead of returning, though, they sailed down the wide river and eventually ended up in the Atlantic Ocean. During their journey, Orellana and his men purportedly were attacked by female warriors, whom they called "Amazons" after the subjects of a Greek myth—a tribe of warrior women from a remote region in Asia Minor who removed the right breast of their daughters so they could shoot bow and arrows more easily. According to the myth, periodically the Amazons mated with men of neighboring tribes; they returned or enslaved sons, and nurtured only the daughters. Tales of women warriors in the South American rain forest reached civilization, and eventually the name Amazon was bestowed on the river and surrounding forest.

20 June 1970

Alan and I board our plane this morning in New York City. As we head south for Belém, I chatter nonstop about Brazilian food, the living conditions, the animals. After a while Alan's eyes glaze over and he tunes me out. Realizing I have overloaded his circuits, I begin to read Theodosius Dobzhansky's 1950 article "Evolution in the Tropics." His descriptive words are perfectly chosen:

> Becoming acquainted with tropical nature is, before all else, a great esthetic experience. Plants and animals of temperate lands seem to us somehow easy to live with, and this is not only because many of them are long familiar. Their style is for the most part subdued, delicate, often almost inhibited. Many of them are subtly beautiful; others are plain; few are flamboyant. In contrast, tropical life seems to have flung all restraints to the winds. It is exuberant, luxurious, flashy, often even gaudy, full of daring and abandon, but first and foremost enormously tense and powerful. Watching the curved, arched, contorted, spirally wound, and triumphantly vertical stems and trunks of trees and lianas in forests of Rio Negro and the Amazon, it often occurred to me that modern art has missed a most bountiful source of inspiration. (209)

Now I too am lost in my own thoughts, visualizing Amazonian life. *Exuberant:* two-meter-wide giant lily pads, strong enough for children to lie on. *Luxurious:* green on all sides, from mosses to canopy trees. *Flashy:* iridescent purple, green, and blue hummingbird feathers shimmering in the sunshine. *Gaudy:* turquoise, black, and orange poison dart frogs. *Daring and abandon:* raucous squawking of parrots flying over the canopy. *Tense and powerful:* emerald tree boas squeezing life from birds before swallowing them whole.

CHAPTER TWO

23 June 1970

Today a scientist working at the Guamá Ecological Research Area introduces us to his friend Paulo, an elderly Brazilian gentleman who spent decades as a missionary working with Indians along the Amazon. Alan and I spend a delightful afternoon with Paulo in his apartment decorated with baskets, blowguns, and feather necklaces. He claims that his library of books about the Amazon is the best in Belém. Paulo seems gentle and scholarly. His skin is like parchment. His legs are unsteady. Thrilled to have a captive audience, he relates his Amazon experiences and tells us what to expect. His eyes twinkle as he speaks fondly of the Indians, the forest, the river. His voice cracks as he says he wishes he could return.

After a while he excuses himself, totters into the kitchen, and reappears with a tray supporting three tall pilsner glasses of cold beer, beads of condensation running down the sides of the glasses. Alan casts me a glance as if to say, "May I?" I nod, and he lifts a glass off the tray. Alan is being treated as an adult, and he loves it.

For dinner we have water buffalo steak, which is as tough as I remember it from last year. The trick is to take small bites. After chewing for a while, your jaws are sore and you have to swallow the mangled, only partially masticated morsel. Water buffalo were introduced to Belém as a dairy experiment. Their milk contains more fat than does cow milk, and the animals are ideal for the local swampy conditions. Brazilians have not yet developed a taste for water buffalo milk, however, so the ranchers have resorted to producing steaks.

26 June 1970

We fly to Manaus, 1,930 kilometers up the Amazon. After getting a room at a modest hotel, we taxi to the National Institute of Amazonian Research (INPA) office to make arrangements to stay at the Ducke Reserve twenty-five kilometers to the northeast. Our request is handled very formally in a conference room, in consultation with four INPA officials. After much discussion and two rounds of *cafezinho*, we're granted permission. Unfortunately, however, the truck won't be going out for another two days. We have an enforced vacation, which already has me agitated about losing valuable field time.

We first wander down to the large duty-free section of the wharf. Manaus became a free-trade zone three years ago in an effort to stimulate development in the upper Amazon. Already the town attracts visitors from all over the country seeking bargains. Mounds of U.S. blue jeans line

46

one area. Nearby are radios, tape recorders, and other electronic equipment. We gravitate to the camera section, as Alan had saved up money to replace his old Kodak. After considering every available 35 mm camera, he chooses a Canon.

Alan tries out his new camera on the floating markets that line the waterfront. Dozens of dugouts full of produce, live chickens, and loaves of bread float on the water. Each vendor is eager to make a sale, and they actively compete with each other for the attention of potential customers. We have dinner at a quaint little seafood restaurant where we both order the traditional *caldeirada,* a delicious stew of fish, octopus, shrimp, potatoes, onions, eggs, and of course *farinha,* the toasted manioc flour.

In 1852, when Manaus consisted of only a few huts on the Rio Negro several kilometers from where it empties into the Amazon, government officials set up camp there to watch over the newly created province of Amazonas. By the following year, Manaus was connected to Belém by steamships that cruised up and down the Amazon carrying natural resources from the rain forest. One of these was rubber, a product that would transform the Amazon Basin.

By the late 1800s, European and North American manufacturers were buying all the Amazonian rubber that could be produced. Most of it came from Brazil. They clamored for more. Speculators bought up huge tracts of land and searched for rubber trees along the Amazon. Most entrepreneurs lived either in Manaus or Belém, from where they directed their operations. Prosperity from the rubber boom, which lasted from about 1890 to 1915, extended far beyond the rubber barons. It transformed Manaus and Belém into modern cities with efficient systems of waterworks, electricity, garbage collection and disposal, and telephone service. Manaus boasted marble and granite government buildings, huge private villas, public gardens, a library, a museum, and luxury that rivaled that of Paris. The crowning glory of Manaus was its opera house, called the Amazonas Theater. Completed in 1896, it took twelve years to build the opera house in the middle of the rain forest. Local wood was used, and materials were imported from Europe: tile dome, pillars of cast iron and marble, bronze chandeliers, gold leaf, paintings and sculptures, wrought-iron staircases, and red velvet-covered mahogany chairs.

The Amazonian rubber boom was short-lived, however. In the 1870s the British, as one of the world's largest consumers of rubber, were anxious to end the Brazilian monopoly on latex. They sent Henry Wickham to Brazil in the hopes of domesticating wild rubber and starting up a plantation. Up until that time, wild trees scattered throughout the rain forest were tapped for their latex. Wickham soon gave up on the idea of laboriously planting rubber trees in the jungle. Taking the easy way out, in 1876 he gathered rubber tree seeds from Santarém and transported over sixty thousand seeds to England. Rewarded for his deed, Wickham was knighted by the British Crown. Eventually seedlings were transported to Ceylon (now Sri Lanka) and Malaysia. Those that survived formed the beginning of the great rubber plantations of the Far East. In 1900 four tons of rubber

Rubber tree being tapped for latex.

were exported from those plantations. Five years later the figure had risen to 145 tons. By 1922 rubber from the Asian plantations accounted for 93 percent of international sales. The plantation rubber, sold at much lower prices than the wild Amazonian rubber, destroyed the Brazilian market. Manaus saw a mass exodus of its wealthy and cultured citizens, speculators, and prostitutes. The opera house was boarded up, the docks and warehouses deteriorated, banks closed, and the city stagnated. By 1928 the lights literally went out in Manaus when the city became unable to pay its electricity bill.

ALAN AND I admire the tile mosaic on the ground leading up to the extravagant opera house and the marble columns at the entrance, but we're unable to go inside because of restoration work in progress. We return to the waterfront and watch the vultures scavenge for scraps of fish in the market. Alan seems subdued and comments that he has never seen real poverty before. I understand, for I remember my first glimpse of Quito two years ago.

5 July 1970

We've had an enjoyable but disappointing stay at the Ducke Reserve. One night I played Duellman's trick on Alan. We saw the bright red eye shine of a South American bullfrog ahead on the trail. I explained to Alan that while I kept my light in its eyes, he should circle around behind it, and then grab with both hands and hang on. It worked. The frog uttered its catlike screech. Alan shrieked in panic and dropped the frog, but not before he'd been covered with slime.

Alan saw some of the unusual ways tropical frogs reproduce. We found leaf frog egg masses attached to leaves overhanging a forest pond. Alan found a male poison dart frog carrying a tadpole on its back. We also found a gladiator frog nest with tiny black-and-white eggs floating on its surface.

We searched in forest, fields, and banana patches for salamanders. I emphasized to Alan that you have to think SALAMANDERS. You can't daydream. But hard as we thought SALAMANDERS during our many hours of searching, we found none. To maintain enthusiasm and optimism, I continually found myself telling Alan, "This is going to be the night. We'll find salamanders tonight"; or, "Moisture and temperature conditions are finally perfect. Tonight the salamanders will be out foraging." But it hasn't happened.

6 July 1970

We return to Manaus this morning, without salamanders. After checking the schedule for the local boats, we buy tickets for a *gaiola,* the most commonly used form of river transportation among the locals. A *gaiola* is a wooden multideck cruiser that makes regular trips between towns along the Amazon. We'll get off at Óbidos, about 535 kilometers downriver from Manaus. What we don't know (and apparently everyone else does) is that not only do you rent hammock space for sleeping, you must provide your own hammock! Immediately upon boarding, everyone joins in a scuffle to secure a good spot for the stringing of his or her hammock. Alan and I quickly claim two narrow, hard benches as our beds. They will provide personal space, but I doubt either of us will sleep tonight.

At the moment we're not thinking about sleep. Sending flames of yellow, orange, and red across the sky, the sun sets over the Amazon. A cool wind caresses our bodies and transports river smells to our noses. The choruses of cicadas on the riverbank grow louder.

10 July 1970

We survived the *gaiola* trip and have been exploring the quaint community of Óbidos. So far we've seen abundant frog life but no salamanders. I'm getting discouraged but am trying not to let Alan know. Maybe there simply are no salamanders in central Amazonia. But how will I ever know if we simply looked in the wrong places, if we were here at the wrong time of year and the salamanders just weren't active, or if in fact they do not occur here?

This evening as Alan and I walk to a wooded area, the locals line the dirt streets and stare at us. Is it our full collecting regalia: headlamp, long-sleeved shirts, baggy pants, and rubber boots? Or is it just that strangers, especially North Americans, are an oddity here? Alan finds the stares unnerving.

Once past the gawking onlookers, we shine our lights into the vegetation and are startled by a huge boa constrictor, its tan and reddish brown blotched, heavy body draped over a branch. "Wow!" shouts Alan. "A live boa constrictor!" I can't resist the temptation to impress my little brother, so with both hands I reach up and firmly grab the snake behind the head. The snake immediately coils its thick body around my arm.

"Alan, grab the snake!" I yell. I have visions of the snake releasing my arm and constricting my neck instead.

Alan hesitatingly grips the snake and tries to unwind the pulsating rope of muscle. Meanwhile the snake squeezes my arm so hard I think my bones will be crushed. Alan and the boa are a fairly even match, so it takes awhile to peel the snake off my arm. After what seems an eternity, my arm is free. We fling the snake into the undergrowth and jump backward. Alan forces a grin and suggests that we stick to salamanders.

A few minutes later, Alan is peering into the inner leaves on a bush, thinking SALAMANDERS, when he jumps backward and gasps, "Oh my god!" Ten centimeters from his nose, in the focused light of his headlamp, three large hairy tarantulas slowly wave their collective twenty-four legs in the air, seemingly at him. We take a few pictures before continuing our search.

After several salamander-less hours, we return to our room. I feel miserable, and not only because of no salamanders. Yesterday while Alan was exploring Óbidos, I spent the afternoon sitting in the grass, watching lizards defend their territories. Unbeknownst to me, the grass was crawling with chiggers. Now the chiggers are sucking fluids from me. My entire body is covered with red welts that quickly grow in size and redness as I frantically scratch them. Last night I awoke umpteen times, my body on fire from scratching. A cold shower provided only temporary relief. I took four cold showers during the seemingly endless night and thrashed on my hard mattress contemplating chigger biology.

Chiggers are tiny mites. The female lays her eggs on moist ground. After the reddish orange immatures hatch, they attach themselves to a vertebrate host, where they remain for a few days to a month. Contrary to popular belief, immature chiggers do not burrow into your skin, suffocate, and die. Instead, they insert their mouthparts into your skin, inject saliva, and suck lymph and semidigested tissue. Your body reacts to the foreign substance of the mite's saliva by setting up an allergic reaction, characterized by almost intolerable itching. Eventually the chiggers fall off. If they are fortunate enough to fall in suitable habitat, they continue development as free-living mites, eating tiny arthropods from the soil. If they fall onto carpet or between the sheets, the human host unknowingly has sweet revenge as the chiggers die.

12 July 1970

During the 110-kilometer boat trip downriver from Óbidos to Santarém, we cruised close to the bank and saw turtles basking on logs, caimans sunning on sandbars, and brightly colored birds flitting amidst the lush green vegetation. We observed day-to-day life along the Amazon—people bathing, washing clothes, and brushing teeth in the river; mothers nursing infants, toddlers chasing dogs, and elderly men reminiscing on the beach;

children plucking papaya, *plátanos,* and palm nuts from trees surrounding their thatched homes built on stilts.

Santarém, founded as an Indian mission in 1661, is now a major city situated midway between Manaus and Belém, located at the point where the Tapajós River empties its clear blue-green waters into the brownish waters of the Amazon. The Portuguese colonial town is a mixture of a busy port with the hustle and bustle of goods being loaded and unloaded, and a sleepy village with lovely cobblestone streets and horse-drawn carts.

Alan and I find a small hotel at the edge of town and decide to stay for five days. It'll be easy to get around here, as the forest is nearby. Manaus and Óbidos didn't pan out, but maybe we'll find salamanders in Santarém.

16 July 1970

"Alan, come quickly! I found a salamander!" I shout with glee. It's about time. It's just where it should be, perched on a leaf about a meter above the ground.

Upon closer inspection, however, I realize my small elongated brown find is actually a slug. Chagrined, I suggest that we leave the forest and search the curled banana leaves near our hotel. I'm still not convinced that there aren't any salamanders here.

An hour later we still haven't seen a salamander, so we visit a pond and record mating calls of the giant monkey frog. This is Alan's favorite Brazilian frog, ever since we found one clinging to the faucet in the bathroom shower back in Belém. Giant monkey frogs walk in slow motion, as if on tranquilizers, and their big brown eyes bulge out from their dark green heads.

Men from the Mayoruna tribe along the Brazilian border with Peru use giant monkey frogs' skin secretions as a drug for "hunting magic." Captive frogs are harassed until they release defensive secretions from glands in their skin. The secretions are then dried. Before a hunting excursion, the man inflicts burns on his arms or chest and spreads the dried powder into the open wounds, where the drug rapidly enters the bloodstream. Repeated and intense vomiting, elevated pulse rate, and incontinence follow and last up to an hour. The recipient then lapses into a state of listlessness, sometimes described as a feeling of being very drunk. This state lasts from one to several days. Eventually the person awakes and feels godlike in strength, euphoric in mind, and confident of a successful hunt because his senses are sharpened.

Giant monkey frog, perched on shower faucet.

18 July 1970

We fly from Santarém to Belém today, over vast expanses of green forests and winding rivers that disgorge their contents into the Amazon. Our three-week trip was wonderful, one that neither of us will forget. But I'll always wonder whether there really are no salamanders along the Amazon, or whether they were just out of sight, snickering at us.

This evening we have a consolation meal of *pato no tucupi,* one of my favorite Brazilian specialties: duck served in a yellow broth made from the juice of manioc root and the herb *jambu.* Alan especially likes the numbing effect of the *jambu.* During dinner I outline to Alan our goal for the last two weeks in Belém—to tie up some loose ends for my masters thesis.

25 July 1970

I've been totaling the numbers of species in each of the habitat types. The results reveal that both frogs and lizards prefer the less wet forests. I've found twenty species of frogs and fifteen species of lizards in the terra firme (high ground) forest. In the varzea (swamp forest, flooded daily), I've found twenty-two species of frogs and fifteen species of lizards. In contrast, in the igapo (permanently flooded forest) I've encountered only thirteen species of frogs and eight species of lizards. The one species of salamander is found in all three habitats.

This afternoon Alan and I make one last trip to Ver-O-Peso to stock up on unusual gifts for friends: small glass bottles of "perfume" that purportedly attract love, although the fluid smells like a mixture of sweat and urine to me; packages of unknown herbs that, when boiled into a tea, bring happiness, love, and money; and tiny glass vials with beads, bird

Alan and Cerpa.

feathers, and bits of colored stones. We're not sure what benefits accrue from possession of these vials, but everyone was buying them so they must be good for something.

Then we visit the animal market. Alan falls in love with a green and yellow parrot, who chatters nonstop at us in Portuguese. We talk with the vendor, who assures us it would be no problem to import the parrot to the United States. "Gringos do it all the time." After signing all the paperwork, we follow the vendor's instructions and take the bird and the paperwork to a government office, where we get more papers and buy stamps for the official documents. We're legal now. On the way home Alan christens his parrot "Cerpa," after his favorite Brazilian beer. This evening we stay in and chat with Cerpa. He has quite a vocabulary, including certain Portuguese words that shouldn't be used in polite company.

3 August 1970

Our departure day has arrived. Cerpa is traveling in a small cage inside a padded carry-on. Alan and I are quiet during the flight. No doubt his thoughts are parallel to mine—contemplations and reflections on the past six weeks. Our time together has been special. Alan was only nine years old when I left for college. Since then I've seen him only two or three weeks each year. This has been a unique opportunity to get reacquainted. Alan has been a tremendous help this summer, and he provided companionship that gave me the courage to strike out on an unknown adventure.

After clearing immigration, we claim our luggage and wheel the cart to customs, where we declare Cerpa. Although the agent says all our papers are in order, Cerpa must stay in routine quarantine in New York City for forty days at a cost to us of $10 per day. Alan and I gasp; we don't have $400. Alternatively, we can donate Cerpa to the Bronx Zoo, and the zoo will pay for quarantine. We have no choice. Eyes brimming with tears, we hand over Cerpa and slowly leave the customs area. We comfort each other in the thought that many people will enjoy watching Cerpa at the zoo, especially those who understand his Portuguese.

3

FIELD COURSE IN COSTA RICA

S OON AFTER I returned from Brazil, I applied for an ecology field course in Costa Rica—a course that would prove to be the most stimulating one I took in graduate school. Rising before dawn, we censused howler monkey troops—and learned about their characteristic defensive behavior. During the day we watched hummingbirds slurp nectar from showy red flowers; dung beetles roll their treasures across pastures; "Jesus Christ" lizards run across the surface of the water. At night we mist-netted bats and recorded frog calls. We (four women, nine men) were students from thirteen universities, participating in a field course of the Organization for Tropical Studies (OTS). The two-month-long course exposed me and my twelve fellow students to a wide range of tropical habitats and diverse organisms, from climbing vines and orchids to tent-building bats. Our intellectual curiosity was piqued and expanded through group and individual field projects, discussions with faculty and visiting scientists, lectures, and day-to-day interchange with each other. We formed academic associations and friendships that last till this day.

OTS was established in 1963 as an educational and research consortium of six North American universities and the University of Costa Rica. Professors from these seven universities shared the common goal of developing a center where students could gain firsthand field experience in tropical biology. They all agreed that a consortium could better provide the breadth of resources required to educate a cadre of tropical biologists than could any single institution. Over the years, more than fifty academic and research institutions from the United States, Puerto Rico, and Costa Rica have joined the consortium. More than three thousand students have participated in OTS field courses focusing on tropical ecology, forestry, agriculture, and conservation biology. Many of us have come away dedicated to pursuing research in the tropics.

14 April 1971

As I slump into my plane seat en route to Costa Rica for the OTS course, I reassure myself that whatever didn't get done will either take care of itself or disappear. During the past three months, I finished writing my master's thesis and successfully defended it, suffered a bout of mononucleosis, and passed my Ph.D. qualifying exam. After my OTS course in Costa Rica, I'll fly to Ecuador to begin thirteen months of fieldwork at Santa Cecilia for my doctoral research.

With my newly acquired Portuguese, I've forgotten the Spanish I learned in Ecuador two and a half years ago. Back to the books. *No hablo español. No entiendo. ¿Como estás? Muy bien, gracias. Buenos días. ¿Donde está el baño?*

15 April 1971

Our first day in San José begins with a lecture on Costa Rica, a small country about the size of West Virginia. Chains of rugged volcanic mountains stretch nearly the length of the country. On the eastern side, the Caribbean coastline is relatively smooth, the coastal plain is wide, tides are small, and rain falls nearly year-round. In contrast, a narrower plain runs along the Pacific coast, which is often rugged and rocky, with many gulfs and peninsulas.

On his fourth and last voyage to the New World, Christopher Columbus landed on the Caribbean coast near what is now Puerto Limón, Costa Rica, on 18 September 1502. The Spanish named the land Costa Rica, which means "rich coast," because local Indians told them tales of nearby gold deposits. Although early Spaniards didn't find gold, many of them stayed on. They tried to enslave the resident Indians to work the land, but fierce resistance and the death of many Indians through European-introduced diseases forced the Spaniards to cultivate their own land. Costa Rica remained a Spanish colony until September 1821, when all of Spain's colonies in Central America declared independence. Costa Rica abolished its army in 1948 and since then has been known as "the little country without an army." We are told that Costa Ricans are extremely proud of this fact and of their long heritage of democracy.

We also hear lectures on the geological history of Costa Rica, climate, and geographical characteristics. Our last lecture of the afternoon concerns health hazards: sunstroke, diarrhea, insects, and blisters. It all sounds fairly benign until we get to snakebite. Of the approximately 120 species of snakes in the country, sixteen are venomous. We are told not to be frightened of venomous snakes. Just respectful.

20 April 1971

We're in the province of Guanacaste, several hours northwest of San José, where we'll visit two field sites in dry forest habitat. One is a large working farm, Hacienda La Pacífica, located about five kilometers north of the town of Cañas. In the late 1950s, part of the land at La Pacífica was cleared to grow medicinal plants for a Swiss pharmaceutical company; but when this venture failed, La Pacífica was turned into a highly diversified agricultural enterprise. Crops of cotton, rice, sorghum, corn, soybeans, and fruit now dot the landscape, and cattle graze in pastures. Unlike most other working farms in the province, at La Pacífica over a quarter of the 1,330 hectares have been left as native forest in an attempt to strike a balance between exploitation of natural resources and conservation of those same resources. Our second site is Finca Taboga, an experimental agricultural station operated by the Costa Rican Ministry of Agriculture. Taboga is located about fifteen kilometers south of Cañas. Both sites are tropical dry forest, with wetter evergreen forest along rivers and streams. It's the end of the dry season here now.

YESTERDAY ONE of the instructors lectured about diversity of Costa Rican bats. There are 103 species known from this tiny country, as compared to about forty in the entire United States. Depending on the species, the bats may have big or little eyes, big or little ears, big or little mouths, big or little feet, even big or little brains. Some look very much like the little brown bats common in the United States. Others, such as leaf-nosed bats, have bizarre faces: nostrils surrounded by a fleshy fold and a spear-shaped leaf rising above and behind the nostrils. Not just for show, the leaf functions as a dish antenna to focus echolocation. Especially peculiar is the wrinkle-faced bat. Large bulging eyes peer out from its flat naked face, covered with wartlike outgrowths, folds, and flaps of skin. A deep fold of loose skin on the chin, drawn over the face when the bat is roosting, hides its face from view, almost as though it were embarrassed about its appearance.

Whereas almost all species in the United States eat insects, Costa Rican bats have diverse diets. During flight some species pluck figs from trees, sleeping birds and lizards from branches, insects from leaves, or swimming fish from water. Others snatch flying insects, hover over flowers to feed on nectar and pollen, swoop to the ground to snag calling frogs, or lap blood from sleeping victims.

When they're not feeding, bats spend most of their time sleeping. Costa Rican bats exploit an amazing variety of roost sites, not just attics and caves. Some sleep in rock crevices or exposed on shaded tree trunks. Some roost in colonies in hollow trees, others individually in foliage. One species sleeps in the rolled-up emerging leaves of wild plantain and must find new retreats every few days as the leaves mature and unfurl. Tent-building bats modify banana and palm leaves to form protective shelters. With their teeth they cut a line down each side of the leaf midrib, causing the sides of the leaf to collapse. Several or even dozens of sleeping bats hang together from a single midrib, protected inside the drooping leaf.

Less is known concerning social behavior of Costa Rican bats, but what we do know is tantalizing. Whereas individuals of some species stay together as pairs for long periods of time, males of other species defend territories and maintain harems. Females of common vampire bats form stable groups of up to a dozen individuals that roost together, feed in the same area, and even share food by regurgitating blood for each other. Male vampires are less social and compete with each other for dominance over groups of females.

THIS MORNING we start a field project on howler monkeys at Finca Taboga. Howler monkeys live almost exclusively in tree canopies, where they feed on buds, leaves, fruits, and flowers. Troops hang out in fairly small areas, which they defend with loud territorial calls. The best time to find troops of howler monkeys is at dawn when they announce their locations by roaring. A howling chorus begins when a male utters an accelerating series of deep grunts that grade into prolonged roars. Females join in with higher-pitched roars, creating a ruckus that can be heard over a distance of several kilometers. We'll collect data on the ages, sexes, and numbers of animals in the troops, and then compare these data with another set that we'll take when we return in June during the wet season.

Before dawn we hike to an area where many howler troops live. As the sky lightens, we hear roars from many directions. Each of us chooses a direction and heads out to find the troop. Using binoculars, we record numbers in each sex and age class.

My troop has two adult males, five adult females, three juveniles, and one infant. The infant clings to its mother the entire three hours of my observation. Both lethargic males remain draped over branches, looking bored with the world. Several of the females and juveniles munch on leaves.

As I get up to leave, the real reason why our instructors assigned us this project suddenly hits me in the face—almost literally. Our clever professors want us to experience firsthand a characteristic howler monkey behavior. My backpack falls noisily onto a pile of dried branches. One of the large male howlers above me, no longer bored, reacts by throwing a pile of freshly produced feces at me, barely missing. Partly horrified, partly amused, I quickly hike over to the designated meeting place to share what I thought was a unique experience. For the next twenty minutes, the other students straggle in with their own howler stories. One hadn't dodged the barrage of feces quite so effectively as I had. Hard nuts landed on another student's head. Branches bombarded a third. A fourth was sprayed with urine. The main conclusion from our morning's project is that howlers should be observed only from the side, not from beneath.

23 April 1971

Last night we mist-netted bats at Finca Taboga and caught many of the species we'd learned about during lectures, including nectar, fruit, insect, and blood-eating species. Hardest to untangle was the common vampire bat. Equipped with long razor-sharp upper incisors, these bats live on the blood of other mammals, including humans and cattle. A bat lands on or near the intended victim. It then crawls to a relatively naked patch of skin where it can get a good supply of blood near the surface—around the eyes, lips, ears, feet, base of tail, or anus. It sinks its sharp teeth into the skin and scoops out a small piece of flesh without waking its victim. The bat's saliva has an anticoagulant, which causes the blood to flow freely and allows the bat to lap from the wound by capillary action. Vampires can be a serious public health and agricultural threat not just because they carry rabies, but also because the wounds they cause may continue to hemorrhage and become infected.

Everyone's favorite was the imposing false vampire bat, the largest bat in the New World with a wingspan wider than the length of my arm. As we extracted the handsome beast from the net, he threatened with open jaws lined with large canines and shearing molars used for chewing birds, rodents, and other bats. (The "vampire" part of the name is a misnomer, in reference to the belief of early explorers that this huge fierce-looking creature must be "the" vampire and must surely suck blood from its victims.) After taking photographs, we released "Bruno." As he flew off, I wondered

False vampire bat, securely held by a glove-protected human hand.

if I would have nightmares of a monstrous bat swooping down, jaws poised to sink knife-sharp teeth into my flesh—revenge for the agony and terror "Bruno" experienced while entangled in the mist net, handled by bare-skinned, wingless giants, and blinded by strobe lights.

WE CONTINUE to learn about the local fauna. My favorites from today are the dung beetles busily extracting their chunks of cattle dung from the mother lode. Dung is rich in nutrients, so it's not surprising that many scarab beetles take advantage of this plentiful source of food. Odors wafting from a freshly dumped pile of dung attract beetles from all directions. Many species patiently shape their chunks into round balls that they roll across the pasture to underground burrows. Often the male and female work together to roll the ball, which is larger than themselves. Others dig burrows next to dung piles and carry their shares to the bottom. Once the dung has been delivered to the burrow, the female lays her eggs on the ball. Upon hatching, her young have a bountiful nutritious food source. In some species the adults snitch a bit of dung for a meal.

Different species of dung beetles prefer different types of dung. One tiny species goes after bird droppings. Several rainforest species collect monkey dung from leaves high in trees and then plummet to the ground clutching their treasures. In a pasture we find one fresh cow pie with ten different species working on it. We're told that a pile of horse dung may disappear in three days from the combined activity of half a dozen species of dung beetles.

28 April 1971

We started our individual research projects several days ago. Mine focuses on the spatial distribution of certain amphibians and reptiles. Animals are rarely distributed randomly with respect to others of the same species. Usually they're either clumped (as in flocks, schools, or breeding aggregations), or they're rather evenly spaced (as when territories are defended, or when food is scarce and each individual needs a certain minimal area for foraging). I plan to study spacing patterns of anole lizards in Guanacaste, poison dart frogs at the Osa Peninsula, and dink frogs at San Vito.

Here at La Pacífica I'm observing copper anoles along a fence line. My study site consists of fifty fence posts, three strands of barbed wire running between the posts, and vegetation within two meters on either side of the fence. Five times each day I map the location of each lizard and measure the distance between individuals. Thirty-two lizards are residents of this area. Males maintain more or less equal distances between other males by defending territories. They extend their dewlaps and vigorously bob their heads up and down in a display that announces their presence and warns intruders. Most of the females hang out within the territories of the males.

I must confess that in addition to watching anoles, I'm enjoying watching the resident leaf-cutter ants. They're just as industrious as the ones I've watched in Ecuador and Brazil. They even look the same. Curiously, I haven't seen a lizard try to eat a leaf-cutter ant. Perhaps they know better. I picked up one that was carrying a bit of orange flower to get a better look at it, and the ant promptly sank its mandibles into my finger.

6 May 1971

We're on the Osa Peninsula now, a frog haven of hot and humid tropical wet forest on the Pacific coast in the far south of the country. Yesterday Roy McDiarmid, our course coordinator, gave us a lecture on his research here concerning two common frogs that live side by side along the streams: plantation glass frogs and La Palma glass frogs. Last night we waded in the stream and watched the frogs for ourselves.

Glass frogs truly deserve their name because many species have transparent skin on their undersides through which the liver, beating heart, and other internal organs are visible. These delicate green frogs lay their eggs on leaves above running water. Males of both species call from the undersides of leaves at night to advertise their territories and to attract females. After eggs are deposited on the undersides of leaves and are fertilized by the males, the females take off. The males are left to attend the offspring and call in other females to lay additional clutches on the same leaf. Although most males attend fewer than three clutches at a time, some real studs have up to eight, each from a different female. Plantation glass frogs lay about fifty eggs per clutch, La Palma glass frogs about thirty. After attending their eggs all night, at daybreak male plantation glass frogs move to surrounding vegetation and curl up on the undersides of leaves, where they spend the day sleeping. In contrast, male La Palma glass frogs stay with their eggs day and night, poised for defense against small wasps and other egg predators.

Which species is more successful? It turns out that adults of both species produce about the same number of tadpoles. They just do it in different ways. Plantation glass frogs lay more eggs than the other species, but a higher percentage of eggs are eaten by predators, perhaps because they're left unguarded during the day.

11 May 1971

Cereal, beans, and rice for breakfast, then I'm off to continue my study of spacing patterns. This time I'll watch poison dart frogs, the fascinating little creatures that lay eggs on the ground and carry their tadpoles to water. The species here on the Osa Peninsula is the granular poison dart frog, so named because its skin is covered with small bumps. These frogs have bright red bodies, smaller than the diameter of a nickel, and blue legs.

I soon learn that male granular poison dart frogs call throughout the day, each advertising his territory to other males and attempting to entice females. They often call from elevated perches, which may allow their calls to be heard from greater distances than if they were earthbound and may help them to keep tabs on the surrounding area. Because this species is territorial, I predict the frogs should have a fairly regular distribution within the habitat. Sure enough, my measurements of distances between seventeen pairs of calling males reveal that the minimum distance is 3.1 meters, the maximum 4.8 meters. That means a male probably defends an area of at least a 1.5 meter radius, an area in which he'll have exclusive access to females and to insect prey.

If one male wanders into the territory of another, the resident calls out a challenge and physical combat often ensues. In order to watch a battle more closely, I gently place one male on the ground about a half meter from another male and then crouch down. Immediately the resident male calls. Both frogs raise up high on their front legs and charge toward one another. They wrestle fiercely for nearly ten minutes, until the intruder breaks off and hops several meters away. The resident male, looking very self-important and pleased with himself, returns to his log and resumes calling.

13 May 1971

Hunkered down on the ground, I watch a male granular poison dart frog calling from an exposed tree root. Soon he turns 180 degrees, raises his body up high on his front legs, fills his vocal sac with air, and once again energetically belts out his advertisement call. Within a few minutes a bright red, blue-legged female hops over a log to within three meters.

He continues to call. The female forages for insects in the leaf litter, then gradually approaches the male. She certainly seems coy. Once she's within a few body lengths of the male, he approaches her, then turns and hops in a different direction. She follows him. Whenever the female lags more than about twenty centimeters behind, the male stops, calls, and waits for her to catch up. The male leads the female for fifteen minutes until he crawls into a dried, partially curled-up leaf. She follows him inside. In awe, I watch as the frogs court each other in an elaborate and very sensual manner. Much of the time the male calls softly as the female rubs her head against his head and chin, then turns and raises her back end in front of his head. Following the sixth of these sequences, the male turns and touches his rear end to hers. I watch her expel three eggs. The male moves slightly, presumably releasing sperm onto the eggs. Both frogs sit next to the eggs for a few minutes, then Dad hops ten centimeters away and calls loudly as if to brag about what he has just accomplished. The female stays with the eggs for about thirty minutes, then hops away. Dad remains near his eggs and calls for the next two hours.

This evening I find him sleeping near the eggs. I borrow the eggs for an hour, examine them under a microscope, and determine that they are indeed fertilized—fertilized without normal frog-style mating behavior.

Mating behavior in frogs and toads normally involves the male climbing onto the back of the female and clasping her either in her armpits or around her waist with his front legs and feet. While the female is being clasped, she deposits eggs and the male then releases sperm onto them.

But I observed no clasping behavior in these poison dart frogs. For granular poison dart frogs, the complex "foreplay" may function to ensure that both partners are committed to the result: fertilized eggs, which the male then guards. Elaborate courtship may synchronize the timing so that the eggs are fertilized as soon as they are released by the female.

Helmeted iguana, in a frozen pose against a tree trunk.

IT'S SUCH great fun to sit motionless in the forest and watch as animals go about their business. Today while watching the frogs, I see a brown figure scurry across the ground—a helmeted iguana. It dashes partway up a tree trunk a meter from me and then freezes. Its brown-splotched body is perfectly camouflaged against the bark. After a few minutes it methodically moves its outrageously crested head back and forth, as if to scan its surroundings. Perhaps it is waiting for a large unsuspecting insect to walk by. Or perhaps it is watching out for its predators.

Later I see something large flying slowly along the path toward me—an electric-blue pair of wings lazily gliding and flapping through the air. This shimmering display belongs to the morpho, a huge butterfly with a wingspan much broader than my hand is long. As it dances through the forest, I wonder how I would feel in the body of a morpho. The butterfly lands on a large leaf near me and folds its wings together. The extravagance is hidden. All that remains are the mundane brown underwings.

20 May 1971

My last few days at the Osa Peninsula continued to be successful as I watched the courtship of three additional pairs of granular poison dart frogs. Each pair displayed the same elaborate tactile courtship but no clasping behavior. This type of mating behavior in frogs has never been observed in the field, so I plan to write up my observations for publication.

WE'RE NOW at about a thousand meters elevation, at Finca Las Cruces near the town of San Vito in southeastern Costa Rica. Although most of the surrounding landscape has been converted for agriculture, a small patch of rain forest bathed in nearly continual cloud cover remains at Las Cruces. A fairly open forest canopy allows light to penetrate to the abundant ferns on the forest floor and to the mosses and bromeliads that cover the tree branches. In 1963 Robert and Catherine Wilson moved from the United States to Finca Las Cruces, where they created a magnificent botanical garden composed of ornamental plants from all over the world. The Wilsons welcome OTS courses to work in their garden, so we will make use of this unique resource.

During our first orientation walk, one of the students finds a larva of the giant swallowtail butterfly—the classic bird-dropping caterpillar. Mottled olive green and brown with white blotches, it looks just like a bird turd. When the student pokes it, the caterpillar everts its "stink horns" (projections near the head associated with glands) and gives off a foul-smelling odor, obviously meant to deter predators.

28 May 1971

This morning each of us sits in front of a patch of flowers in the botanical garden and watches hummingbirds. We're surrounded by yellow and red pinecone-like flowers of wild ginger, showy passion flowers, green flowers curving up from the sturdy red bracts of wild plantain, and dainty bright yellow "rattlesnake plant" flowers peeking out from a series of large yellow bracts structured very much like a rattlesnake's rattle. Our objective is simple: watch closely and learn.

We see eleven species of hummingbirds visiting ten species of flowers. Several kinds of flowers are quite popular, receiving forty-three to sixty-three visits, while others in the garden receive none. Some of the hummingbird species, for example the rufous-breasted hermit, visit only one species of flower. Others, such as the white-tailed emerald and the rufous-tailed hummingbird, visit several different kinds. We see the two contrasting foraging modes of hummingbirds. Some hummingbirds visit, but don't defend, sequences of small isolated clumps of flowers, scattered about the landscape. They appear to revisit their "traplines" when enough

Lobelia, pollinated by hummingbirds with very curved bills.
Photo by Peter Feinsinger.

new nectar has accumulated to make the revisit worthwhile. More bellicose individuals, sometimes males of the same species or other species entirely, stay at a single large clump of flowers and defend it against all intruders. We measure the length of the flower tubes and from the literature obtain measurements of the average bill lengths of the hummingbird species. Just as we expected, hummers with short bills sip nectar from short-tubed flowers. Those with long bills slurp from long-tubed flowers.

I've been continuing my study of spacing by measuring nearest neighbor distances of about a hundred calling Agua Buena dink frogs. My study site of dense vegetation growing along the edges of roads isn't very exciting. But that's where the frogs are. They seem to prefer the dense clumps of plants, whose bases provide ideal calling sites as well as protection from predators. Within the suitable habitat, however, males seem to space themselves at random.

7 June 1971

Rainy season has begun in the northwest. We're back in Guanacaste, and what a difference the rain makes. Temperatures are cooler. Vegetation is green and lush. And the frogs are active.

Last night we heard the deafening whooping calls of the Mexican burrowing frog, a call reminiscent of a vomiting college freshman who's had too much to drink. These comical frogs have plump, loose-skinned bodies propped on short fat legs, and pointed pea heads with tiny black eyes. When males call, their entire bodies inflate, resembling balloons about to pop. Much of the year the frogs remain underground in burrows they dig with their hind feet. The tadpoles look just as bizarre as the adults. The wide mouth is bordered by barbels and extends across the entire front of the broad, flat head, much like a catfish. Although they eat mainly algae, if conditions become crowded and food becomes limited, the tadpoles sometimes use their unusually large mouths to eat their comrades instead.

This afternoon I spend a delightful few hours watching "Jesus Christ" lizards along the river. The common name stems from the fact that these large brown semi-aquatic lizards run on their back legs across the surface of the water. Juveniles, much more agile than the large clumsy adult males, can run up to twenty meters across the surface without sinking. The trick is that they run very quickly on large hind feet outfitted with flaps of skin along each toe. The lizards run primarily when frightened, so whenever one senses my presence and freaks out, I'm treated to a performance.

Male Jesus Christ lizards resemble miniature sailfin dinosaurs, with large crests on their heads, backs, and tails. An adult male can reach a meter in length, three-quarters of which is tail. Females are much smaller and have only a small crest on the back of the head. Jesus Christ lizards sleep on vegetation overhanging the water at night and drop below when disturbed. They eat just about anything that fits into their mouths—fruits, flowers, insects, shrimp, fish, hatchling lizards, small snakes, birds, and mammals.

8 June 1971

The head of a white maggot bobs up and down through a small opening in my wrist. Overjoyed by my predicament, one of the course instructors calls everyone over and lectures us on the biology of my wrist visitor—a bot fly larva.

Bot flies are stout, hairy, black parasitic flies, almost beelike in appearance. In the tropics their main hosts are cattle and other large mammals (including humans), which they exploit in a unique and clever way. A fertilized female bot fly catches a mosquito or some other bloodsucking flying insect and attaches her eggs to its abdomen, then releases her captive. When this insect then alights on a host (for example, me) to feed, the warmth of the skin induces the eggs to hatch into tiny larvae. The larvae, or bots, crawl down the bloodsucking insect's legs, burrow into the host's skin, and once settled in they feed on tissues and fluids. The larva constructs a breathing hole in the skin, through which it extends its snorkel-like spiracle to obtain air. A boil-like lesion eventually forms. If allowed to run their course, in a human host the larvae take about fifty to sixty days to mature, at which time they exit, fall to the ground, and pupate. Eventually an adult fly emerges from the pupa. It then mates. If it's a female, it catches a mosquito and lays her eggs on its abdomen; the mosquito sucks blood from some other unsuspecting host, and the cycle begins again.

The cook for the course, a self-professed expert on dealing with bot fly larvae, rallies to my cause after the lecture. He explains that you don't want to grab the maggot with tweezers and yank it out, because the unwanted guest will hold on to the inside of its breathing hole with its strong hooks. If the body snaps in two and part is left inside, secondary infection is likely. The cook suggests three alternative techniques for covering the breathing hole so that the creature will have to emerge partway to breathe: a piece of raw meat, a slab of butter, or a piece of masking tape. I choose the tape. After a few hours the cook removes the tape and grabs the larva with tweezers as, gasping for air, it extends its body out of the opening. He puts the larva in a small glass vial with alcohol, winks, and tells me to keep it for good luck.

10 June 1971

Now I see why the instructor was so eager to discuss my bot fly. Our group project for today is to return to our howler monkey site at Finca Taboga and repeat our census of troop structure. In addition, we are to survey the monkeys for bot flies. We awaken at 4:30 A.M., then spend the next several hours craning our necks toward the canopy. With binoculars glued to our eyes, we count the number of swollen bot fly sores we see on each monkey. Luckily for the howlers, we see evidence of fewer bot flies than the instructors expected. All of us are now vigilant, remembering our previous experiences, and handily avoid the objects or liquids the howlers rain down on us. We compare the composition of troops during April with the composition now and find no real difference—further evidence that the instructors' covert reason for the project was to subject us to the defensive behaviors of howlers.

16 June 1971

We drove back to San José three days ago, then spent two days writing and typing our individual project reports. After a late-night farewell party, I board my plane to Quito, Ecuador. En route I marvel over what I've learned in the past two months. My head is spinning with ideas that will form the foundation for years of research to come. My souvenir vial with the bot fly larva is packed in my suitcase. I wonder if I'll ever return to Costa Rica.

The Many Ways
to Beget a Frog

PHYSICALLY EXHAUSTED but mentally energized by the OTS course in Costa Rica, I staggered down the steps of the plane and crossed the runway into the busy airport terminal in Quito. It felt good to be back in Ecuador. It'd been three years since my first encounter with tropical frogs at Santa Cecilia. At that time I had been amazed by the diversity of the fauna, from the gaudy color patterns of treefrogs to the bizarre shapes of the Surinam toad and the egg-brooding horned treefrog. Even more fascinating, however, had been the wide variety of ways these frogs reproduce: eggs developing out of water, frogs carrying their tadpoles to water, females carrying eggs stuck to their backs. Now I was returning with National Science Foundation support, for thirteen months, to take a closer look at these frogs and their fascinating variety of life histories. The research would provide the basis for my Ph.D. dissertation.

Because my adviser, Bill Duellman, was well aware of my propensity to get lost in the forest, he scrounged some funds to support a field assistant for me. John Simmons, an undergraduate student working in the Herpetology Division at the museum, was thrilled to take a breather from calculus and chemistry to accompany me on a tropical adventure. John and I returned to Muñozlandia to stay with our hosts, Ildefonso and Blanca Muñoz. They had built me a small, one-room wooden cabin, painted it white, and topped it off with a shiny tin roof. John lived in one of the older bamboo and thatch huts. For our houses, three daily meals, and weekly laundry service we each paid $5 per day.

24 June 1971

Times have changed. There is now an airstrip at the newly founded oil town of Lago Agrio, sixteen kilometers east of Santa Cecilia. If space permits, Texaco allows locals to fly to and from Quito on their small plane, so this morning we fly directly from Quito. Several of the town prostitutes are our traveling companions. The women eye me suspiciously, conclude that I'm no competition, and then ignore me. I feel awkward and very unglamorous. I'm wearing no makeup and my clothes aren't particularly attractive from a male's point of view. I retreat by staring out the window most of the flight. There are beautiful views of first the snow-covered Andes and then the carpet of green vegetation that covers the eastern slope.

One of Ilde's Texaco buddies, Scotty, meets our plane and gives us a quick tour of Lago Agrio before driving us to Muñozlandia. Scotty hails from Oklahoma. His rugged frame, leathery skin, and squinty blue eyes are classic traits of the experienced oilman who loves adventure and the thrill of new places just as much as he loves his considerable tax-free income.

Muñozlandia in 1971. My house is the larger white structure with the tin roof; the smaller white structure with a tin roof to the left is the outhouse. The laboratory is the large thatched building behind the latter. The Río Aguarico flows in the background.

Lago Agrio is a small, filthy oil town springing up next to the camp where Texaco personnel have relocated their operations from Santa Cecilia. The Texaco camp appears clean and comfortable by jungle standards. Town is another matter. The streets of Lago Agrio are dirt, and because it rained recently we are soon ankle-deep in mud. Pigs roam freely, rooting in the garbage. Scrawny dogs compete with them for scraps. The Río Aguarico that borders one side of town doubles as an open sewer for human wastes and a bathtub for residents. The oilmen are mostly husky, rugged Texans or Oklahomans, with booming southern drawls. Their six-foot-plus frames tower above their Ecuadorian counterparts. Most of the women in town are prostitutes, taking advantage of the golden opportunity. Very few children live in town . . . as yet. There are no schools or churches.

Scotty drives us to Muñozlandia in his flaming orange heavy-duty four-wheel drive pickup. We bounce along the mud road slashed through the jungle, with the shining silver pipeline always within sight. With construction of the road from Quito to Lago Agrio, colonists have flooded in from all over the country. They've replaced the lush forest with *yuca* and *plátanos*. Many of the local Quechuas have abandoned their homes along the river in order to relocate next to the road. They no longer rely solely on their piraguas for travel. Now they hitchhike.

Santa Cecilia itself has changed dramatically since I left three years ago. After Texaco relocated to Lago Agrio, the Ecuadorian army claimed the base. The soldiers are uncomfortable with the forest crowding in on them, so they've cleared away the vegetation from around their compound. Even Muñozlandia has expanded. The largest and most impressive new building is a round structure made of bamboo and thatch—Ilde's bar and dance floor.

But some things never change, such as Ilde and Blanca. I'm looking forward to being their foster daughter for the year.

5 July 1971

I plan to study reproductive ecology in what we now realize is the most species-rich assemblage of frogs known anywhere in the world: eighty-one species in an area of about three square kilometers. In comparison, there are only eighty species of frogs in the entire continental United States and Canada combined. Florida, the state with the greatest richness, can boast only thirty-one species of frogs. Why is the diversity of frogs so high at Santa Cecilia? Part of the answer is the geographic location. Because Santa Cecilia lies between the lowland Amazon Basin and the cooler eastern slopes of the Andes, it provides a home for widespread frog species and is also well within the range of species that spill over from the nearby eastern slopes of the Andes and those typical of the Amazon Basin.

How can so many species coexist? My guess is that the eighty-one species coexist, in part, through their many different ways of reproducing. Perhaps as a result of this diversity, more species can pile up in a small area than if, for example, all followed the temperate-zone norm and laid their eggs in water and passed through a tadpole stage. My research will consist of two aspects. First, I'll characterize each species' reproductive pattern: number of eggs deposited, size of eggs, number of days required from laying until hatching, size of hatchlings, and type of development (tadpoles versus direct development from egg to froglet). Secondly, I'll document the details of where and when each species breeds.

I've set up my field schedule by dividing the next thirteen months into blocks of twenty days each. During each time block I'll record calling activity by males, reproductive condition of females, and presence of eggs for as many species of frogs as possible. In addition, during each time block I'll observe species' composition, abundance, and activity in four different areas of primary and secondary forest and at eight aquatic sites.

I've spent several days surveying the potential aquatic breeding sites and have chosen the eight that reflect the wide variety available to the frogs: five temporary water bodies (one set of ditches, four seasonal swamps) and three permanent (one chronic swamp, one pond, and one lake). I'll use existing paths in the four forest areas, three of which are fairly close to Muñozlandia. The fourth, dense primary forest three kilometers away, is a hike of two hours along a meandering, muddy trail.

John and I found the permanent swamp last night by homing in on a loud chorus of treefrogs. We've named it "Heliconia Swamp" in honor of the striking plantain plants that rise up more than two meters above the water surface. Wild plantain (*Heliconia*) has large banana-like leaves and showy brightly colored inflorescences reminiscent of bird-of-paradise plants: bright orange-red and yellow bracts from which yellow flowers curve upward. During the day hummingbirds dominate the swamp, defending clumps of flowers, sucking out their nectar, and inadvertently pollinating the flowers. Accumulated water in the sturdy bracts houses mosquito and beetle larvae. At night the leaves provide calling sites for a variety of treefrogs and egg-laying sites for leaf frogs.

The swamp is nearly impenetrable, so John and I have returned today to cut several paths around and through it. We spend quite awhile trying to figure out the shape of the swamp from the edge and finally conclude that we wouldn't make very good surveyors. As we wonder how to proceed, John suddenly shrieks and plunges into the water. "Ants!" he yells. "I'm covered!" Awhile later, once he extracts the last biting ant from underneath his clinging wet clothing, we realize that he's accidentally hit upon the best way to proceed: through the water. So I join him. With machetes we clear a narrow path the length of the swamp, then cut several perpendicular paths across to the other side. Several wasp stings later, as I climb

Wild plantain, *Heliconia*.

back onto dry land, I slip on a log, grab the first handy trunk to steady myself, realize too late it's a spiny palm, and receive a handful of black spines. Despite this inauspicious beginning, the swamp should be a great site because it's large enough to attract high densities of breeding frogs.

28 July 1971

Not unexpectedly, it has taken a few weeks for John and me to settle into a comfortable working relationship. At first I felt awkward because I'm not paying John to help me and thus didn't want to exploit him. But we're both easygoing. We've worked out the kinks and already have become best friends. John has a unique sense of humor. He says his self-appointed task is to "provide comic relief and keep Marty humble." We're not out to prove anything to each other. Furthermore, our roles here are very different. This is my research, and I call the shots. John is here to help me, but from his point of view, he's also here to sit back, kick up his feet, and take stock of his life and future. Already we seem to have an unspoken agreement that we must give each other space, yet support each other fully. We have no other colleague here.

Our first month has been productive. The laboratory tables are covered with plastic containers housing eggs and tadpoles. Rather than raise tadpoles to froglets as I did three years ago, now I just raise the eggs to the hatching stage, measure the newly emerged tadpoles, and then release them where I found the eggs or gravid females.

Plastic bags hang from the bamboo rafters in one corner of the lab. Each bag contains a leaf and a clutch of eggs from a leaf frog suspended above six to eight centimeters of water. The eggs resemble large white pearls at first. Then, when the embryos are a few days old, I can see the tiny black eyeballs and the tail fins through the capsules.

While carrying the male piggyback, a female leaf frog searches the shrubbery overhanging the water for a suitable leaf on which to deposit her eggs. The male has rough pads on his thumbs, which help in holding on to the female during this sometimes lengthy and bumpy ride. Eventually she finds an acceptable site and lays her eggs on the surface or outer tip of a leaf. In one species here, the brownbelly leaf frog, the female first releases a small mass of empty jelly capsules, followed by the eggs and then additional empty capsules. The empty jelly capsules probably serve as "plugs" that provide protection from the sun and dry air, and they may also provide fluid for the developing embryos and a buffer against predators. After fertilizing the eggs, the male folds the leaf around the eggs to form a closed nest.

Clutch of brownbelly leaf frog eggs, found in a rolled-up leaf. Note the empty jelly capsules on the top and bottom of the clutch, and the embryos' pairs of little black eyes.

On another table several clutches of dink frog eggs sit on moist soil in plastic refrigerator dishes. These eggs are large (3.5 millimeters) compared to eggs that are laid in water (1.0 to 2.0 millimeters). Dink frogs usually lay fewer than ten eggs, in moist secluded sites under leaf litter or beneath logs on the ground. The eggs are endowed with large quantities of yolk, providing all the nourishment the developing embryos need until they emerge from their capsules as miniature replicas of the adults. When fully developed, the tiny froglet rips through its jelly capsule by means of an "egg tooth," a horny projection on the tip of its snout.

Strings of marine toad eggs develop in a bucket on the floor. Toads lay their eggs in two strings, one from each ovary. Within a string, each egg is connected to the one before and after it, like beads on a necklace. Marine toad eggs are less than 1.5 millimeters each. The other day I painstakingly counted the number of eggs in a pair of strings from one female toad: 5,984 perfectly formed black-and-white pearls. If predators didn't eat huge quantities of eggs and tadpoles, all of Santa Cecilia would be overrun by marine toads in no time!

Tonight at Ilde's party in his new bar, John and I meet the five army officers from the Santa Cecilia base. All are friendly and at least superficially interested in our work. During a tour of the lab, Capitán Mario Durán seems especially intrigued with the leaf frog embryos wriggling inside their jelly capsules. He asks if some night he might accompany us to a swamp. We have fun dancing and trying to communicate in my very limited Spanish and his even more limited English.

6 August 1971

John and I hike up to the far primary forest area after dinner. Partway up the trail we both need to change batteries in our headlamps. Just as we extract the used batteries and are fumbling in our packs for the new ones, we hear very loud, heavy breathing from the bushes directly behind us. It's an animal, and whatever it is, it's BIG and it's MAD! Terrified, we load our headlamps and take off running along the muddy trail. My legs feel like cooked spaghetti, my hands are cold and clammy, and my neck is hot and sweaty. Once we slow down, recover our breath a bit, and reach a reasonable blood pressure, we try to puzzle out what the beast might have been. Neither of us has a clue. "It's an Asthmatic Monster," declares John.

After a successful field night, we leave the site about 1:00 A.M., tired and apprehensive about retracing our steps past the Asthmatic Monster. Sure enough, in the same place along the trail, we hear heavy breathing. "Run!" I gasp. Three minutes later I'm tangled in a tree root and fall facedown in the mud. John wheels around, thinking the creature is about to swallow me. He yanks me back onto my feet and off we gallop in utter panic.

20 August 1971

Tonight John and I force ourselves to revisit the primary forest site. We eat an early supper so we can walk the three kilometers before dark—

ostensibly to save headlamp batteries, but the real reason is we hope to avoid running into the monster in the dark. A ways off the path, but in the general area from where we heard the heavy breathing a few weeks ago, we see a huge white Brahma bull glaring and snorting at us. The neurons fire and we both realize at the same instant that here, in living flesh, is our Asthmatic Monster. Although we'll always have to be careful to avoid attracting the monster's baleful attention, we're glad to have identified it, since the known threat is always easier to face than the unknown.

23 August 1971

I turned twenty-five today. John surprised me at breakfast with the "World-Famous Marty's Birthday Songbook." Inside are his lyrics about life in the jungle set to familiar tunes: home where the cockroaches roam, days full of heat and at night dirty sheets, collecting frogs in muddy bogs, the burp of a ten-foot herp, fungus and bug bites.

Tonight we stuff ourselves on a rich chocolate and yellow layered cake that Blanca made, and then take our full bellies up to the fence-line trail and work until after midnight. The frogs surprise me with an orgy, a frenzy of calling, mating, and egg-laying activity. In grand style we vocally compete with the frogs by singing the lyrics that John composed to the tunes of "Home, Home on the Range," "Sloop J. B.," "Sweet Betsy from Pike," and "Clementine."

Back in Muñozlandia we gravitate to the kitchen for more birthday cake. As we wolf down the sugar, Ilde's pet monkey watches us intently. Do monkeys eat cake? Our sleepy and blurry eyes focus on the cockroaches scuttling across the dishes, the counters, the table, the cake. I comment to John that they act superior, as if they know they'll rule the earth someday. John rolls his eyes and counters that at least in Muñozlandia, they may have to compete with rats.

29 August 1971

Tonight Mario (Capitán Durán) joins John and me for a swamp survey. His presence gives the fieldwork a new dimension. Somehow it seems more fun, more exciting to share our finds with him. Mario responds like a little boy in a candy store, thrilled about every frog, lizard, or snake we find. As I explain my research, he seems genuinely interested and asks perceptive questions. The highlight of the evening is watching a pair of jaguar leaf frogs deposit and fertilize a clutch of white pearly eggs on a leaf above the water. After I tell Mario about the eggs' main predator, cat-eyed

Pet monkey, kept in the kitchen at Muñozlandia.

snakes, he insists that we search the vegetation for snakes with the intent of removing them to protect the eggs. When I point out that the snakes have to eat also, Mario reflects a moment and then nods in agreement.

Later Mario invites us to the officers' mess hall, where we spend the next three hours, until 3:15 in the morning, talking and drinking Coke. In mangled English and Spanish we discuss religion, Ecuadorian politics, frogs, and John's girlfriend back in Lawrence. When John leaves for a moment to investigate a frog calling nearby, Mario offers to give me daily Spanish lessons in his office. I readily agree, for I need to communicate more effectively in Spanish. And I must admit that I enjoy being with this dashing thirty-five-year-old army captain.

21 September 1971

Heavy rains have fallen recently. This afternoon as the rain starts, I count the individual drops falling on my tin roof. They become more and more frequent until they're indistinguishable from each other. Soon the rain pounds on the tin so forcefully I can't hear myself think. I feel the rain closing in on me. I'm trapped. Hours later the raindrops once again become distinguishable and eventually disappear. The silence brings relief to my scrambled nerves. As I open the door, I'm bombarded by the almost suffocatingly pungent smell of wet jungle vegetation.

The heat and humidity are starting to get to me. My leather shoes are fuzzy with green mold, even though I periodically rub formaldehyde over them. My damp and clammy sheets always smell musty. Sometimes the sultry air seems so thick I wonder how we can breathe. The heat leaves me lethargic by late afternoon. I'm revived only by a cold shower. Sometimes I take three per day. Fortunately, there's an endless supply of water flowing through the split-bamboo flume system from the spring above Muñozlandia.

Rain has stimulated frogs into breeding activity. The choruses of hundreds of pond-breeding frogs and toads are deafening, each species giving its own characteristic call. Why should a male join a chorus and compete for females with other males of his species rather than go off to call alone? One of the functions of a chorus is to enable females to cue in to the breeding site and the waiting males. The volume of sound produced by a chorus acts as a magnet, attracting far more females than would an isolated calling male. So even though he might rarely get the chance to court one of the females, each male still has a better chance of mating if he joins a chorus than if he calls alone. Females of most water-breeding species at Santa Cecilia have already ovulated by the time they arrive at the pond. They choose a male, enter into clasping behavior, and they're ready to lay eggs within an hour or two.

In contrast, individual male dink frogs chirp their insectlike calls while scattered throughout the forest. If a male is lucky, a female eventually approaches him, he clasps her, and they remain together for several hours or even days until the female ovulates. Because eggs are expensive to produce, it's advantageous for a female to delay ovulation until she's found an acceptable mate to fertilize her eggs. A female dink frog presumably has a more difficult time finding the ideal partner than does a female toad or treefrog that can choose from among hundreds of males congregated at a single pond.

INSTEAD OF doing fieldwork during a torrential downpour tonight, John and I play Ping-Pong with Mario and the other officers at the rec hall on the base. For the past three weeks, Mario has given me hour-long daily Spanish lessons focusing on grammar, vocabulary, and pronunciation. We're working on the three essential verb tenses: present, simple past, and future. In addition to improving my communication skills, I've had fun getting to know the captain. He's engaging, has a great sense of humor, and is a true gentleman.

10 October 1971

When I tire of thinking about breeding frogs, I switch my focus to the reptiles here, which are almost as fascinating. Green-and-brown dwarf iguanas scramble through the vegetation, impersonating miniature dragons with spiny crests running down their backs. Emerald tree boas coil around branches, lying in wait for unsuspecting birds. Flashes of red, yellow, and black rings slither through the undergrowth. Was it a coral snake or a coral snake mimic? Glowing red eye shines of spectacled caimans outline the perimeter of the lake at night. South American yellowfoot tortoises stumble along the forest floor on their short, stumpy legs.

Ilde has a matamata turtle that neighboring Quechuas caught in the river. It's his pride and joy, and he loves to show it off to visitors. No other turtle in the world is quite as bizarre, with its flattened body, broad head, mouth poised in a perpetual grin, and fleshy proboscis projecting from the

Head and neck of a matamata turtle, one of nature's more bizarre-looking creatures with a fleshy proboscis and a mouth poised in a perpetual grin.

snout. The turtle spends hours in the murky water of its concrete pen not moving a muscle, then suddenly lunges out to strike at a fish that swims too close.

I especially enjoy watching lizards forage. Most lizards here are opportunistic feeders. That is, if it's the right size, they'll eat it, their only rule being "never eat anything bigger than your head." Still, the methods used to capture prey are quite diverse. Recently I spent an afternoon watching lizards in a forest treefall gap. In the open area, several ameivas actively searched for prey. Ameivas are moderate-sized, very active ground-dwelling lizards with long tails. Males are brilliantly colored reddish brown and metallic green; the back legs are green with small blue spots. Frenetically, the ameivas scuttled about in the leaf litter, poking their heads in between the fallen leaves looking for insects, spiders, or other small moving prey. They are called "actively searching predators." In contrast, at the edge of the gap, I watched a small brown anole perched head-down on a tree trunk, waiting for something to move to within reach, at which point the anole darted after it. Like the matamata turtle, the anole is a classic example of a "sit-and-wait" predator.

12 November 1971

Dilapidated buses chug back and forth from Quito to Lago Agrio, each bringing more colonists. Considerable forest has been destroyed to install the 495-kilometer pipeline that carries oil from its home near Lago Agrio, up, over, and back down the Andes to the Pacific coast. Currently the pipeline has the dubious distinction of being the highest major oil pipeline in the world, crossing the Andes at nearly four thousand meters. I view the shiny silver monster snaking along the road as a major eyesore, but the locals seem to have incorporated it into their lives already. Women spread their laundry along it to dry. Children run and play on it. People of all ages sit on it and socialize day and night.

Low-lying depressions alongside the pipeline attract breeding treefrogs after puddles form, and high grass and thick weeds provide plenty of retreat sites for them. Insects with aquatic nymphs or larvae also lay their eggs soon after puddles form. Within days the water is a veritable organic soup of wriggling, swimming, diving, and dancing organisms. Mosquito larvae are innocuous to the tadpoles. Other insects, such as dragonfly nymphs, are voracious tadpole predators. Birds wade through the puddles by day and gobble up tadpoles, and snakes extract their share at night. Although the treefrogs lay many small eggs, only a few tadpoles are likely to survive the gauntlet of predators. The hot tropical sun exacts its share of damage

Pipeline along the road between Quito and Lago Agrio.

also, leaving behind masses of decaying eggs and tadpoles on bare ground. Fortunately, since these treefrogs breed throughout the year, an individual frog probably has multiple opportunities within its lifetime to replace itself.

6 December 1971

Today Ilde throws a party for his Texaco friends in celebration of one of the biggest public holidays in the country: *6 de deciembre* (6 December). Before his friends arrive, Ilde educates me about the holiday.

My history lesson begins with the late 1400s, when the Inca Indians from Peru penetrated northward and conquered the many different tribes of highland Indians living in what is present-day Ecuador. They united many of their subjects and taught them the Incan language, Quechua. By the 1530s the Inca Empire had two great centers, ruled by two brothers: Huáscar at Cuzco, Peru, and Atahualpa at what is now Quito, Ecuador. In 1532 Atahualpa won the civil war the brothers had fought against each other for the previous five years. Less than a year later, the ruthless Spanish explorer Francisco Pizarro and his army of fewer than 180 men ambushed Atahualpa and killed six thousand Incas, thus conquering the huge Inca Empire in Ecuador and Peru and opening the way for Spain's subsequent colonization of much of South America.

Pizarro traveled south to conquer and plunder Cuzco, while one of his lieutenants, Sebastián de Benalcázar, headed north through the Andes to do the same in what is now Ecuador. On 6 December 1534, Benalcázar marched into the great northern Inca city just after it had been burned by one of Atahualpa's generals—destroyed so that the Spanish could not pillage the gold and other riches. Benalcázar founded the town of San Francisco de Quito on the site of the ruins and ashes. The founding of Quito is now celebrated annually on 6 December with festivities that include bullfights, parades, and street dancing.

Scotty and his friend Joe come for the celebration. Months ago I saw them both as swaggering braggarts, chauvinistic and arrogant. In fact, most of the Texaco men I've met had struck me similarly. Now I realize that for many it's all a facade, a shell that enables them to survive each day in the jungle, where each man must constantly prove his worth and strength. Away from the peer pressure of all their Texaco buddies, Scotty and Joe are gentle, intelligent, considerate human beings. Scotty has two young kids and a wife who teaches elementary school back in Tulsa. Contrary to my initial assumption, he's hoping to save enough money from this jungle stint so that he can retire and spend more time with his family. Joe, who has no wife waiting for him back in Houston, says he, too, is getting tired of oil exploration adventures and is almost ready to settle down. He says he hopes his high school sweetheart will still be available in a few years, as he doesn't remember how to court a woman any longer. Joe is suffering through a bout of dysentery, so his spirits are especially low at the moment.

It's hard for me to cheer him up because I'm so confused I don't know what to think or feel. Recently my friendship with Mario has evolved into romance. John was surprisingly perceptive. A few weeks ago he told me that either Mario was falling in love with me, that I was falling in love with him, or both . . . to which I retorted, "You're crazy! What an unlikely match—captain in the Ecuadorian army and Ph.D. candidate in biology!" Inside, though, I knew we were attracted to each other and becoming more emotionally involved than just friends.

Mario is worried about whether his family would accept me. He's Catholic. I'm not. His family's idea (and his?) of the perfect wife is a homemaker spending all day nurturing his kids. How would my family respond? Would they worry that Mario would stifle my career goals? Would Mario and I be able to surmount the cultural and educational barriers and respect each other as equals? Would he give me the freedom and independence to pursue long-term fieldwork? Which culture would we live in, his or mine? If mine, could he adapt to a very different lifestyle? If his, could I get a university position? And if so, could I function effectively and happily in the more rigid, male-dominated academic scene of Ecuador? My head spins with questions and doubts. Have we fallen in love because of being lonely in this isolated place for so long? We're both in vulnerable positions, away from family and friends. If our surroundings had been different, would we still have been attracted to each other?

24 December 1971

At 5:30 this morning I'm rudely awakened by Colombian Christmas music blaring from the tape recorder in the kitchen. Ilde says the Christmas celebration will officially begin at 8:00 this evening and dinner will be at 11:00 P.M. He explains that he is telling me in advance so I can get all my work done in plenty of time and be free to participate full-time in the festivities, leaving the frogs alone for the next two days. I agree, somewhat grudgingly, to surrender myself to his social scheme.

Guests begin to arrive about 9:00 P.M., and by midnight we have a crowd of more than fifty people: army officers, representatives from all the oil and construction companies based in Lago Agrio, eight prostitutes, and the one schoolteacher from the newly constructed school in Lago Agrio. Bowls of fried *yuca* and *plátanos* are liberally scattered around the bar because Ilde says one needs grease while drinking. And he makes sure that everyone drinks to, and beyond, his or her capacity. Dinner, finally served at 2:30 in the morning, includes chunks of salty pork roasted over an outdoor spit, baked potatoes, and succulent *choclo* (corn on the cob).

I talk for a long time with one of the prostitutes from Lago Agrio, Rosa, a girl about sixteen years old. She tells me that she, her mother, and her ten-year-old brother have been living in Lago Agrio for the past six months. Rosa's mother was never married, and Rosa has never met her father. Her brother has chronic headaches and dizziness, but Rosa's mother can't afford to send him to a doctor. Rosa and her mother are working in the world's oldest profession as a way to survive. Rosa tells me her dream is to meet a rich oilman who will take her away from Lago Agrio. She says all the prostitutes dream the same dream, but so far none has been successful. Our conversation gives me a new perspective on the "night women of Lago Agrio."

Ilde's dance floor gets a good workout. The eight prostitutes, the schoolteacher, and I dance nonstop as the ratio is about six men to every one woman. Ilde's shirt is saturated with sweat, and he dances with a terrycloth towel around his neck to soak up the copious droplets. One of Ilde's dogs, the black one named Negra, wanders unsuspectingly into the bar while forty of us bounce up and down to the bunny hop. She panics and bites me on the leg. There isn't much blood and no one seems particularly upset, so I rejoin the bunny hop line. Negra, however, is temporarily banished from the bar.

The drinking, dancing, and eating continue all night to midmorning. By then most guests have gone home, and just family is left. We open presents, then I retire to my cabin and fall into a deep sleep. A little after midnight, I awake to something running across my feet. My flashlight reveals a large brown rat at the end of my bed. It jumps to the floor, runs under the bed, and out again. I grab my umbrella and chase it, taking random whacks. It runs back under the bed. Crouching down, I see a twitching nose protruding from a nest of confetti made from about $100 worth of Ecuadorian paper money I had stashed in a cloth snake bag behind the suitcase. I open the door and chase the rat out of my house, knowing it will return before daybreak. Although I doubt they will be accepted in Quito, I spend the next hour angrily taping together shreds of moldy bills since I can't sleep anyway.

1 January 1972

I don't know how Ilde and Blanca can manage another big party so soon after Christmas, but we had an even bigger one last night for New Year's Eve. Wives from Quito were here to welcome in the new year with their husbands stationed at the army camp and in Lago Agrio. All were invited to Muñozlandia.

I began New Year's Eve by working for three hours at Heliconia Swamp. When I returned, I learned that a tragedy had taken place. A friend of Ilde's, René, has been staying in Muñozlandia for the past several months. His wife, eight months pregnant, is here to spend New Year's with him. She had severe cramps and spasms all afternoon. René drove to Lago Agrio to get the doctor, but they didn't return in time. The military nurse and Blanca delivered a dead baby boy. Blanca wrapped the baby in a blanket and one of the workers made a little wooden box for him. He was buried in Muñozlandia without delay.

The party started at about 11:00 P.M., though everyone was depressed about the miscarriage. René's wife wanted to be alone, so René came to the party by himself. Conversation was stilted and awkward for a while, but then at midnight a handmade rag doll representing the old year was burned. One of Ilde's daughters read the testament of things the Old Year left behind. For Mario, she said the Old Year left him "some frogs so that he might further the progress of science." For Marty, "a Spanish/English dictionary so that she wouldn't have to walk so far to learn Spanish." After a few more drinks, everyone seemed to be in a party spirit. People drank heavily and danced wildly. Finally at 3:30 A.M. I returned to my cabin.

WHEN I WANDER into the kitchen for breakfast this morning, I find Ilde and Blanca still entertaining guests in the bar. René is spilled over a tabletop, unable to stand on his own two feet. Ilde calls from the bar, inviting me to come and join them for a beer. I agree, not realizing that his invitation is an extension of the party. Before I can escape, more guests arrive and we spend the entire day dancing, drinking, and eating. I quit by early evening, but Ilde continues throughout the night—thirty-six straight hours of partying.

21 January 1972

This afternoon, during my Spanish lesson, Mario tells me that he's being transferred to Quito next week. We vacillate between feeling panicked and numb, as we both sense this relationship is "the real thing." He has no choice but to obey orders. We talk about the positive and negative effects the separation might have on our relationship.

FROGS ARE out by the thousands at Palm Pond, our large permanent pond in mature forest: tiny treefrogs *peeping* from fronds of spiny palms, leaf frogs *clucking* from tree branches, slender-legged treefrogs *boop-boop-booping* from the canopy, narrowmouth toads *buzzing* and *baaaahing* from cavities around tree roots, and South American bullfrogs *whooping* from the ground. Each has a unique advertisement call that functions to identify the species, broadcast the individual's location, and announce reproductive readiness. Species with similar calls don't call from the same pond at the same time. During the countless hours I've spent at these ponds, I've never seen a female go to the wrong species of calling frog. Their ears are "tuned" for the appropriate call; the right one comes in loud and clear through what seems to me to be just a raucous cacophony of disorganized noise.

I walk back home from Palm Pond about 2:00 A.M., engrossed in my thoughts of Mario's imminent departure. The moon is shining brightly enough that I can see the bordering vegetation, so I turn off my headlamp to save battery juice. After about twenty minutes, for some unknown reason I turn on my light. Less than three meters in front of me, lying coiled in a ready-to-strike position, a huge bushmaster viper faces me. I screech to a halt and then step backward slowly, slowly, not taking a breath until I've put a few more meters in between us. I watch the snake for a few minutes while my heart begins to slow down from its furious pounding, and then take a wide detour. The pounding of my heart in reaction to the snake reminds me of the experience picking up my very first snake at Santa Cecilia three years ago. How I've changed. That was the most docile and innocuous snake imaginable—a snail-eating snake. Yet, I was terrified. Now I'm experienced at handling snakes. I've even picked up many fer-de-lance vipers. This experience, though, is truly frightening because of the sheer size of the snake and the fact that I almost stepped on it. A close call indeed. I'll not be walking at night again without my headlamp on. The snake's scientific name, *Lachesis muta,* translates into English as "silent fate"—an appropriate name for so venomous a snake.

5 February 1972

Mario left two days ago for Quito. Between tears we both promised each other we'd write often. I'll visit him in Quito several times between now and July. That's the best we can do. Thinking back over the past five months, I realize how much my relationship with Mario has affected my work. Being in love has given me heightened energy, enthusiasm, and motivation.

A FEW DAYS ago Ilde proudly announced that he was going to make banana wine. Homemade blackberry and blueberry wine can be quite good, I recalled from the States, so I optimistically looked forward to Ilde's brew.

Once the process began, however, my optimism quickly dissipated. Ilde began by hanging several bunches of black rotting bananas from the kitchen rafters. These bananas were so far gone you wouldn't even dream of using them for banana bread. He placed several wide buckets underneath. Over the next few days, juices from the rotting bananas dripped down into the buckets, where they continued to ferment. Ilde eventually strained the juice to eliminate the dead flies and rat turds. He then carefully poured the liquid into empty beer bottles.

Tonight Ilde invites some friends over and ceremoniously opens a bottle. He proudly pours equal amounts into shot glasses. Hoping my intestinal tract will endure this insult, I swallow my first sip. It's sweet and thick. I think about the objects I saw floating in the buckets.

Somehow I choke it down. I put the empty glass on the table. Big mistake. Instantly, Ilde picks up the bottle and aims it toward my glass. Realizing I can't politely refuse, I try at least to indicate that I want only one inch worth. But instead of saying *"una pulgada,"* I say *"una pulga."* Everyone at the table roars hilariously. Ilde pounds the table, slaps me on the shoulder, and informs me that a *pulga* is a flea, and there are certainly no fleas in his banana wine! As quickly as possible I beg off from yet another glass, saying that I have to go watch frogs. Of course this brings further laughter from the group, but I'm spared another sip of Ilde's banana wine, fleas or no fleas.

As I walk along the jungle path, thankful that I've escaped drinking more banana wine, I almost brush against a spectacular grasshopper perched on a leaf. It's nearly seven centimeters long, lime green, and covered with long, sharp spines. I've never seen anything like it before, so I stop and take some pictures. The grasshopper has chosen a very artistic background for itself: a bright green nettle covered with yellow hairs.

Eventually I decide that since the night is dry and very few amphibians are out and about, I'll return home. After walking for an hour, I have a nagging feeling that I'm not where I want to be, so I turn around to retrace my steps. I remember something Bill Duellman told me almost four years ago: It's easy to overlook forks in the trail when you're carefully scanning vegetation for animals. Now that I'm paying attention to the trail, I see numerous alternate paths. Where did I go wrong? Wandering one way, then another, I realize I'm hopelessly lost. Am I ten minutes from home—or two hours away? After focusing my panicked brain on the question of whether to stay put and wait for morning or to extricate myself from the maze, I decide to wander for another thirty minutes.

I try various paths, but nothing looks familiar. Suddenly I see the same lime-green spiny grasshopper on the same green hairy nettle. It was on my left side going up the trail, so now that it's on the right side of the trail I know where I am. Forty minutes later I leave the forest and walk the final stretch back along the runway.

21 February 1972

Last week there was a military coup in Quito, and President Velasco Ibarra, commonly referred to as "El Viejo" (The Old One), was exiled. General Guillermo Rodríguez Lara declared a military dictatorship.

John and I went to Quito the following day to buy batteries. While there I tried to fathom public opinion concerning the coup, but the people I spoke to either had no opinion, didn't want to talk about it, or felt it was for the best without being able to explain why. Perhaps Ecuadorians are apathetic because they are so used to political takeovers.

An article in the Sunday *New York Times* begins, "Politics in Ecuador are never what they seem." The article points out that Velasco was ousted by a military coup for the fourth time in his forty-year political career. Since June 1970 he had been ruling as a dictator with the ostensible support of the armed forces. It was commonly rumored that Velasco was ruling for the military because the military leaders were too embarrassed by the mediocre performance of the previous military junta, which ran the country from 1963–66, to take complete responsibility themselves. Apparently their greed for direct control finally overcame their embarrassment. The presidential elections that were scheduled for June have been suspended. Supposedly the armed forces desperately want to keep Assad Bucaram, a populist demagogue, from becoming president in a few months. It remains to be seen whether the military has stepped in to maintain the status quo or whether they will truly attempt to lead the country in new directions. The answer to this question will have important ramifications for Texaco, which expects to make Ecuador the second most important oil-exporting country in Latin America (Venezuela is first). The article ends, "Ex-President Velasco said he'd be going back to Buenos Aires. He has spent so many years in the Argentine capital, out of power and out of favor, that he owns an apartment there."

MY VISIT with Mario was short but eventful. He asked me to marry him and I said yes. He wanted me to stay in Ecuador, not finish my dissertation, and marry him this summer. After a lengthy discussion, he realized that giving up my degree is out of the question and he apologized for being unreasonable. We agreed that I'll return to Lawrence in late July with the goal of finishing my dissertation in May so that we can get married in June. Mario plans to continue in the army for another three years so that he won't lose his monthly pension. After that, he'll probably take over the family winery. We'll live in Cuenca and I'll hope to get a position in one of the universities there. From my standpoint, it's a win-win situation: I'll finish my degree and marry the man I love. I'm not sure, however, that Mario feels as comfortable about the plan. I have a nagging feeling that he resents my career goals.

4 March 1972

Today John and I join Ilde and Blanca for a wedding celebration at the home of some Quechuas who live nearby. The house is a typical one-room thatched structure perched on stilts. We climb up the ladder and find about twenty Quechua men milling around, many of them already quite inebriated. Naked children chase a pathetically scrawny dog. A woman dressed only in a torn cotton skirt swings back and forth in a hammock while nursing a toddler. In one corner two young men play monotonous music on a homemade drum and a wooden three-stringed violin. The bride and groom look to be fourteen to sixteen years old at most, and neither one seems to be particularly happy about the event. The bride wears a faded orange dress, and the groom wears a nondescript blue shirt and stained brown cotton pants.

Off to one side of the room, eight women sit in a circle. They talk and laugh as they chew hunks of raw *yuca*. After masticating for a few minutes, each spits the accumulated saliva and chewed *yuca* into a large hollowed-out gourd. Ilde explains to me that they are making *chicha,* a fermented drink. The contents accumulated in the receptacle will be set aside and left to ferment for a few days, after which the *yuca* fibers will be strained out. Enzymes from the women's saliva help to speed the fermentation process. *Chicha* is also made from corn and other plants, but in this part of the Amazon Basin, *yuca chicha* is most commonly consumed.

Just as Ilde finishes his explanation, the bride's mother appears and offers us some *chicha*. She dips a small gourd into a larger container and hands it first to me. There's no way to refuse, so I take a sip. The *chicha* is strong and bitter, unlike anything I've ever tasted. The woman is surprised I don't drink more, but passes on the gourd to John. He takes a tiny sip (actually, I think he fakes it) and hands it back to her. She passes it to Ilde, who obliges by guzzling.

For the next several hours, we either sit on the bamboo floor soaking in the unfamiliar sights and sounds of the Quechua wedding feast or we dance to the indigenous music. Several of the young men attempt to teach me their dance, a monotonous rocking back and forth to the beat. I enjoy the dancing, though, because when I'm dancing I'm not offered *chicha*. Whenever I stop dancing, around comes the bride's mother with her gourd of fermented *yuca*. I assume it would be impolite to refuse, so I don't.

Our hosts seem disappointed when, after several hours, we rise to leave. The bride's father invites us to return. He explains that the celebration will continue throughout the next fifteen days, a time designated for family and friends to offer advice to the newlyweds. There will always be music and *chicha* available.

18 March 1972

Exhausted, I collapse onto my damp, mildewed sheet. The constant heat and humidity are depressing. My leather shoes and belt sport impressive colonies of mold. My writing paper is damp and limp. My clothes reek of fungus.

An hour later I'm up again, madly chasing a rat that's been gnawing on a bar of Ivory soap. "Scram, you damn beast!" I shout as it squeezes out through an opening in the roof. By the time I return to bed, my sheets are damp again. "Oh, for a good night's sleep," I think as I doze off.

My hand brushes against my stomach and I feel peach fuzz. More fuzz on my thigh. What's happening to my body? I grab my flashlight and peer under the covers. GROSS! My entire body is covered with greenish gray fungus. I try to scrape it off with my Swiss Army knife. The long filaments fall off, but there's a stubble left, stubbornly adhering to my skin. I peer into my pocket mirror and scream in horror at the fuzzy green monstrous face peering back at me.

My scream wakes me from the nightmare. After checking to make sure my body is still fungus free, I lie awake, eyes wide open, wondering which is worse: the real-life rat who makes nightly visits or the fuzzy green fungus of my vivid dream. I've been living in the hot and humid jungle for almost nine months. Am I finally going crazy?

26 March 1972

During the past twenty-day time block, I've added information on the development of several frog species, bringing the total to fourteen. The lab table is covered with containers of wriggling embryos, ready to burst through their protective capsules. My data so far show a definite trend for fewer eggs, larger egg size, longer developmental time, and larger hatchling tadpole size for treefrogs that lay their eggs on leaves above water as compared to those that lay their eggs directly in water.

Fieldwork has been exciting. We found yet another fer-de-lance viper in the secondary forest, making it the most commonly encountered snake here. The other night I found a large female egg-brooding horned treefrog. As I picked her up to measure her, I noticed a tiny miniature of her on a leaf. And then another, the same size, a meter away. These two little ones must have just recently freed themselves from Mom. Like juveniles of most species, the head was proportionately too large for the body. As was the proboscis extending from the snout. We found hundreds of leaf frogs *clucking* from leaves overhanging a large pond. A few clutches of pearly white eggs had already been deposited on leaves. Cat-eyed snakes lurked amidst the vegetation, searching for dinner.

One evening, when about halfway to the primary forest, we heard the Asthmatic Monster and then saw the huge Brahma bull in the middle of the trail. He snorted and lumbered toward us. Spying an escape route, John and I bolted to our left and squeezed under the fence. Change of plans. We decided to cut a trail through a tangled bamboo thicket and follow the call of our mysterious laughing creature. For months now John and I had tried to locate and identify the animal that made loud cackling noises in the canopy. John guessed it was a mammoth frog. I thought it was a giant nocturnal bird. Every time we heard one, we would shine our headlamps in the direction of the laugh, but the noise would stop. This night, our original plans thwarted, we were more determined than ever to solve the mystery. We crept up to the target bamboo, turned off our headlamps, and stood motionless for twenty minutes until it finally laughed again. We shone our lights in the direction of the laugh. Silence. Fifteen minutes later it laughed

Treefrog eggs hanging from a leaf above water. The embryos are about ready to hatch and will fall into the water below where the tadpoles will continue to develop.

again. This time our lights revealed a large spiny rat perched on a branch, his entire body vibrating as he jeered down at us.

TONIGHT I suddenly come face-to-face with a weevil frozen in position on a leaf by the fungus that shrouds it. I recall the many previous times I've encountered beetles, flies, wasps, moths, and other insects cemented to leaves in contorted positions, their exoskeletons sprouting white fungal filaments. It strikes me that this apparition is the origin of my fungus nightmare. The gruesome process begins when the insect inadvertently ingests the spore of a particular fungus. Germinating inside the insect, the spore produces a tangled mass of threadlike tubules (hyphae) that invade the host's body. As its tissues are digested, the insect scrambles about erratically, eventually settles onto a flat surface such as a leaf, and dies. The exoskeleton breaks open and the hyphae exit, showering spores around the rigid victim. So far as I know, the fungus doesn't attack humans except in dreams.

1 April 1972

The rain never stops. Today while walking home in midafternoon from the farthest forest swamp, I'm caught off guard by a sudden downpour. Wind whips through the vegetation. Branches bend at ninety-degree angles, snap, and crash to the ground. Further along, the Río Aguarico is already cluttered with logs and other debris that fell in upstream. The water level is rising. By the time I near Muñozlandia, the rain has slowed to a drizzle. Instead of cool relief after the storm, though, there's just an increase in the oppressive humidity. The heavy smell of jungle vegetation clogs my nose. I enter my room and discover the roof has sprouted a leak—right over my bed.

One of the benefits of a rainy spell is an increase in breeding activity. So far Heliconia Swamp attracts the most species: twenty-five, although only sixteen species use the swamp for breeding. On any one night, I've seen and heard a maximum of ten species calling, each from its characteristic calling site: ground, shallow water, or vegetation. One night six species laid eggs—the most I've seen breeding simultaneously at one place so far. The fact that three lay their eggs on leaves above water and three lay their eggs in water means less demand on potentially limited sites. Some only lay eggs following heavy rains; others are happy with light rains. The breeding patterns of other species seem to be related more to the presence or absence of other frogs than to the weather. If a certain species is present and calling at the swamp, a closely related species may be absent, although it calls the same night at a nearby swamp where the first species is absent. Perhaps the first species to arrive at the swamp discourages other species that have similar calls or similar requirements for egg laying or calling sites.

Rain seems to stimulate arthropods also. The other night while in bed, I felt something huge but lightweight crawling on my arm. I shook it off and grabbed the flashlight. There, crawling on my sheet was an enormous but harmless tailless whip scorpion. It was jet black. Its front pair of walking legs were over half the length of my hand. I shuddered as I coaxed it into a plastic bag and released it outside. These long front legs are "feelers," used as touch and chemical receptors for locating prey, much like the antennae of other arthropods. A tailless whip scorpion searches for prey by walking sideways with its front legs extended—presumably what this one was doing on my arm. Once it locates a prey item, it grabs the animal, tears it open, and sucks the body fluids from the hapless victim. John and I refer to these creatures as the "big and uglies."

THE PAST few days have been traumatic. Bill Duellman came to Santa Cecilia for a visit. He offered me a two-year research assistantship to support myself while I write my dissertation back in Lawrence. When I told him that I plan to finish in one year and return to Ecuador to marry Mario, I got stony silence. Shock? Disapproval? He says I can take the offer or leave it, but if I accept the assistantship I must commit for two years. I don't know what to do. If I turn down the offer, I'll probably ruin our professional relationship forever. Plus, on returning to Kansas if I don't have an assistantship, I'll have to teach introductory biology labs. Teaching would be time-consuming and might prevent me from completing my dissertation in one year. But if I accept the assistantship for two years, will Mario wait for me?

28 April 1972

After much agonizing, I accepted Bill's offer of support for two years. Breaking the news to Mario was painful, especially because I hadn't consulted him about the decision. Not unexpectedly, he accused me of putting my career before our relationship. Perhaps I am. At any rate, he reluctantly agreed to wait for two years.

10 May 1972

John and I are getting very sick of rice. We're served rice for lunch and dinner every day without exception, and often for breakfast as well. Blanca packs rice into a cup and carefully maneuvers the contents onto the center of the plate. Frequently she tops off the mound with a dab of ketchup. We refer to an exceptionally large mound of rice as a *"Chimborazo de arroz,"* Chimborazo being the beautiful snow-covered volcano visible from Quito; *arroz* is Spanish for "rice." A few days ago John and I speculated that we are being served the same mounds of rice at subsequent meals (yes, we often leave the mounds intact on our plates). To test our hypothesis, we've been introducing foreign objects such as beans (also omnipresent) into the rice mounds. Sure enough, the same mounds—complete with beans—appear the following meal.

There have been a few occasions, however, when the rice has been a welcome sight. Recently we were served a huge mound of rice next to a chicken neck in a sauce of boiled potatoes and peanut butter. Deathly allergic to peanuts (a half teaspoon of peanut butter would kill me), I had a good excuse for not eating the chicken neck. I had told Blanca of my allergy months ago, but apparently she forgot. That night I gratefully filled up on rice.

John and I are served chicken foot soup periodically, and we've found a good use for the rice on such occasions. By mixing rice with the greasy broth, both taste better. We're not sure what we're supposed to do with the feet, so we simply avoid them.

16 June 1972

People ask me, "Aren't you afraid to be out in the forest by yourself at night?" Philosophically, I agree with my adviser that it's not wise to do fieldwork alone. Anyone, male or female, could sprain an ankle, sink in soft mud, or get bitten by a venomous snake. Without a companion to help, you might be in serious trouble. Practically, however, it isn't always possible. John has been away for weeks at a time, and I've had to go out alone. So, my view is that you do what you have to do—sensibly. I don't take chances, and I watch carefully where I'm about to put my hands and feet. As long as I have a spare flashlight (and extra batteries and an extra bulb) and a clear path (without too many forks), the only thing I fear is people. I admit I have felt nervous when I've heard jaguars snarling nearby, but rationally I know the snarling is just part of their hunting behavior. And they don't normally hunt anything as big as a biologist. Other humans, though, are a different story because they're unpredictable.

Tonight I have a run-in with drunken soldiers in the middle of Heliconia Swamp. I hear rustling noises and then loud crashing through the vegetation. Soon several very drunk voices yell, *"¡Alta! ¡Manos arriba!"* ("Stop!

Hands up!") There, standing at the edge of the swamp so as not to get their feet wet, are five teetering soldiers from the army base, all pointing their loaded rifles at me. Without asking who I am, they say I don't have permission to be out at this time of night. I'm outraged enough, naive enough, and, yes, stupid enough that rather than raise my hands (which at the time were holding a treefrog and a millimeter ruler), I yell at them.

"I know your commander Major Alvarez, and if you don't leave me alone immediately, I'm going to tell him that you are out here drunk, trying to frighten me!" I'm so scared I'm shaking, but the soldiers never know it. They mumble apologies and stumble off.

29 June 1972

As we walk back home along the runway tonight, we see an inspiring sight in front of us. Reventador, an active volcano about eighty kilometers west from here, is erupting. The reddish orange lava flowing down the mountain is as bright and spectacular as if we were next to it. Imagining the heat emanating from it makes me feel a bit warmer and I forget about being wet. John and I sit in the middle of the runway and in awe watch as the lava continues to spill out and flow down under its own power. We feel terribly insignificant.

THE OPPORTUNITY to pick up and handle so many amphibians and reptiles over the year has impressed on me their diversity of defenses. Often the first line of defense is crypsis, or blending in with the environment. A green frog, lizard, or snake in the trees may blend into its leafy surroundings so successfully that a potential predator is unaware of its presence. The same is true for a brown frog, lizard, or snake on the mud. If the animal is detected, though, a backup defense comes into play. Many species attempt to flee by swimming, crawling, hopping, running, or slithering. Leaf frogs trick the potential predator by suddenly ceasing to look like a frog. A green leaf frog resting on a green leaf is very difficult to detect. Once the frog jumps, though, suddenly the contrasting colors on the flanks leap into view. One species here has orange flanks with vertical purple bars; another has cream flanks with brown spots. The predator presumably cues in on this sudden flash of contrasting colors. But when the frog lands, it holds its legs close to the body. Once again the colors disappear, and the frustrated predator has lost its search image.

Once detected, some species stand their ground and bluff. As I learned during my first visit to Santa Cecilia, the egg-brooding horned treefrog threatens by opening its cavernous yellow-orange mouth. Many of the lizards likewise inflate their bodies and open their mouths wide. Once attacked, an amphibian or reptile has several potential defenses. A toad inflates its lungs with air and puffs up its body, making itself difficult to handle. Other species release smelly, sticky, or otherwise nasty substances onto the aggressor: snakes defecate, frogs slime, and toads pee. Leaf frogs roll over on their backs, curl up, and play dead. Lizards and snakes that have spines, fangs, and claws become aggressive. They jab, bite, and scratch. Caimans lash their strong tails.

The first line of defense isn't always crypsis, however. Sometimes it's just the opposite. Poison dart frogs advertise their toxicity with bright colors as if to say, "Don't eat me, I'm poisonous." Likewise, the alternating red, yellow, and black bands of a coral snake advertise its venomous nature. Birds are potential predators of both snakes and frogs, and birds have color vision. Experiments have shown that some species of birds learn from experience to avoid the bright colors associated with distasteful or toxic prey. Other species avoid the warning colors of coral snakes and their mimics instinctively from birth.

18 July 1972

I've come up with a framework of ten modes (or patterns) of reproduction for the assemblage of seventy-four of the eighty-one species of frogs known from Santa Cecilia. The other seven species are extremely rare, and their reproductive patterns remain mysteries. The modes are distinguished from each other by a combination of where the eggs are deposited, in or out of water, and whether the eggs hatch as tadpoles or as miniature adult frogs. For each of the modes, I've characterized the range of egg and clutch size, and for many I have data on larval development and a good idea of the major causes of mortality for the eggs and tadpoles or froglets.

My observations and data suggest that the different species divide up the available breeding sites at Santa Cecilia. Forty-one species of frogs that have aquatic larvae were associated with my eight focal aquatic breeding sites. No species laid eggs in all eight aquatic sites, and the maximum number of species breeding synchronously at any one site was ten. Many frogs don't use aquatic sites at all since they lay direct-developing eggs on land. Of these species, some are found predominantly in primary forest, others in secondary forest or disturbed areas. The very nature of the diversity of reproductive patterns results in extensive dividing up of the resources. Quite possibly eighty-one species couldn't coexist if all of them deposited their eggs in water and had aquatic tadpoles.

19 July 1972

John and I have been packing up belongings from our jungle homes and laboratory, saying good-bye to friends, and making farewell visits to each of our study sites. Ilde and Blanca have been like parents to us. We'll miss them. The year has been satisfying and fulfilling in so many ways. We both feel we know ourselves better: our capabilities, limitations, needs, desires, hopes, and dreams. We lived in such close quarters and had so many shared experiences that we'll always be like brother and sister. I've matured as a scientist over the year. I no longer feel like a neophyte, but rather like a seasoned researcher. Living in such an isolated place for so long while doing my dissertation research has had its pluses and minuses. The major plus is the total immersion in the fieldwork. The major minus is reduced intellectual stimulation from peers and mentors. By the time I return to Lawrence, I'll be about fifteen months behind on the literature. New ecological theories to understand. New ideas to test. New viewpoints to ponder.

22 July 1972

The last day in Quito I picked out my engagement ring—an emerald in a lovely yellow gold setting. John and I bought last-minute souvenirs for friends, family, and ourselves. We splurged on food, from steak dinners to second helpings of banana splits. We never once ate rice.

With a combination of anticipation and regret, we board the plane to Miami. I have three bulging data notebooks waiting to be massaged into a dissertation. After a ten-day vacation in Pittsburgh, I'll return to Lawrence and spend the next two years thinking and writing about the many ways to beget a frog.

IN NOVEMBER of that year, after barely four months of separation, I received a letter from Mario, calling off the engagement. He'd decided it wasn't going to work after all. Two years was too long to wait, and he'd realized how important my career was to me. I fired off a letter asking if we could discuss his decision in person when I visit at Christmastime. His response was a telegram simply saying, *"Pensé mucho para decidir favor no venga."* ("I've thought a lot and have decided please don't come.") Initially devastated, I eventually realized that Mario was right. I probably would not have felt fulfilled in the life he envisioned for us. Furthermore, I needed freedom and independence to begin my career without the constraints of a confining relationship.

WANT SOME RESPECT?
WAVE A VIPER.

AFTER FINISHING my Ph.D. at the University of Kansas, I spent
two years on a postdoctoral fellowship in ecology with Dr. Stan
Salthe at Brooklyn College in Brooklyn, New York, but escaped
one summer for follow-up work at Santa Cecilia. In 1976 I accepted a faculty position as Tropical Amphibian Community Ecologist in
the Department of Zoology at the University of Florida, in Gainesville.
Finally I was a college professor.

MY SECOND year in Gainesville, Dave Pearson, an ornithologist from Pennsyl-
vania State University, invited me to participate in a floral and faunal survey
in Ecuador's Oriente near the Peruvian border, an area to be designated
the Yasuní National Park. Dave organized and led the expedition. Our group
included four professional biologists from the States, two Peace Corps volunteers, two Ecuadorian forestry specialists, an Ecuadorian biologist, two
cooks, and a boatman. With financial support from World Wildlife Fund and
the backing of the Ecuadorian government, we were to compile a preliminary species list of the plants, mammals, birds, amphibians, and reptiles
from the primeval-looking blackwater swamps, periodically flooded forests, and uplands of the area. Supposedly we were the first nonindigenous
people in the region since the era of rubber tree tapping, eighty years earlier. The area had been avoided because of the Huaorani Indians.

The Huaorani (pronounced Wow-rá-ni), a group of between 1,200 to 1,500 people who speak a language related to no other known tongue, live in a vast and largely unexplored stretch of the Amazon Basin that begins south of the Napo River and extends more than 185 kilometers south and east to the Peruvian border. *Huaorani* means "the people." A derogatory term often used for this tribe is Auca, the Quechua word meaning "savage." Until the 1950s, the roving small clans of Huaorani were almost completely isolated. They killed any outsider who ventured into their territory.

In 1956 Huaorani warriors speared and killed five North American missionaries. One of the missionaries had an older sister, Rachael Saint, who vowed to carry on her brother's work by civilizing the Huaorani. In 1957, with the backing of the evangelical Summer Institute of Linguistics and the Ecuadorian government, she bribed some Huaoranis with gifts and made contact. Rachael established a settlement along the Curaray River, where she exposed the Huaorani to their first taste of Western civilization—the good and the bad. There she built a chapel where she taught the Huaorani about God and the "evils" of nudity, shamanism, and extramarital sex, and she started a school where she taught Spanish to the children. She taught the Indians that killing other people was wrong. And she convinced many clans to give up their nomadic lifestyle.

Due to Rachael's influence, by 1977 most of the Huaorani had decreased their hostility toward outsiders—most of the time. Two small splinter groups, though, were still nomadic and mistrustful of outsiders, including other Huaoranis. Reports of spearing raids still surfaced periodically. Government officials didn't think the splinter groups currently roamed the area we would be surveying, but they couldn't guarantee anything.

7 September 1977

Over the past two days, the four North American biologists have assembled in Quito: Dave Pearson (ornithologist), Louise Emmons (mammalogist), Robin Foster (botanist), and myself. Joe Anderson, a Peace Corps volunteer collecting insects for the Smithsonian Institution, will join us and inventory insects. We'll meet the second Peace Corps volunteer, Bob Trimmer, in Lago Agrio, and our Ecuadorian associates southeast of Lago Agrio in Coca, an oil town at the end of the road.

Several hours late, the National Parks truck picks us up at noon, and we're on our way. Two hours into the trip, a huge landslide blocks the road. Fortunately, crews of men with heavy machinery are already hard at work removing the rubble. The foreman estimates it will be another four hours until we can pass, so despite a heavy drizzle, we head out to explore the nearby cloud forest. Cool and misty, the forest is quite a contrast to the lowland forests with which I'm familiar from Belém and Santa Cecilia. The vegetation is lush, with epiphytes (nonparasitic plants growing on other plants) clinging to every tree trunk and branch—mosses, orchids, and bromeliads. Lots of dink frogs are calling. Joe finds metallic green tiger beetles, scarab beetles, and spectacular butterflies.

When we reconvene at the truck, we wake the driver and point out that one of the tires is flat. So at 6:00 P.M. we put on the spare and drive on to Baeza and get the flat repaired. Baeza is a lovely colonial town, founded in the mid-1500s. Until the pipeline road from Quito to Lago Agrio was completed five years ago, Baeza was quite isolated, accessible only by horse, mule, and oxcart. The old parts still have cobblestone streets, but already the town has expanded and modernized since I first visited in 1972.

An hour after leaving Baeza, we get a second flat tire. There's nowhere to get it repaired before Lago Agrio, so we'll just hope for the best. A little farther down the road, the driver tries to pass a bus and we land in a ditch. Just as we think that nothing else can go wrong, the generator weakens and the headlights dim to almost nothing. We drive the last twenty-five kilometers to Lago Agrio at a snail's pace, with Dave sitting on the hood, illuminating the road ahead with his flickering headlamp. The sight of his gangly frame faintly outlined against the dimly lit road would be comical if we weren't all concerned for his safety. I'm impressed that Dave jumped up on the hood without hesitation. Another expedition leader might have asked for a volunteer, but Dave took on the job himself. We're in good hands.

Main street in Lago Agrio, 1977.

Hot, dusty, and exhausted, we check out the only three passable hotels in Lago Agrio, but none has any vacancies. Dave suggests we go to the Texaco oil camp and plead for floor space. We luck out. They offer us the billiards room, where we throw our sleeping bags onto the floor. This is a side to Lago Agrio that I haven't seen before. I'd always suspected that the Texaco guys lived comfortably. My suspicions are now confirmed. In stark contrast, the town's other inhabitants still deal with outhouses—at best— and free-roaming pigs.

8 September 1977

After a large American-style breakfast of bacon and eggs, pancakes, and orange juice in the Texaco cafeteria, we get the flat repaired. Bob, the Peace Corps volunteer based in Lago Agrio, offers to let us drive his truck to Coca since ours is falling apart. Just outside Lago Agrio, though, his "indestructible" truck threatens to throw a piston, so we backtrack and repack our equipment into the National Parks truck. We're finally on our way out of Lago Agrio a little after noon. On the first of two ferry crossings of the Río Aguarico, the barge becomes detached from the ferry and we drift for a while before getting reattached. Then, just as we approach the second ferry, our truck battery dies. Is this expedition cursed? We pile out and push the truck onto the ferry. A friendly local jump-starts our engine.

We finally reach Coca but find no vacancies in the one passable hotel. Once more we go to the local Texaco camp. We're moving up in the world: they offer us two rooms—air-conditioned and with showers! Coca, officially named Puerto Francisco de Orellana, is a port town at the junction of the Coca and Napo Rivers. Although some semblance of the town has existed since the 1500s, it is now a rough boomtown and quite unenticing.

A cold shower revives me. As I pick up my glasses afterward, one of the tiny screws from the frame falls out and rolls down the drain. The lens crashes against the porcelain. Fortunately the lens is plastic. Now what? I'm practically blind without my glasses. In a stroke of genius, I recall that I have some twist-ties in my box of plastic storage bags. I extract the wire from one and jerry-rig my glasses back together.

While drinking cold beers, we laugh about our mishaps over the past thirty hours. Our standard joke now when anything goes wrong is "I bet Darwin never had these hassles." After supper Louise, Joe, and I walk around the Texaco compound and find ten species of frogs, all easy to identify because they also occur at Santa Cecilia.

10 September 1977

Yesterday was wasted because Flavio, the Ecuadorian biologist, didn't show up until late afternoon. We wandered around Coca, bored and annoyed at the delay. All of us are anxious to be on our way. I think everyone is a bit perturbed with me also, because I led the group into a grassy area next to the airstrip to look for frogs and now everyone is scratching furiously from tiny ticks and chiggers.

OUR FIRST delay this morning is waiting for the replacement spark plugs for the outboard motor we'll need for the dugout. Finally at 1:00 P.M. we load all our backpacks, duffel bags, and cardboard boxes of food into the truck and drive down to the river, where we wait for another hour. After getting our passports stamped, we load into a small boat and a ten-meter long dugout and set out for Añangu (Quechua word for "ant"), an oil camp a ways down the Río Napo.

11 September 1977

Dave wakes us at 6:15 and, amazingly, we're back on the Río Napo by 7:00 A.M. We stop an hour later at a little Quechua village for breakfast of boiled *plátano*, *yuca*, and canned sardines. After many more hours perched on the wooden seats, we reach Nuevo Rocafuerte in late afternoon. Nuevo Rocafuerte is Ecuador's easternmost town, located where the Río Yasuní empties into the Río Napo. In 1542 Francisco de Orellana and his group of about fifty men paddled down the Río Napo past this exact spot on their way to become the first Europeans to travel the length of the Amazon River to the Atlantic Ocean. There isn't much in Nuevo Rocafuerte other than a small army base, a small Capuchin mission, about twenty houses, and one greasy spoon restaurant. No beer or soft drinks are available, and supply boats come by only very rarely.

The Ecuador-Peru border sits near the mouth of the Río Yasuní. Here, each country has a little cabin that flies its national flag. We had to get special permission from the military to enter this area because Ecuador is a bit paranoid about the border. During the past century, Peru has gradually infiltrated and claimed much of what had been Ecuador's Oriente. In 1941 a major border dispute broke out. Once again Ecuador lost out when leaders from various Latin American countries met in Río de Janeiro, Brazil, and worked out a settlement that gave most of the disputed territory to the more powerful Peru. To this day, however, Ecuador still claims the land, and in fact every map of the country made in Ecuador includes the disputed territory as part of Ecuador. Every Ecuadorian with whom I've discussed the dispute strongly believes that the land is theirs and that someday the forest will be returned to them.

12 September 1977

After a breakfast of freshly caught fish, rice, fresh pineapple, and papaya, we show our passports to several more officials and then we all load into the dugout. Anticipation of the unknown experiences ahead of us surpasses even the feeling I had as a child on Christmas morning. All six of the North Americans are dressed in old, stained drip-dry pants and T-shirts in preparation for fieldwork. Flavio, the Ecuadorian biologist, and the two Ecuadorian forestry specialists are still dressed in snappy "street clothes." Flavio, acting rather self-important, still carries his fine leather briefcase. Secretly, Louise and I can hardly wait until he slips and falls in the mud. So far we have the impression that none of the three is excited to be along on the trip. All they do is giggle, tell dirty jokes, and talk about women. They've shown little interest in the landscape and natural history around them. There must be enthusiastic and capable Ecuadorian field biologists. How did we get stuck with these three? Still, we're hoping that once we get into the forest, we can get them more enthusiastic about the inventory.

For the next seven and a half hours, we chug about 150 kilometers up the Río Yasuní. The river is about 130 meters wide at the mouth but narrows considerably as we go upstream. With unbroken forest along both banks, this is the most spectacular canoe trip I've ever taken. Large river turtles bask on logs. Bright red passion flowers, purple trumpet vine flowers, and blue morning glories add splashes of color to the green walls of vegetation. Dave seems to have a sixth sense for spotting birds, identifying them under low light conditions, and recognizing their songs. We see three species of macaws, lots of parrots, several species of kingfishers, an egret, Muscovy ducks, and loads of white-rumped swallows. We're most excited about seeing several hoatzins, unusual-looking birds about the size of small chickens.

Hoatzins are mostly brown with large baby-blue patches around the eyes and a stiff bristly crest, an exaggerated spiked haircut. These birds are unusual in their biology as well as appearance. When the chicks hatch, they have claws on their wings. Until they learn to fly, the baby birds use these claws to climb around in the trees. Although the claws fall off as the birds mature, adults use their wings to clamber about on branches in a very un-bird-like manner. Hoatzins have a digestive system that's unique among birds and even somewhat cowlike. The birds eat mostly leaves, which are stored and partially digested in a thick muscular compartment called the crop. The food mass then passes to the stomach, where it's further digested. Other birds that eat leaves grind up the food in the gizzard, *after* it has been mixed with gastric juices in the stomach.

BY LATE afternoon we stop at a lovely lagoon. In a relatively open area of forest, we set up camp—ten tents of assorted sizes, shapes, and colors. The place is swarming with hordes of ants of many different species. Much of the ground is swampy, so between the ants and the water there isn't much choice in where to pitch the tents. Dinner tonight is identical to the meals Quechuas fixed for me at Campana Cocha in 1968—noodle and potato soup, boiled *yuca,* and rice. No ketchup this time, though. The two men whom we brought along to cook for us seem remarkably unenthusiastic about their tasks. They seem to expect all of us, but especially Louise and me, to pitch in and help. Apparently they don't get the message that the reason we've hired them is to maximize the time we can devote to fieldwork.

My first night out in the Yasuní nets only six species of frogs and one anole lizard. Either amphibian and reptile diversity is low here, or the animals

Río Yasuní, near the mouth where it empties into the Río Napo.

Anole lizard, common in the Oriente of Ecuador.

aren't very active now because it's the dry season. Flavio comes with me and seems interested in the animals, though he doesn't find any on his own. I give him the same pep talk I gave my brother, Alan, years ago in Brazil. To find animals you have to think FROGS, LIZARDS, or whatever. If your heart and soul aren't involved, you'll walk right by the animals and never see them. Flavio looks at me strangely, as though he thinks I'm weird!

14 September 1977

Yesterday I added another seven species of frogs to the list. One of the frogs is a crested toad, my old friend from Santa Cecilia and Belém. But there wasn't a single lizard in sight. And still no snakes. We're all surprised at the seemingly low density of mammals and insects as well.

After an early breakfast, we break camp and head upriver in hopes of finding a more species-rich site. Three hours and about fifty kilometers later, the boatman, Carlos, stops and declares that we can't go any farther because we have just enough gas to make it back to Nuevo Rocafuerte. From the nervous mutters we've overheard from him and from the cooks the past few days, it's clear that Carlos is loathe to go any farther upriver for fear of Huaoranis. We don't complain, though, because this area seems more diverse than the first one, at least vegetation-wise.

By the time we've unloaded the dugout, it begins raining. We set up tents in a driving downpour, then duck inside our respective abodes for the

Crested toad, with large bony flanges on the sides of its head.

next couple of hours. As I know from Santa Cecilia days, it can rain hard even during the dry season. My one-person pup tent really is designed for one person who can store his or her belongings in a car parked nearby. My backpack and duffel bag have to share the limited space with my body— and none of the three of us can touch the wall of the tent without getting drenched. I'm already getting claustrophobic, and we have another ten days left with our tents.

I spend the enforced tent time getting caught up on my field journal and writing a letter home. What words can I use to describe the trip thus far? There are so many impressions of landscape, forest, plants, animals, and colleagues that I can't sort them all out. How can I convey my excitement in a letter to people thousands of miles away, without burying them under a landslide of vignettes?

Tonight I find nine species of frogs and a salamander, but no reptiles. More treefrogs are calling at this site than at our first one, but this might just be a response to the afternoon's heavy rain. The density of ants— army, leaf-cutter, and otherwise—is just as high as at our first site.

Just as I'm falling asleep, my bladder begs to be emptied one more time. I put on my flip-flops and tiptoe out of camp. On my return, I suddenly gasp in pain and shock. Something is stinging my toe. Sure enough, my flashlight beam reveals a huge black conga ant (*Paraponera*) still attached to the toe. I must have accidentally brushed against the ant. I yank the creature off and hobble back to my tent. For the next several hours, sharp bursts of pain shoot through my foot and partway up my leg. My throbbing appendage keeps me awake, and my mind wanders to thoughts of Huaoranis. Do they know we're here? In the distance I think I hear voices mumbling, but I convince myself the noise belongs to some nocturnal animal. A few minutes later, I hear rustling in the bushes and crackling of sticks and leaves. I soon recognize the sounds as footsteps. They're getting louder. Should I awake the others? Just as I muster up enough nerve to take action, I hear Louise say, *"Buenas noches,"* to Flavio. The two have just returned from the nightly search for mammals.

15 September 1977

When I awaken my foot is still swollen, but I can limp about without too much discomfort. I spend several hours in treefall gaps hoping to find lizards basking in sun spots but I see none. There's a noticeable absence of many of the species abundant at Santa Cecilia, perhaps because many of those species prefer disturbed habitats. This area is anything but disturbed.

This afternoon as Robin is pressing plants between sheets of newspapers, he comes across an issue of *El Comercio* with an article about me and "the many ways to beget a frog." The article boasts about the number of frogs at Santa Cecilia, the highest diversity of any comparable-sized area in the world, and describes the unusual modes of reproduction of the frog fauna. Clearly the story was plagiarized from my recent article in *Natural History* magazine as I recognize statements lifted verbatim, translated into Spanish. Flavio reads the article with interest and asks me a few questions about Santa Cecilia.

As a break, in the late afternoon we take refreshing baths in the river, oblivious to any piranhas and electric eels that might be nearby. The water feels wonderful and it's great to feel clean again.

16 September 1977

Bob, Joe, and I spend the morning cutting trails for inventory work. We find several additional species of amphibians to add to the list, the most exciting one being a Muñoz's glass frog, lime green with yellow spots. The specific name, *munozorum,* of course honors Ildefonso Muñoz. Muñoz's glass frog was named four years ago from Santa Cecilia, where it was originally discovered. Ilde is extremely proud of "his" frog. He has one preserved in a vial of alcohol and shows it to everyone who'll look at it.

The trails are productive after dark. A beautiful dwarf iguana sleeps on a branch. A calico false coral snake slithers along the trail. A white-lined leaf frog with bulging eyes watches us from its perch. Most exciting, though, is a beautiful two-striped forest pit viper, pale green with a yellow stripe down each side, draped over a branch. I want to photograph the snake, but I don't have my camera with me. And I forgot to bring a cloth snake bag. So, with long tongs I carefully grab the snake behind the head. As I stroll into camp, I encounter Flavio, the two forestry specialists, the cooks, Carlos, Robin, and Dave swapping stories. Thrilled with my find, I wave the viper in front of them. Robin and Dave *ooh* and *aah* appropriately, but the Ecuadorians act a bit reticent and keep their distance. I gently insert my prize into a snake bag and return to the forest to continue my search.

17 September 1977

This morning the cooks complete their chores with uncharacteristic alacrity. I spend time photographing the viper and some of the other animals we've found. Joe has fallen in love with the bright green leaf frog and asks to keep it as a pet. Although I want to release the frog to live out its existence in the wild, it warms my heart to see someone suddenly turned on to amphibians. Perhaps it's worth the life of one frog if a person becomes so interested in amphibians that he or she becomes a "friend of frogs" and ultimately fights for their conservation.

Dave reveals to me the events of the last few days and the reason for the cooks' new cooperative spirit. At the outset of the trip, as soon as the two cooks saw Louise and myself, they apparently decided that with two women on the expedition, there was no reason for them to perform the more onerous duties of cooking and cleanup. Over the next couple of days, their machismo beliefs had begun to suffer more and more as Louise and I disappeared every night into the forest—and in different directions, too. They themselves were deathly afraid of wild animals, Huaoranis, and spirits of the dark. The crowning blow came when I wandered into camp last night clasping a large viper. Holding on to the last vestige of machismo, they'd exclaimed to Dave, "*¡No es una mujer! ¡Tiene cojones!*" ("She's not a woman! She has balls!")

Later I reflect on the cooks' change of attitude. I'm not surprised that they expected Louise and me to take over their duties. In their culture, women typically cook and clean for the men. But haven't they noticed that Louise and I don't receive, or expect, differential treatment from our male colleagues? We're all in this together, as equals. I can imagine the tales these men are going to tell once they return home!

An afternoon search in the swamp forest nets an additional six species of frogs and a gecko lizard. Carnivorous bladderworts are scattered across the water surface. The only parts visible are the bright yellow flowers. Beneath the surface, however, lurks the dark side of bladderworts—traps that catch tiny arthropods to be digested for food.

18 September 1977

This morning Carlos shoots a white-lipped peccary from a herd of about fifty animals. The cooks go all out for us, and for themselves. Meat for lunch is a treat, as our only protein since leaving Nuevo Rocafuerte has been canned tuna fish and beans. We have chunks of peccary in our carrot and noodle soup, plus fried peccary on a bed of rice. The meat tastes similar to tender pork and is delicious.

Midmorning the two forestry specialists, bored with inventory work, cut a vine overhanging the river and spend the rest of the morning swinging Tarzan-style back and forth over the water. During bath time we all take turns. How exhilarating to swing out high over the stream, then back to the wall of green!

This afternoon I learn the hard way about the gardening activities of ants. While searching for lizards on tree trunks, I see an impressive mass of epiphytes clustered on a branch. It reminds me of a potted basket of exotic houseplants sold at a nursery. I reach up to inspect the clump and am immediately attacked by stinging ants. For the next hour, large itchy welts on my hands and wrists nearly drive me insane. I relay my trauma to Robin over dinner, and he smiles and tells us about "ant gardens."

Indeed, the epiphytes were growing out of an occupied ants' nest built on a tree branch. Most amazing, I think, is that the ants themselves planted the garden. Ants of certain species collect seeds from many different kinds of epiphytes, eat the fruit pulp from around the seeds, and then drop the seeds into their nest. The seeds germinate and the seedlings thrive on the nutrients available in the detritus in the nest. As the plants mature, their roots become part of the nest's framework. Robin has seen ant gardens here with at least six different species of epiphytes emerging from a single nest. The association between ant and plant presumably is mutualistic— that is, both benefit. As I just learned, the ants viciously defend against possible leaf-eaters. In addition, the ants help to disperse the seeds and their nest provides nutrients for the plants. So what do the ants receive in return? The plants may help to hide the ants' nest and thus protect them from ant predators. Also, the ants obtain food from the plants. Although they also forage away from their garden, the ants slurp up the sugar and water oozing out of extrafloral nectaries (nectar glands in plant parts other than flowers) on their garden plants.

White-lined leaf frog. Leaf frogs lay their eggs on leaves overhanging water. When the tadpoles hatch, they fall into the water below, where they continue to develop.

Egg-brooding horned treefrog. Females carry their eggs attached to their backs. Eventually little froglets pop out of the egg capsules.

Tiger-striped leaf frog. When the green frog sits on a green leaf, it is fairly well camouflaged. If a predator detects it, though, the frog jumps and exposes its orange and purple flash colors. Presumably the predator cues in on the contrasting pattern. Then, when the frog lands again on a green leaf and holds its legs close to its body, the contrasting stripes disappear and the predator has lost its search image.

A harlequin poison dart frog sits fully exposed as if to warn, "Don't eat me! I'm poisonous."

A female harlequin frog sits on her boulder at the Río Lagarto.

A male golden toad in the Monteverde Cloud Forest Reserve patiently waits for a female.

A male Darwin's frog in southern Chile broods his wriggling tadpoles in his expanded vocal sac. After the tadpoles metamorphose, they will climb out of Dad's mouth and hop out onto land.

A blue-sided leaf frog waits for action at a breeding pond in Monteverde, Costa Rica.

The bright red iris of a
blue-crowned motmot peeks
out from a black mask.
Photo by Peter Feinsinger.

An Ecuadorian spider sports the
Batman logo on its abdomen.

This dwarf iguana seems to impersonate a miniature dragon.

Rainbow boa, lovely in color and pattern but deadly to its rodent prey.

My study site at the Río Lagarto, Costa Rica. In the early 1980s the area was swarming with harlequin frogs, but by 1988 the frogs had mysteriously disappeared.

A hummingbird-pollinated vine brightens the otherwise dark undergrowth of an Ecuadorian cloud forest near Baeza. Photo by Peter Feinsinger.

Called "hot lips," the pair of bright red bracts of this shrub resemble lipstick-covered lips framing teeth of delicate white flowers. Hummingbirds with short bills slurp nectar from these flowers. Photo by Peter Feinsinger.

A passion flower from Manaus, Brazil, flamboyantly begs to be pollinated. Photo by Peter Feinsinger.

19 September 1977

We leave at 6:15 this morning and paddle about twenty-five kilometers upstream in the dugout. The river is narrow here, so we can easily see animals on both shores. Because we go slowly, and without the motor, we see more wildlife than before, including about twenty caimans and thirty-five turtles basking on the sandbars and logs. A capybara dives from the shore into the water, swims alongside our boat, and then scrambles back up the opposite bank. Capybaras, at about one meter in length, are the world's largest rodents. They look like huge guinea pigs with coarse reddish brown hair. We return midafternoon with plants, vertebrates, and insects to add to our growing inventory list.

Tonight's walk along our trails nets an egg-brooding horned treefrog. Flavio is impressed when I get the frog to display its defensive behavior of a yellow-orange gaping mouth. Snakes tonight include a snail-eating snake and a blunthead tree snake. I also find a fanciful little poison dart frog—black with gold stripes running down its body, a metallic gold throat with a black spot, and metallic blue-and-black-spotted belly and legs. Fascinated by my description of poison dart frogs carrying tadpoles to water, Flavio wants to know more detail: how the eggs stay moist on land, and how the frogs decide where to dump their tadpoles. He's intrigued to hear that Indians in Colombia use the skin secretions from three species to poison their darts.

Baby caiman, lovingly held in a biologist's hand.

Blunthead tree snake—it couldn't bite you if it wanted to!

Interactions with the Ecuadorians have reached a fairly comfortable state. Now that I'm viewed as having *cojones* and they respect Louise and me for braving the forest alone in the dark, the cooks have continued to be more industrious in tending to their cooking and dishwashing duties. The two forestry specialists, though still not overjoyed with the project, have participated more than at first. They've learned from us and we've learned from them. Most satisfying is that Flavio is genuinely excited about the plants and animals—from ant gardens to fruit-eating bats and poison dart frogs.

21 September 1977

The river level has dropped about one and a half meters in the last couple of days. We're worried about getting stranded here. Because the river is fed only by local rainfall, the water level fluctuates dramatically. We've been warned that levels can fall precipitously overnight, making navigation impossible. Purposely tempting fate by getting stranded and running out of food in an area where there might be Huaoranis is not recommended, so we regretfully decide to end the inventory early.

We break camp and head downriver. Soon after starting out, the motor jams, so we stay at putt-putt speed the rest of the way. In a constant hard drizzle, we sit hunkered miserably beneath leaky raincoats. At our slow pace, it takes five hours to return to our first campsite. Just as we arrive, the rain pounds harder. There's no point in setting up tents in the downpour, so, looking and feeling like drowned rats, we remain hunkered in the dugout. We're all wondering if this rain will replenish the water level to the point it was a few days ago. Maybe we could have continued the inventory. Too late now, though. Once the rain subsides again to a drizzle, we drag ourselves onto land and set up camp. After a supper of noodle soup and, yes, more rice and tuna, Joe fries up some crepes. We smear *guayaba* jelly over them and begin to feel rejuvenated.

22 September 1977

We rise at 4:00 A.M., eat breakfast, break camp, and take our seats in the dugout. Today the hot sun beats on us incessantly. At one point we see a huge fallen tree lying across the river ahead of us. Obviously the tree was here on our way upriver, but we didn't even notice it because it was submerged. Now that the water level has dropped, it's exposed. There's no way we can get around or over it. Patiently we wait for forty-five minutes watching the water level drop, until finally with all of us crouched down on the floor of the dugout, we are just able to drift underneath.

Because of the broken motor, it takes us ten hours to return to Nuevo Rocafuerte, with only one five-minute "relief stop." We arrive tired, sweaty, and sunburned, but overjoyed to be on solid ground and off the dugout's hard seats. The thought of wet tents is depressing, so most of us opt for sleeping inside on hard floors. We're hoping that our motor can be repaired tomorrow.

23 September 1977

The first thing we all do this morning is spread tents and the contents of duffel bags onto the ground to dry. The next item of business is washing off the grime and sweat during long baths in the Río Napo. The late afternoon sky is dramatic, the huge billowy clouds changing in form minute to minute. I wish I could paint, but I wouldn't be able to decide which scene to paint first.

We spend the evening sharing notes on our inventories. Louise found eight species of bats, including spear-nosed bats, short-tailed fruit bats, and long-nosed bats; six species of primates, including squirrel monkeys, white-faced capuchins, red howlers, and woolly monkeys; long-nosed armadillo; red brocket deer; woolly opossum; and rodents such as rice rats and spiny rats, capybara, and paca. The latter are large rodents, though much smaller than capybara. A rather small head is connected to a stout body propped up on short legs, and the body ends in a large rump and a tiny stump of a tail. Bird diversity here is amazing considering the short time Dave has been observing: harpy eagles; twelve species of parrots, including five species of macaws; seven species of hummingbirds; fourteen species of antbirds, not surprising considering the super-abundance and diversity of ants here; ten species of tanagers; fourteen species of flycatchers; woodpeckers, toucans, owls, ducks, and trogons. The list goes on and on. I found one species of salamander, three species of toads, two species of glass frogs, two species of poison dart frogs, twelve species of treefrogs, and fourteen other miscellaneous species of frogs. Reptiles included nine species of lizards, six species of snakes, and one caiman.

Robin describes to us the vegetation we lived in for ten days along the Yasuní. He found the lowest plant diversity in the blackwater swamp forest and the highest in the upland forest. A surprising number of plants in the upland forest are associated with ants, both those of the ant gardens and trees that provide shelter for ants. For example, in *Cecropia,* colonies of stinging ants live inside the hollow stems. They get food directly from the tree and in return protect the plant from leaf-munchers and from encroaching vines. Robin explains that because of nutrient-poor soil, the forests on either side of the Río Yasuní are less productive than many tropical forests, such as those around Lago Agrio, Coca, and Nuevo Rocafuerte. Some of the Yasuní's plant species are unique to these stressful conditions. For this reason alone, it is important to argue for their protection.

26 September 1977

After prolonged delays of showing passports at the immigration office and having the military personnel check us out, we finally left Nuevo Rocafuerte two days ago and began our long trip back to Quito. Saying good-bye to Flavio was almost sentimental. He thanked all of us for the opportunity to participate in the inventory and for sharing our love of fieldwork with him.

I SPENT TODAY in Quito shopping for friends and relatives. My suitcase is now loaded with woven wall hangings and wood carvings. My favorite wall hanging is one of egrets woven into an Escher-like design—blue, white, light gray, and charcoal gray birds. On first glance the white birds stand out against the dark background. A second glance reveals that the background consists of egrets of the other colors. The story has it that in the 1960s a Peace Corps volunteer gave some Indians from Otavalo reprints of Escher drawings. Since then the designs have been enthusiastically incorporated into delightful weavings, popular with tourists and biologists alike.

OUR INVENTORY of the Yasuní region was overwhelmingly successful despite the limited time and the impressive number of mishaps early on. A high point of our adventure for me was learning about birds, mammals, plants, and insects from my colleagues. I also learned the intricacies of teamwork. When each person on the team can roll with the punches, maintain a healthy sense of humor, and not take him- or herself too seriously, the team works. Ours did. We all agreed afterward we'd do it again in a heartbeat.

During the ten days, we recorded ove e400 species of plants, an undetermined (but high) number of insects, 25 species of mammals, 177 species of birds, 33 species of amphibians, and 16 species of reptiles—for each group a mere drop in the bucket of what is likely to occur in the area.

As part of our inventory report we made the following recommendations:

- The greatest possible effort should be made to protect the entire watershed of the Río Yasuní, from its origins to where it empties into the Río Napo. All plants and animals within the boundaries of the park should be protected from exploitation.
- The region has high potential to attract ecotourists. Because colonization destroys the forest and many of its animal inhabitants, colonization will also destroy the potential for ecotourism. A buffer zone established around the park borders should be patrolled against colonists and hunters. The vicinity of Nuevo Rocafuerte is the most appropriate place to develop tourist facilities. A biological station that would facilitate and encourage responsible research should be established in conjunction with the park.
- Both the current and future living conditions of the Huaorani who live in the area need to be considered carefully in plans to establish a Yasuní National Park.

THE YASUNÍ NATIONAL PARK was indeed established in 1979 as the largest national park in Ecuador, with an area of over 500,000 hectares. Since then the park's borders have changed several times, but—at least on paper—the total area protected has been kept about the same. In the early 1990s, the boundaries were changed to establish a large reserve for the Huaorani, though the reserve was only about a third of their traditional territory.

Adventurous ecotourists can now retrace the route our expedition took in 1977. From Nuevo Rocafuerte, guides take visitors up the Río Yasuní past the newly established Huaorani villages of Jatuncocha and Tambococha. Times have changed and the Huaorani are no longer isolated. The Huaorani understandably want to benefit from ecotourism, so each village requires visitors to pay a hefty "entrance fee" to see the village and proceed upriver.

There are now two Ecuadorian-run biological stations that operate within the park. Scientific researchers work at these stations in relative comfort, and ecotourists are welcome to visit the stations and interact with biologists. Everyone benefits because the ecotourists help to pay the bill for maintaining the stations and for administering the park.

THE SEEMINGLY impossible has happened recently. In October 1998, Ecuador and Peru signed a treaty recognizing the 1942 Protocol of Río de Janeiro. Ecuador has finally given up its claim to the large expanse of the Amazon region "stolen" by Peru. New maps are being made to reflect the national borders. In general, Ecuadorians seem pleased that the conflict has finally been resolved. They know it was unrealistic to believe they could ever recover the territory. Time, effort, and financial resources that were previously devoted to border skirmishes might now be spent on social and economic programs.

AT THE TIME we carried out our inventory of the Yasuní area, Ecuador didn't have much of a tradition of field biology. A "real" scientist was one who wore a white lab coat and carried out experiments in the laboratory. If the "real" scientist needed animals, someone was hired to go out and do the dirty work of collecting them. It's no wonder that at first Flavio felt that what we were doing was beneath him. In that era, field biologists from other countries did little to help change these attitudes. Whether North Americans or Europeans, most First World investigators went to Ecuador and other Latin American countries to do their own research, took their own students along as assistants rather than enlisting and training promising local students, returned home with their specimens and data, and published their results in U.S. or European scientific journals.

Happily, the situation has changed dramatically. Now there are many highly motivated, scientifically adept young field biologists from Ecuador and the rest of Latin America who spend much of their time sloshing about in the mud for the sake of natural history, experimental biology, and conservation ecology. They consider themselves real scientists, and they are rapidly gaining respect in the international arena.

Expressing in
the Rain

IN THE spring of 1979, I returned to Ecuador with my fiancé, Peter
Feinsinger, whom I'd met my first day in Gainesville two and a half
years earlier. Also a tropical field biologist, Peter had actually applied
for the same job (Tropical Amphibian Community Ecologist) as myself in the zoology department. He's more the community ecologist; I'm
the amphibian biologist. Because our skills and interests were complemen-
tary, the zoology department had hired us both. Our first casual conversa
tion upon meeting each other revealed three more coincidences: we both
play the cello; we were born in the same hospital in Madison, Wisconsin;
and we're both avid rockhounds.

The objective of our first trip together to Ecuador was to find a place
where we could both do our research, Peter on hummingbirds and I on
frogs. We visited numerous sites but in each case were forced to conclude
that any site accessible to us was already too disturbed by colonists to be
suitable for Peter's work, which required a large expanse of primary forest.

Married the next summer, we spent our honeymoon in Monteverde,
Costa Rica, where Peter had done his Ph.D. dissertation research. He
already knew the forest there was suitable for his new project, but I didn't
yet know whether or not I could find something of interest in cloud forest
habitat—until I saw my first harlequin (or clown) frog. We returned to
Monteverde for fieldwork the next two summers, still carefree and childless.

By this time I was thirty-five years old, and we decided the time had come to replace our pet guinea pigs with a child. At the same time, we wished to change our lifestyle as field biologists as little as possible while nurturing our offspring. And we assured each other that the experiences of foreign travel, living in different cultures, and meeting people with diverse backgrounds could only be a positive influence for a child. So in 1982 I became the first female faculty member in the history of the zoology department at the University of Florida to give birth while employed. This process received mixed reviews from my academic colleagues. The graduate students and most faculty members expressed sincere support and enthusiasm for our upcoming event. But there were exceptions. One male professor, on hearing the news, said to me, "Well, I guess we'll see a dramatic drop in your productivity now." A female colleague said, "Are you serious? You're going to have the baby? There *are* other options!"

Determined to prove to my colleagues that pregnancy would not affect my professional work, I never missed giving a lecture in my courses. And, in spite of looking and feeling like a beached whale, I went on every fieldtrip in my vertebrate zoology class—four trips each week for four weeks. Karen was born soon after the end of final exams in the spring semester.

Six weeks later the three of us (and fourteen pieces of luggage) flew to Costa Rica to begin our sabbatical year in the Quaker community of Monteverde (Green Mountain). Our pediatrician had armed us with critical baby medicines and the name of a trusted colleague in San José. We were first-time parents on our way to the tropics.

NESTLED IN the lush mountains of northwest Costa Rica, Monteverde is a dairy-farming community founded in 1951 by North American Quakers. Monteverde's history really begins in Alabama, where four young Quakers were jailed in 1949 for refusing, because of their religious beliefs, to register for the draft. Following their release from prison, they and other Friends looked outside the United States for a peaceful place to live their beliefs and raise their families. Their search led them to Costa Rica, attractive to pacifists because it had just abolished its army. The forty-four colonists chose Monteverde, in the Tilarán Mountains, for its isolation, pleasant climate, fertile soil, and idyllic landscape. Of the fifteen hundred hectares of land purchased, the colonists set aside about a third to protect the watershed above their farms. They tried several crops, without great success. At a potluck dinner, John Campbell brought some cheese he'd made from his cows' milk. The idea caught on and the seeds of cheese production in Monteverde were planted. Today a large modern cheese factory, the *lechería*, produces several varieties of cheese that are sold throughout the country and exported as well.

In 1972 about two thousand hectares adjacent to the community's watershed were purchased through the help of several conservation organizations, and the Monteverde Cloud Forest Reserve was established. The reserve encompasses one of the most beautiful and diverse cloud forests in all of Central America. It has grown greatly in size since then and now extends far over the continental divide toward the eastern lowlands. Depending on the location relative to the moisture-laden Atlantic trade winds, the forest is either wet or very wet. Clouds and mist that bathe the forest foster luxuriant vegetation: tree ferns, orchids, and a huge diversity of trees carpeted with epiphytes. Dwarfed and sculptured by the strong trade winds, an elfin forest sits atop the exposed east-facing upper slopes. Surveys of the reserve have documented more than 500 species of trees, about 300 species of orchids, 400 species of birds, 100 species of mammals, 120 species of amphibians and reptiles, and nearly 500 species of butterflies. A rich environment indeed.

While I was doing my Ph.D. research at Santa Cecilia in 1971–72, Peter had been doing his at Monteverde on hummingbirds and the flowers they pollinate. Peter was one of the earliest in a long succession of biologists to work at Monteverde. Little did he know in 1972 that several years later he would introduce me to his Quaker friends and the forest on "Green Mountain," and that we'd spend many field seasons studying hummingbirds and frogs together in this misty fairyland. And little did I know when I left Costa Rica after my OTS course in 1971 that I would return to the country for many delightful field seasons.

1 July 1982

Several of our graduate students meet us at the airport outside of San José, and from there we begin the drive along the Inter-American Highway. Our only stop is for a late afternoon meal at an empty roadside restaurant. We locate a strategic spot from where we can watch the Land Rover and our fourteen pieces of luggage. Six-week-old Karen begins to fuss loudly. Suddenly a bevy of five solicitous waitresses rushes to our table to placate her. They coo, cluck, and cajole, but to no avail. Finally they decide Karen is cold. We're almost at sea level, the sun outside is bright, and I've uncovered Karen's arms and legs because it's as hot and muggy as Gainesville. She's not cold. She's cranky from the long plane ride. To avoid a scene, however, I acquiesce and dress Karen in a pink-flowered sleeper outfit from the overstuffed diaper bag next to my foot. Of course that doesn't work. She's *hot* now. She fusses more urgently. The waitresses scurry back, scoop Karen into their collective arms, and without saying a word to me disappear into the kitchen.

For the next ten minutes, Peter and I chat with our students about research and try to ignore the all-too-familiar squalls blasting from the kitchen. Before long the five waitresses reappear. One of them dumps Karen in my lap, lifts my blouse, unhooks my bra, and declares, *"Tiene hambre."* ("She's hungry.") I blush at my unexpected exposure but dutifully oblige. Under five sets of watchful waitress eyes, I continue to nurse Karen while eating my chicken. As Peter pays the bill, the women huddle around me and the now-content though still pink-outfitted baby, exclaiming, *"¡Qué linda!"* ("How cute!"). I'm realizing firsthand how much Costa Ricans focus on babies. I can't imagine this scene happening in the States. One particularly matronlike waitress tells me in a whisper always to offer the baby a breast whenever she fusses. If only life were that simple . . .

The next leg of the trip is the three-hour climb up the mountain on a rough dirt road, bouncing over potholes and swerving around curves. Though today the road is difficult at best, and sometimes impassable during the wet season, the trip must have been a nightmare three decades ago. It was just an oxcart trail back in 1951 when the Quaker settlers made this trip with all their belongings.

7 July 1982

Home for the next year is a spacious two-story wooden house surrounded by forest, pasture, and clouds. Though basic and sparse, the furniture will be more than adequate: sofa and chair, kitchen table and chairs, desk, set of dresser drawers, double bed, and a crib borrowed from one of the original Quaker families. Large picture windows overlook an unbelievably lush pasture dotted with moss-covered stumps and logs—a surreal scene as the clouds gently tumble toward the house.

Yesterday we hired Liliana, a thirteen-year-old Costa Rican neighbor girl, to help with laundry and cleaning. I spent the morning teaching her how to wash diapers, and from her quizzical expressions, sighs, and grunts, I gather she finds me obsessive. First we wash the diapers in cold water because we don't have hot water in our semiautomatic washing machine. Then we wring them through a manual roller. Afterward, to kill the germs, we boil the diapers in water and vinegar for ten minutes on the wood stove. We wring them manually through the roller a second time and hang them outside on the clothesline, where, if it's not misting, the sun bleaches and further sterilizes them.

Karen's babysitter is Helena, the older daughter of two of the original settlers. Helena embodies the true spirit of Monteverde: accepting, giving, loving, gentle, creative. Peter has known her since 1971. She is now a close friend to whom we will entrust our daughter five days a week.

EACH OF THE past five days, I used my plastic hand pump and expressed milk, which I stored in sterile plastic bags and froze. I've accumulated enough so that I can be away from home for most of a day. Helena arrives early this morning. While I load my backpack, I watch Helena's hazel eyes sparkle as she sings to Karen, swinging her long dark braids for Karen to grab.

Eager to return to the field, I head off for the Monteverde Cloud Forest Reserve confident that Karen is being well cared for. After nearly two hours of sloshing my way uphill along slick, muddy trails, I search in vain for harlequin frogs for an hour. Then I find a soft moss-covered log on which to perch while I express. Five minutes later the sky explodes with thunder and large raindrops. Unearthing a folding umbrella from my backpack, I reposition myself on the now soggy log, umbrella handle propped under my chin. Rain dribbles off the umbrella onto my shoulders and I manage to pump several ounces of milk, seal up the bags, and store them in the thermos with ice. Now I have forty-five minutes to look for frogs before the two-hour trek home.

Despite an intense search, today's observations total a measly three harlequin frogs. As I trudge home in the rain, I think about Karen and her first day away from Mom. Near the house I hear Karen screaming. Helena is pacing the floor, unable to pacify Karen, who has refused the bottle all day. Karen is hungry and she's mad. All I want at the moment is a hot shower and dry clothes. Instead, Helena fixes me some hot cranberry herb tea and I resume my role as Mom.

9 July 1982

Today I descend in elevation to the Río Lagarto (Lizard River). I set off on my two-hour hike feeling optimistic. At least it shouldn't rain today and I'll be warm.

MY RESEARCH planned for this year concerns the ecology and behavior of harlequin, or clown, frogs. These frogs earned their name for their bright, gaudy, and somewhat comical appearance: black with yellow stripes, polka dots, and irregular blotches. At barely more than half the length of my little finger, these small frogs are active during the day. They're easy to observe because they sit fully exposed on boulders in or near the stream. Despite their local abundance and the ease with which they can be watched, very little is known about them. Finding over fifty frogs today convinces me to do my study at the Río Lagarto and to forget about the reserve.

This site, though more disturbed than the reserve, is a beautiful place to work. Originating in cloud forest near the continental divide, the Río Lagarto flows down the Pacific flank of the Tilarán Mountain range. In my study site, at an elevation of about 1,140 meters, the stream is only one to four meters wide, no more than a meter deep, and is punctuated by many small waterfalls from one to several meters high. Both sides of the stream are bordered by forest, with sparse shrubs, clumps of wild ginger relatives, and bamboo thickets close to the water. The stream bank varies from sand to large boulders or extensive rock faces, providing abundant foraging sites for the frogs during the day and crevices for retreats at night.

From watching these frogs during the past two summers, I've seen that harlequin frogs are extremely aggressive toward one another. One objective of my research will be to study the interactions among males, among females, and between males and females. I hope to provide answers to several questions: Are the frogs aggressive year-round? Why are they aggressive? Who wins encounters?

To begin answering these questions, I'll place a frog (the intruder) fifteen centimeters from an undisturbed individual (the original). After I introduce the intruder, I'll watch from a distance of two meters and record what the frogs do for at least twenty minutes.

Today I begin the manipulations. What fun they are to watch! Because each frog is unique in color and pattern, it's easy to keep the individuals straight. The first manipulation involves a male I've placed onto a female's boulder. She immediately chases him. He jumps down onto the sand and skedaddles into a thicket of bamboo. Another involves two males. Within seconds of seeing the intruder, the original male assumes an alert posture, hops over to the intruder, pounces on him, and slowly rotates his body back and forth over his pinned opponent. This squashing behavior continues for over an hour until finally the intruder escapes and quickly hops away. The original male raises the front of his body high on his forelimbs and belts out a loud call as if to say, "Get out of my territory and never come back!"

I LEARN TODAY that rain isn't the only challenge to expressing in the field. This afternoon as I sit on a large boulder in the stream, just finishing up the second of two expressing bouts for the day, I hear something crashing through the bushes behind me. Terrified, I whip around to confront what is about to attack. Just two feral pigs chasing each other. In the process I tip over the sterile bag of milk. White gold dribbles down the muddy boulder. Have I made the right decision about beginning a long-term field study when Karen is so young?

As I approach the house, rather than Karen's screams, I hear Joan Baez singing "One Day at a Time." Helena greets me at the door, smiles, and says that Karen gave in and accepted the bottle. Despite minor disasters of a bag of milk curdling and one nipple getting scorched while being sterilized, they had a good day together baking banana bread and watching the cows. I hug Helena. This crazy scheme will work after all.

17 July 1982

Instead of watching harlequin frogs every day for the next month, I've decided to spend only two days each week at the Río Lagarto. On the other days, I'll do an experimental study at home with tadpoles and aquatic insects. This change of plans will allow me to spend more time with Karen. Helena will continue to care for Karen on these three home days except for feeding her, which will reduce my expressing demands.

I'll work with meadow treefrogs, small yellow frogs that lay their eggs in shallow water in meadows and pastures. Within twenty-four hours after a heavy rain, hundreds of lemon-yellow males appear from nowhere at the newly formed puddles and ponds and start up their deafening chorus. Females soon arrive and a mating frenzy begins. At the same time, female dragonflies are attracted to the shallow puddles, where they lay their eggs. Over the next few days, thousands of frog and dragonfly eggs hatch, and eventually the voracious immature dragonflies, called nymphs, are large enough to eat their tadpole puddle-mates.

One way that tadpoles might avoid being eaten is by growing rapidly, quickly reaching a body size that is too big for insect predators. All is not utopia, however, for large tadpoles. Just before a tadpole metamorphoses into a froglet, it passes through an ungainly and awkward stage, comparable to human teenagers. At this stage, when the tadpole erupts its forelimbs and begins to resorb its tail, it can neither swim as well as a younger tadpole nor hop as well as a completely transformed froglet.

I'm curious about whether meadow treefrog tadpoles going through that awkward teenage stage are more likely to be eaten by dragonfly nymphs than are similar-sized tadpoles either without legs or with only the two back legs. Also, I wonder if indeed dragonfly nymphs prey more heavily on smaller tadpoles than on larger individuals. These questions should be easy to answer with some simple experiments that I can do right here in the house.

So today Helena, Karen, and I collect meadow treefrog tadpoles of various ages and sizes, plus dragonfly nymphs, from a nearby pond. I line up dozens of water-filled plastic shoe boxes in our spare room and then introduce various combinations of tadpoles and dragonfly nymphs. I'll leave them undisturbed for the next twenty-four hours and then record who was eaten—the first of many sets of experiments.

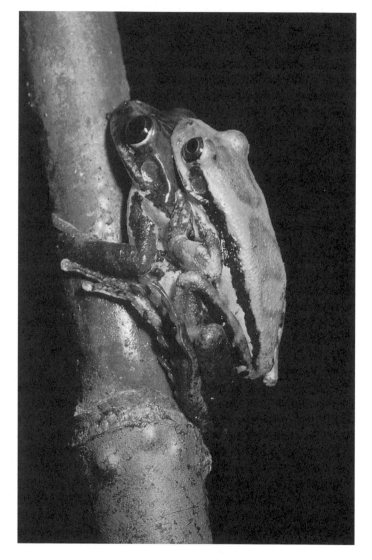

Pair of clasping meadow treefrogs. Males turn from dull yellow-brown to bright lemon yellow when ready to breed.

26 July 1982

We're in San José for a week, jumping through the bureaucratic hoops in order to obtain our temporary residency visas. This evening we go to the Bar Lido. The head waitress recognizes us from past years and leads us to the far booth. She takes Karen to the kitchen, and when the two return, the waitress is also carrying our standing order: beers in frosted glasses, shrimp cocktails, and popcorn. Eventually Peter stuffs Karen into the blue-and-white seersucker baby carrier strapped across his chest and we walk to our favorite seafood restaurant. By the time we arrive, with an extra walk around the block for good measure, Karen is asleep. She sleeps on Peter's chest throughout the meal, with a white linen napkin protecting her billiard-ball head first from dribbles of French onion soup and later from cocktail sauce.

17 August 1982

Not surprisingly, my experiments with meadow treefrog tadpoles and dragonfly nymphs reveal that small tadpoles and four-legged individuals were most frequently eaten. The few four-legged tadpoles that survived had climbed out of the water and clung to the side of the plastic shoe box, out of reach of the dragonfly nymphs. In nature, once a tadpole sprouts all four legs, it may be able to escape aquatic predators by climbing out of the puddle and hanging out in moist grass nearby. But what chance has a small tadpole that must stay in water because its lungs are not yet developed and it can't hop about on land? The cruel reality is that tadpoles are an important source of food for aquatic insects, fish, and birds. Most never survive to become frogs.

The past several weeks have been especially rewarding. I've completed a study and enjoyed the more relaxing pace of working at home three days each week. But Karen is nearly three months old now. I've lost some of the weight I gained during pregnancy and thus have more stamina for the long hike down to the Río Lagarto on a regular basis. I must admit that I'm antsy to begin more intensive fieldwork. Each day as Peter leaves for the field before sunrise and returns late afternoon, I envy his freedom to immerse himself entirely in his work.

For one of my projects, beginning today and once each week until the end of next June, I'll walk slowly along the stream and record behaviors of all the frogs I see interacting with each other. These observations, under natural conditions, will provide additional information to answer my questions concerning when and why the frogs are aggressive, and who wins. I'll keep track of everyone as individuals by taking Polaroid pictures.

During today's census, I find a drab greenish yellow and black-spotted male getting squashed by a strikingly handsome black-and-yellow-striped male in what looks like a slow-motion replay. The battle is more violent in another pair, as a black male with a large yellow blotch on his head has his forelimbs wrapped around the neck of a yellow-and-black-speckled male and is yanking him backward. After twelve minutes both frogs lose their balance and tumble off the boulder. The speckled frog quickly rights himself and flees.

28 September 1982

Peter returned to the States last week and will be gone for six weeks more. Life is moving a little slower in the mornings, but overall Karen and I are managing quite admirably by ourselves. Tonight, however, I sorely miss Peter's help.

This morning a tour guide called and invited me to give an after-dinner lecture to a group of Audubon nature tourists who are bird-watching at Monteverde. He asked me to broaden their Costa Rican experience by showing slides of the diversity of tropical amphibians. Helena had agreed to stay with Karen but called thirty minutes before I needed to leave home to say she was sick and unable to come. I call the hotel to cancel my lecture, but the tour leader pleads that I come with Karen and the cook will watch her for me. Against my better judgment, I wrap Karen in a raincoat and we set out in the cool, misty evening air.

When we arrive, the cook hesitantly takes Karen and I begin my talk on "The Many Ways to Beget a Frog." Karen is *not* pleased at being held by a strange woman who's pacing back and forth the length of the small kitchen. Karen fusses, then cries, then screams so loudly that no one can hear me. Embarrassed, I interrupt my description of poison dart frogs carrying their tadpoles to water, retrieve Karen, and lecture the second half of the hour with Karen strapped to my chest, smiling contentedly at me. Afterward I offer to answer questions. For the next ten minutes, I respond to: "How can you stand to be away from your baby during the day?" "Do you hope she becomes a biologist?" "Aren't you nervous about being in Costa Rica with such a young baby?" Clearly my personal life is more interesting to the bird-oriented tourists than are the reproductive peculiarities of Ecuadorian frogs.

Our hike back up the hill through softly swirling mist seems magical. I look into the night sky and see my first "moonbow": a diffuse ring of pinkish yellow light encircling the moon. My lungs expand with breaths of cool, clean air. Yes, I answered the tourists' questions truthfully. I am very content in this isolated spot away from the stresses and deadlines of Gainesville, Florida. Monteverde is the ideal community for combining motherhood and field biology. Because there are so few outside demands on my time here, I feel in control of my life. Every new mother should be so fortunate.

30 October 1982

I'm thrilled at having located such a dense population of harlequin frogs along the Río Lagarto. Some days I see more than a hundred frogs during a census. And they're so easy to watch. A field biologist's dream come true.

Behaviors of the frogs are fascinating, especially interactions between males and females. Males almost always pounce on females without any courtship preliminaries and grip them in the armpits in a typical mating position. Rejecting these advances, the attacked female responds by kicking to dislodge her unsolicited baggage and by rocking back and forth to dump him off. One female squeezed into a rock crevice and wriggled back and forth as if trying to scrape off the male. Equally dramatic is the response of a female toward a male that suddenly invades her space. She chases the male, pounces on him, and vindictively bounces up and down on his back, vigorously slamming his head against the ground.

This morning while sitting on a boulder watching frogs, I have an eerie feeling that someone or something is watching me. Glancing nervously over my shoulder, I see an otter less than ten meters away, standing on hind feet peering at me. I turn around to see if the male harlequin frog has escaped from the irate female, and by the time I look behind me again the otter has vanished.

12 November 1982

Recently one of my graduate students, Alan Pounds, joined us in Monteverde and has been helping me with the weekly census. Last week at the Río Lagarto, we found a nearly dead harlequin frog with a hole in its hind leg through which we could see wriggling white maggots. Memories of my bot fly during the OTS course more than a decade ago triggered terrifying thoughts. What if these maggots also eat humans? Thirty minutes later, we found another moribund frog with a hole in its hind leg, again with maggots. By the time we left, we had found five more. Our population had been attacked by parasites, but what were they?

We took five victims back to Monteverde and placed them in plastic shoe boxes lined with several layers of paper towel. By today the maggots had consumed most of the flesh and internal organs of the frogs and the frogs died. The maggots crawled in between the layers of paper towel, where we're hoping they'll pupate.

14 November 1982

It worked! The larvae have pupated. Now the wait to see if they'll survive, and if so, what will emerge from the pupae?

TODAY IS a long day at the Río Lagarto. Midmorning after I express, I rummage through my backpack for my water bottle. Damn, I forgot it and I'm already thirsty. This is not good, because the more water I drink, the more milk I produce. And if I don't express enough milk for Helena to give to Karen, my time in the field is curtailed. I glance at a harlequin frog sitting on a wet boulder and think, "How lovely to be a frog and never have to drink." On their underside, frogs have an area called a seat patch that's especially permeable to water. By merely sitting on wet surfaces, they absorb water into their bodies.

After finishing the day's observations, I slowly plod home along the dirt road exposed to the baking sun, feeling very dehydrated. A marine toad sits in squishy mud by the side of the road, soaking up water through its seat patch. Sitting exposed in the middle of the day, the warty toad isn't as vulnerable to predators as it seems. Huge parotoid glands protruding from the side of its head are filled with potent toxins that ooze out of pores when the toads are molested. A dog that bites into a toad and gets a mouthful of these white secretions is quickly deterred and may even die.

Although these parotoid secretions protect toads, people have long known of their medicinal properties. Eighteenth-century physicians used powder made from dried toads to reduce fever. The Chinese make a powder, called *Ch'an Su*, from toad secretions. They use this powder for treating heart ailments, drying boils and abscesses, and healing ulcers. Indian folk healers in Veracruz, Mexico, use toad secretions in their medicinal preparations and "love magic" potions. It seems odd that parotoid secretions are so widely used as medicines until you realize they contain epinephrine and norepinephrine—chemicals known to stimulate the human heart and help the body deal with stress.

But medicines aren't the only use humans have found for toad parotoid secretions, some of which contain strong hallucinogenic chemicals. Ancient cultures of Mesoamerica are thought to have used toad secretions as hallu-

A marine toad soaks up water through the skin on its underside. Note the large poison-filled parotoid gland on the side of its head.

cinogens during religious ceremonies. Haitian witch doctors include toad secretions in their concoctions designed to induce near-death comas and to create zombies of their victims. And in my own backyard, in southern Arizona and in California, foolhardy people get high by smoking dried parotoid secretions of Colorado river toads.

1 December 1982

The first of the pupae metamorphosed today, producing a hairy black fly about a centimeter long. I've preserved it so that I can send it to a fly expert in the States and have it identified.

These flies seem to be one of the few predators on harlequin frogs, whose skin contains tetrodotoxin, one of the most potent of all animal toxins known. [Curiously, pufferfishes also contain tetrodotoxin. Puffers are considered a delicacy in Japan, but must be skinned very carefully prior to being cooked. Every year brings reports of fatalities caused by eating improperly skinned puffers.] The bright black and yellow colors of harlequin frogs warn potential predators they are poisonous. Because of their toxicity and warning coloration, they sit exposed on boulders all day, seemingly impervious to predation. Yet their conspicuous behavior may make it easier for parasitic flies to find them.

25 December 1982

Christmas this year is truly a community experience. Six weeks ago everyone who wanted to participate in the gift exchange entered his or her name into the gift draw box and then drew the name of someone else. The idea is to make the gifts by hand. Everyone has been creating and finally Christmas is here.

First we have a Quaker meeting at the schoolhouse. Meeting is a special time of contemplation when participants commune silently with God and nature or share thoughts with the rest of the group. Often at the regular Sunday meeting, the hour drifts along in silence except for the noises of the children, who are always forgiven no matter how much they fidget and whine. Today several people speak aloud: how wonderful it is to have family, friends, and visitors nearby; how thankful they are to live in this idyllic spot; how much they hope that peace will envelop the world. The feeling during and following a meeting is always one of warmth, love, and acceptance. If everyone could share and live Quaker beliefs, what a different place the world would be.

Contributions to the potluck dinner range from tuna pizza to tamales (ground corn and pork wrapped in plantain leaves) and from deadly chocolate fudge to a multilayered cake, each layer separated from the next by a thick layer of *dulce de leche* (thick syrup made from milk and sugar). As everyone savors the last bit of sugar, Santa (one of Helena's brothers decked out in full regalia) rides up on horseback. Dipping into his huge red pack overflowing with gifts, he calls out the name on each package. Everyone, without exception, seems thrilled with the handmade gifts of clothes, toys, paintings, pottery, or furniture.

18 February 1983

Earlier this month we drove to San José and picked up my parents, who will visit for three weeks. We spent a few days relaxing at the beach, where Karen loved the black volcanic sand (and ate more than her share). At Volcán Irazú, the highest active volcano in the country, we felt transplanted to another planet in the bare landscape of volcanic ash and craters. Cascading waterfalls and gaudy flowers in lowland forest were lovely, but we were glad to leave the heat and humidity behind.

We've been back at Monteverde for a week, where my folks are impressed with the lush cloud forest. Dad, who spent several years on the island of Mindanao in the Philippines as a guerrilla during World War II, finds many similarities in the vegetation between Mindanao and Monteverde. Mom, on her first visit to a tropical environment, is thrilled to walk amidst bamboo, tree ferns, and orchids.

Predictably, Mom shares my dislike for the sinister-looking scorpions in our house. I've warned her that at night when I stumble into the bathroom, I inevitably find one lying in wait. They scurry out from behind dishes in the kitchen cupboards. And they hide out in our underwear in the drawer and in our shoes and boots. Rule number one: Use a flashlight when walking around the house at night. Rule number two: Be on guard in the kitchen. Rule number three: Shake out your clothes and shoes before putting them on.

Ever since we moved here last July, I've worried that a scorpion will crawl into Karen's crib, she'll roll over on it, and it will sting her. Or she'll see one and grab it to play with or eat. I'm the only one, however, who's been stung so far. While I walked across the bedroom floor in bare feet, a scorpion that was skulking in a crevice between two floorboards whipped out his stinger and nailed my little toe. My foot throbbed for the next twenty-four hours.

Despite my innate fear of scorpions, I must admit they are fascinating creatures. They appear prehistoric for good reason. Except for size, they've changed little in the past 425 million years. One early ancestor, unearthed from Wyoming, was a meter in length! With a shudder, I imagine one of our Monteverde scorpions, the size of my index finger, expanded to a meter. Scorpions stun their prey by injecting poison through a stinger at the tip of the tail, then clawlike mouthparts pulverize the victim. Finally the prey's body parts are liquefied and predigested in an enzyme-filled cavity before they enter the gut. Females give birth to miniature scorpions rather than eggs, and the babies ride piggyback on the mother for several days.

Today I take Mom, Dad, and Karen to the Río Lagarto to see harlequin frogs. With Karen strapped to my back, I take the lead as we wander along the stream bank. Suddenly a green vine snake lazily draped over a tree branch ahead of me sways ever so little. I freeze. Ever since I can remember, my mother has had a phobia about snakes. She would never enter the snake building at the zoo, and I was never allowed to keep garter snakes as pets. How is she going to react? I have to point it out to her, because if she sees it unexpectedly she'll panic. I turn and calmly announce that there is a harmless beautiful vine snake three meters away that I want her to see.

Her voice quivers as she bravely says OK. With her feet firmly planted on the ground, she leans forward and cautiously peers into the brush. After a few seconds she turns around, her face ashen. She says she's seen enough, but forcing a smile she admits that it's attractive—in its place.

Of much greater interest are the next two animals we encounter. At a large rock face, I reach into a crevice and extract an ivory-colored, oval-shaped reptile egg. It hatches in my hand and out pops a wet, wide-eyed

Marty and Karen, off to watch frogs. Photo by Peter Feinsinger.

anole lizard. It cocks its head, looks around, then scampers away into the unknown. I pick up a black female harlequin frog with a yellow heart-shaped pattern to show to Karen. She grabs it from me and immediately tries to stuff it into her mouth. Mom rescues the frog (and Karen) just in time.

The highlight of the day for Dad occurs while we're eating our cheese sandwiches on the stream bank. He sees a long column of jagged leaf fragments cruising along the ground. "Leaf-cutter ants!" he announces. He's thrilled to watch ants efficiently snipping out pieces of leaves, struggling back down the plant stems to the ground with their awkward cargo, communicating with their neighbors by batting antennae as they march toward a large mound of dirt, and then disappearing into the opening of their underground nest.

I TALK WITH Mom about my evolving philosophy concerning my current roles. Ten months ago I naively thought that with the help of a baby-sitter and a part-time housekeeper, life as mother, wife, and field biologist would be relatively routine and straightforward. Wrong! Unexpected minor crises are to be expected. Priorities must be flexible. Karen gets sick and she becomes top priority. My weekly frog census will have to wait a day or two. Peter's experimental plants are withering from an unexpected lack of rain. So that he doesn't lose the months-long experiment, he must spend Sunday doing what sounds like a joke—sprinkling water on his plants in the cloud forest. My role as wife assumes top priority, and I take over Peter's maintenance chores for the day. The harlequin frogs inexplicably change behavior and tolerate their neighbors. The field biologist part of me must set aside other demands and spend the day making observations or the opportunity will be lost. I'm not totally comfortable with my philosophy, but I see it as a compromise. When one role assumes top priority, I can't allow my other two-thirds to feel guilty. They will have their turns tomorrow or next week. And I mustn't feel guilty then. Mom nods sympathetically and assures me that I'm doing a fine job.

14 March 1983

Having studied this population of harlequin frogs since 1980, I'm amazed at how long individuals remain in one place. Some frogs have stayed on the same boulders for two years. We know that some amphibians have homing abilities. That is, if displaced from their home site, they return. After harlequin frogs have jumped out of the way of feral pigs snuffling and rooting in the leaf litter, do they return to their displaced

A female harlequin frog peeks out from its crevice in a rock face.

sites? Or what if a tree falls and frightens them into hopping upstream or downstream? Sudden cloudbursts cause temporary flooding. If a frog is washed downstream, does it return to its home site?

I began to test for homing ability two years ago by picking up frogs and carrying them either ten meters upstream or ten meters downstream before releasing them. Then one week later I censused the stream bank and recorded locations of all individuals. Although some frogs had had to climb over or crawl through massive treefalls to return home, they did it. There was no difference in the tendency between males and females to home, nor in the success of homing from upstream versus downstream. Residents (individuals known to have stayed within 1.5 meters of a spot for at least the previous ten days), however, were much more likely to home than were transients (individuals I had not seen before).

As part of a follow-up experiment to compare homing success during the dry season (now) and the wet season (next June–July), last week I moved forty-four frogs ten meters either upstream or downstream. Three days later I found twenty-five individuals that had already returned to within one meter of their capture spot, most at their identical crevice or boulder. Today, one week after displacement, I find another six frogs that have returned. Thus, 70 percent of the frogs homed; most of the individuals that did not home were probably transients. It'll be interesting to see if the frogs show a different pattern during the wet season.

I've been sampling insects and measuring physical characteristics of the frogs' habitat. During the wet season, I'll repeat the measurements to check for any obvious differences between the seasons. I'll also be able to compare sites from where frogs homed back to, versus those to which they did not return.

18 April 1983

Karen wakes up this morning with a fever of 104°F and a red rash on her belly. We flip through our medical encyclopedia and diagnose her symptoms as roseola. Peter draws a tepid bath and immerses a listless baby, who immediately responds with bloodcurdling piercing screams. While Peter attempts to lower Karen's temperature, I run down to the community phone to call the pediatrician in San José. The sudden illness frightens me, and I feel guilty that we've taken our infant daughter to a remote place so far from medical care. If we were back in Gainesville, she could have seen the doctor by now.

Halfway down the hill I run into Lucky, Helena's mother and one of the original Quaker settlers here. She has raised seven children at Monteverde, so I ask her what she did when her kids ran temperatures of 104°F. Her response is reassuring. "I never knew what their temperature was because I never had a thermometer. I just soaked them in cool water." She is so matter-of-fact that I feel relieved.

The pediatrician says that yes, the symptoms strongly suggest roseola. Indeed, he says we should do just what we did, give Karen a tepid bath to reduce the fever and the rash will soon disappear. If not, call him back.

Although there is a small clinic about five kilometers away, we're a long way from expert medical care. At least we have a car and could drive to a real hospital in about three hours. What did the Quakers do in times of emergency thirty years ago? What do people who live in any isolated rural area do in times of emergency? They do their best. And they live with the consequences of inadequate medical care.

My worries dissolve as I walk through the front door and see Peter holding Karen, who grins and reaches out to me. Her fever has subsided, her rash has nearly disappeared, and she almost seems her usual perky self. We lucked out this time.

28 May 1983

I leave home at 7:30 this morning dreading what might be stored in the ominous sky packed with thick gray-black clouds. Two hours later I arrive at the Río Lagarto just as the heavens explode with thunder, lightning, and lashing rain. My umbrella is useless. I'm soaked. And cold. But the worst is the lightning. I scramble up the bank to distance myself from the river and collapse onto the slippery mud slope. If lightning strikes, surely it will hit a tree and not me. Each explosion seems closer. Why didn't I stay home today? I could have worked on data summaries and enjoyed the lightning display over the pasture from the safety of my dining room. I hunch over and bury my head between my knees. While staring at the soggy ground, I see the leaf litter move slightly. Out walks a male Hercules beetle, reminiscent of the ones from Ecuador.

It seems an eternity but is barely two hours before the lightning fades into the distance and the torrential downpour subsides to a sprinkle. I return to the river and find that the harlequin frogs are doing the same: emerging from their crevices, peering out to reconnoiter the situation, and venturing onto the surrounding ground and boulders.

Male Hercules beetle from Monteverde. Males fight among themselves for dominance and for access to females by locking horns. Photo by Peter Feinsinger.

As I RETURN to Monteverde late afternoon, I think about how important friendships are here. Our graduate students are a focal part of our lives, from the social interactions during Sunday brunches at Bill's cabin and lasagna dinners at Greg and Kathy's hexagon house, to the evening research discussions around our kitchen table. Strong bonds of camaraderie develop among biologists doing long-term fieldwork in an otherwise isolated spot. Thinking back over my year spent in Santa Cecilia doing my dissertation research, I'm reminded of how starved I was for intellectual stimulation. The situation here at Monteverde seems ideal. Our graduate students can immerse themselves completely in their research, but they have many opportunities to discuss their observations and results with each other, with Peter and myself, and with other resident and visiting scientists.

My most treasured friend here is Helena. Loving, patient, and responsive to Karen's needs and demands, Helena is a perfect second mother. She also seems to know just what I need and supports me in my effort to combine field biology and motherhood.

18 June 1983

This afternoon, just as we're about to hike the seven kilometers to Santa Elena for our weekly ritual of beer and fried fish dinner, I feel a throbbing, aching sensation under my toenail. Something is alive in there, moving and creating pressure. Helena, here to baby-sit Karen, takes a look and declares I have parasites. Having grown up with them, she knows these particular critters well. As I gasp in pain, she patiently extracts them with a sewing needle and the tweezers from my Swiss Army knife. I have one sore foot when the process is over. Only the thought of cold beer and greasy fish keeps me going as I limp along the mud road to Franklin's restaurant.

Over beer we discuss the biology of my unwelcome toenail parasites, called jiggers or chigoe fleas, found only in the tropics. The larval stage develops in sandy soil and eventually metamorphoses into tiny adult fleas. A fertilized female attaches herself to the foot of a human or other terrestrial mammal. She rapidly burrows into the soft skin between the toes or under the toenail, where she feeds on blood. Expanding to a diameter of about five millimeters, the female produces several thousand eggs over a period of a few weeks. The eggs that fall out onto sandy soil hatch into larvae. Many of the eggs, however, are wasted because they don't land on soil. In the case of human hosts, many eggs end up between the sheets or inside socks. After producing her eggs, the female dies within the host. Sepsis is common when the female dies, often causing blood poisoning and infection. Thus, the females must be removed before they die, by first enlarging the entrance hole, as Helena did for me. At least we can remove our female jiggers. Pity the poor pig or cow that can't! Since the best way to pick up jiggers is by walking barefoot in areas used by farm and domestic animals, I vow to quit going barefoot outside.

29 June 1983

Today is my last of the forty-five weekly observations of aggressive behavior. Besides chasing, pouncing, squashing, and wrestling each other, the male harlequin frogs exhibit a most unusual foot and forelimb waving behavior. One frog faces another frog, raises a front foot and sometimes the entire forelimb into the air, and slowly rotates it in a circular motion. Presumably a form of communication, this bizarre behavior is often exhibited by a male just before he pounces on and squashes another male or after he has finished the squashing, but sometimes both males wave at each other during the aggressive encounter.

Body size does not determine the outcome of fights. Little guys are as likely to be victorious as big guys. The deciding factor is usually whether the frog is an intruder or a resident. In most cases the resident wins the battle, with the intruder eventually retreating or being chased from the area. Not surprisingly, a resident advantage is nearly universal among territorial animals, whether they be frogs, lizards, birds, or mammals. Since the resident has more to lose, he or she may invest more energy and effort in the encounter.

Although fights between female harlequin frogs are similar to those of males, they lack wrestling and are shorter and less intense. Aggression between females is intriguing because such behavior is extremely rare in frogs. Perhaps females defend foraging sites. A female needs to find plenty to eat if she is to develop a large clutch of eggs for the following wet season. Alternatively, perhaps the females defend retreat sites from each other. Or, as one of the graduate students suggested, perhaps they are simply cranky old bitches because of being harassed constantly by males.

Among the forty-one mated pairs of harlequin frogs I found during the year, eight females were attempting to dislodge the male. I watched three of these pairs for over four hours each, with the female still trying to rid herself of the boorish male at the time I left. In the other five instances, the males eventually dismounted and the females responded with a vengeance by creeping up behind the departing male, pouncing on him, squashing him, and pounding his head against the ground. My more militant female colleagues would *die* to see this! From watching mated pairs on successive visits, I have records of minimum times pairs stayed clasped together. (Minimum because I don't know how long pairs had already been together when I first found them, nor how long they stayed together after the last time I saw them.) The record is thirty-two days for one pair! Most frogs and toads clasp for only a few hours or a day at most.

Recently I finished up the last of 632 staged encounters between frogs, and the observations reveal differences in behavior throughout the year. Clearly the seasonal changes and the function of aggression relate to reproduction. During the six-month dry season, males clumped together in the wettest areas and they were rarely aggressive. Immediately following the first rains of the wet season, however, they became intolerant of each other.

Throughout the year, on any given day I always found many more males than females—up to ten times as many. Assuming an equal number of both sexes in the population, the remaining females must wander up into the woods or remain hidden in retreat sites. From a practical standpoint, what this skewed sex ratio means is that males compete with each other for females. Thus, it makes sense that males defend territories that provide them with exclusive access to whatever female happens to wander through the area. The skewed sex ratio probably also explains why males clasp females for such an unusually long period of time, and why they go after any female they see, including ones that are not yet receptive. Even if the female is not ready to lay eggs, it might be advantageous to nab her now because he may not have another opportunity. This situation, however, results in a conflict of interest between the sexes because the female could easily find a willing male to fertilize her eggs once she is ready. Males seem to be winning this battle between the sexes. Persistence and tenacity pay off for the male, while the female has the burden of lugging around a male for weeks before she is ready to lay her eggs. No wonder she takes it out on a male who is stupid or wimpy enough to dismount!

4 July 1983

A week ago I moved another thirty-six frogs either ten meters upstream or ten meters downstream. Since so many of the frogs had already homed by day three in the dry season, I censused at intervals of one day, three days, and one week to get a better idea of how quickly the frogs return home.

Amazingly, after one day I found that seven frogs were already back in their original spots. After an additional two days, another seven were home. And today I find eleven more that returned to within one meter of their capture spot. That makes a total of twenty-five frogs that homed, or 69 percent of the animals that I displaced—no difference from the dry season.

So why do some frogs home? Two possibilities are because the home spot contains a lot of food or because it provides good shelter and ideal moisture conditions. Yet my data from sampling insects and comparing the physical qualities of sites reveal no trends. Perhaps frogs home simply because it's familiar ground where the resident has learned the precise locations of the good spots for food, emergency shelter, or moist micro-habitats. Although I can't explain *why* frogs home, it's clear that some individuals stay at home, while others roam the countryside. And there is no correlation with gender or size of the frog. Perhaps someday we'll learn the answer, but the *why* questions in biology are always the most elusive.

15 July 1983

Peter and I harbor mixed feelings as we board the plane today clutching several full data notebooks, Karen, and an overstuffed diaper bag. It's been an exciting and rewarding sabbatical year, but we're also looking forward to interacting with our colleagues back home.

It'll also be good to have quick access to medical care for Karen. Several days ago the lab in San José presented us with the results of Karen's stool sample: she has giardiasis. The culprit is a protozoan parasite, *Giardia,* that causes diarrhea, cramps, and weight loss. We've started her on medication, and her intestine should be free of parasites with time. The more frightening revelation is that she tested positive for tuberculosis. We'll have her retested back in Gainesville. If she indeed does have TB, Peter and I will have to deal with our guilt for having taken her to a dairy community and inadvertently exposed her to the debilitating disease.

From the standpoint of research, I couldn't have asked for a better population of frogs. They cooperated in allowing me to watch their daily activities, and I was able to gather information on over a thousand individuals. Secure in the knowledge that these frogs are so abundant, I plan to return to the Río Lagarto in future years to unlock more of the secrets of harlequin frogs.

ONCE AGAIN we lucked out with Karen's health. Subsequent TB skin tests in Gainesville indicated that the one done in San José had been a false positive. The giardiasis was cleared up in time, and we had a healthy toddler who had survived her first tropical experience.

Our year in Monteverde was special, and it surely molded Karen's being. Karen was irresistibly fascinated by animals at an early age, although at first she only wanted to eat them. We often found her in a corner of the house, happily crunching on june bugs. Between the ages of eight and thirteen months, Karen would awaken us in the morning by her imitations of roaring howler monkeys and cooing ruddy pigeons, uttered with great pride as she bounced up and down in her crib. And then there was the influence of Helena, a social butterfly, flitting from one end of the community to the other, helping and visiting friends, always with Karen in tow. Perhaps that explains why Karen makes friends easily.

I spent many hours that year expressing in the field, sometimes under difficult circumstances: with ants swarming nearby, during lightning storms, and at night with my headlamp propped on the ground. The frozen milk became my lifeline to the freedom I needed to do fieldwork. To this day I feel a tremendous sense of satisfaction and accomplishment at having combined long-term intensive fieldwork with motherhood.

DR. WILLIAM L. DOWNES JR., a world expert on parasitic flies, identified our black hairy flies as members of the family Sarcophagidae. The species, *Notochaeta bufonivora*, seems to specialize on frogs as hosts in Central and South America.

7

LOST GOLD OF THE
ELFIN FOREST

S A CHILD I loved to raise tadpoles and I still do. So for my next project I chose to work with tadpoles, or *cabezones* (big heads) in Costa Rican slang, of the meadow treefrogs of Monteverde. I was interested in the ways these tadpoles cope with their highly unpredictable environments: temporary bodies of water, ranging from small ponds to water-filled cow hoof prints. Often the shallower sites dry up before the tadpoles can transform into froglets. Even if they don't dry up, these puddles are often short on food. Sometimes the best morsels available are other tadpoles, and in fact meadow treefrog tadpoles are cannibalistic. They readily eat each other as well as eggs of their own species.

Although I had planned to do a series of experiments with meadow treefrog tadpoles over the next several years, after the first year I was lured away by my first sight of golden toads—a spectacle of amphibian show-stoppers in gold and Day-Glo orange. I intended to switch entirely from *cabezones* to golden toads, but unforeseen circumstances drove me back to the tadpole experiments while waiting for the toads' next show.

SUMMER 1986

25 May 1986

"How much longer till we get to Costa Rica?" asks Karen ten minutes into our first plane flight for the day. I explain that first we must go to Miami and get onto a bigger plane that will take us to Costa Rica. The ride on the big plane will last several hours. With a puzzled expression, Karen asks, "Mommy, is it just your ami, or is it other peoples' ami too?" The couple across the aisle chuckles.

This is the first leg of what I can tell is going to be a long trip. Karen (barely four years old), her brother, Rob (eighteen months), and I are on our way to join Peter, who has been in Monteverde for several weeks setting up his research project on hummingbirds and plants. Our suitcases are filled with clothes, toys, and books; two cardboard boxes are bulging with plastic containers for housing tadpoles.

The flights go smoothly, although they seem longer than usual because of the challenge of keeping two small children amused. Eventually we land in the airport near San José and pass through immigration. I quickly grab two luggage carts. When I spy the first suitcase cruising toward me, I order Karen to sit on the floor with the three carry-ons, dump Rob in her arms, and demand, "Don't let go of Rob no matter how much he cries." By the time I grab the suitcase off the conveyer belt, another passenger has swiped both of my empty carts. I desert the kids, carry-ons, and suitcase and dash off to find a cart. None left. Frustrated, I elbow my way back through the crowds of people only to see my carry-ons and suitcase sitting alone. No kids. After a frantic search, I find Karen chasing Rob through the crowd, both kids laughing hysterically, expending pent up energy. Finally I manage to consolidate kids and luggage. We're the last to clear customs. By this time I'm hot, exhausted, and quite eager to share parental responsibility. Suddenly Karen screeches, "Daddy!" There's Peter, looking worried that we'd missed the plane. After hugs and kisses, we pile into the aging Land Rover and head up the mountain toward Monteverde.

6 June 1986

Recently the kids helped me unpack my plastic bowls and cups—containers for raising *cabezones*. Long ago I'd discovered that the most mundane plastic household items are often more useful for fieldwork than overpriced specialty equivalents from scientific supply houses. A plastic turkey baster is an efficient tadpole scooper. Plastic shoe boxes make excellent terraria for keeping pairs of frogs until they deposit eggs. Plastic bowls can simulate small pools. Clear plastic drinking cups provide short-term housing for single tadpoles, although after a bad experience I'm now cautious about which kind I use. In preparation for an experiment last year, I had placed each of sixty tadpoles in a separate clear plastic cup with springwater, fed them, and left them to acclimate for twenty-four hours. Thirty cups were regular-strength and thirty were extra-strength, same brand. When I returned the following day, almost all the tadpoles in the extra-strength cups were belly-up and dead. All thirty tadpoles in the regular-strength cups were happily swimming laps and munching down their tadpole chow. Apparently, chemicals released from the extra-strength cups had poisoned the tadpoles. The take-home message: Be kind to your friends be they humans or tadpoles, and use only regular-strength plastic cups for your parties and for your experiments.

The first question I want to answer is a simple one: If the puddle begins to dry up, can meadow treefrog tadpoles speed up their development? If so, they would increase their chance of metamorphosing in time to escape before the puddle vanishes. I'll raise one group of tadpoles in bowls with a constant amount of water, and another in bowls with less and less water, imitating a puddle that's drying up.

This afternoon Karen, my budding young tadpole biologist, gleefully wades into the pond with me and helps collect *cabezones*. We keep 144 tadpoles all at the same stage of development and assign eight to each of eighteen beige plastic bowls. Each day I'll change the water in the bowls so that accumulated wastes won't affect growth and development, and every third day I'll decrease the amount of water in those bowls designated as "drying-up puddles." I'll dump eighty milligrams of a prepared tadpole chow called Frog Brittle into each bowl daily.

20 June 1986

All went well with the experiment until yesterday, when I caught Rob using his juice cup to even out the water levels of the bowls. Not knowing for how long he'd been performing this act of kindness to the tadpoles, I decided to take no chances. Karen and I spent the afternoon releasing all the tadpoles back into their pond, then collecting 144 new tadpoles from a different pond. I spent the evening re-creating the experiment—in a place inaccessible to Rob.

MIDMORNING, AFTER considerable consternation and mild panic, we surrender the house to an invading army of ants. Our house is literally alive with raiding parties and columns of reddish brown army ants with a mission—to grab every small moving creature they can find. Thousands of ants march purposefully along the floor, up the walls, over the counters, and along the rafters. Before long they occupy every room of the house. Scorpions, crickets, and spiders frantically dart helter-skelter, but their escape tactics are futile.

Early evening we return to a clean house. Having secured the insects, scorpions, and spiders as booty for later consumption, the ants have marched elsewhere. At least for a short time, our house will be free of scorpions. A great natural form of pest control. Karen comments that she's glad army ants don't raid homes at night and that she wasn't sick in bed today.

7 July 1986

We're in San José getting exit visas. And enjoying restaurant meals as a break from the limited range of variations on "tuna glop" we concoct in Monteverde. Last night we started out at a great little bar we've nicknamed the "Boca Bar." A *boca* (Spanish for "mouth") or *bocadito* (little mouth) is an appetizer served with beer. At this bar you can choose from among thirty-five different *bocas* with every round you order, including popcorn, fried banana chips, French fries, slices of avocado, slivers of cooked carrots, slices of soft white cheese, bite-sized cross sections of hot dogs, and fried tidbits of beef and onions. The *bocas* are great, but actually the best part about Boca Bar is the ambience. Three walls are lined with small booths, each with its faded velveteen curtain that ensures privacy. Couples self-consciously wander into the bar, sidle over to a booth, and quickly close the heavy curtain. Waiters coming to take orders or to deliver beers and *bocas* always knock on the wall discreetly and then wait a bit before opening the curtain.

At a nearby restaurant we began with *cebiche,* one of my all-time favorite foods of Latin America: a cocktail of shrimp, fish, or other seafood marinated in lemon juice, onions, and herbs. When I started working in Latin America in the late 1960s, *cebiche* was generally prepared with raw seafood. Now, however, the shrimp or fish is usually cooked before being marinated, because of the risk of cholera. Each country, and in some cases different regions within the country, has its own unique way of preparing *cebiche,* but all varieties are delicious. After the *cebiche* we feasted on mounds of *arroz con pollo* (chicken and rice). Unlike *cebiche, arroz con pollo* is quite standardized: a pile of saffron rice mixed with canned peas, onions, spices, and shredded chicken, topped with dabs of mayonnaise and ketchup. *Arroz con pollo* is always good. Not terrific, but good.

5 August 1986

Over the past two weeks, the *cabezones* have been transforming. Sure enough, the first to erupt their front legs and absorb their tails were those from the bowls with decreasing water levels. So it looks as if meadow tree-frogs do indeed have the flexibility to speed up their development in a deteriorating environment. Today the last slowpoke sprouts its front legs, ending the experiment. To celebrate, the kids and I have a party with chocolate cake, after which we release all the froglets at their pond. All three of us giggle as the froglets squirt out of the plastic bags in all directions and disappear into the high grass. No matter how often I see it, I'm still fascinated by the magic of metamorphosis. How unlikely that an algae-eating blob that is mostly intestine with a prim little mouth at one end and a finny tail at the other end, propelling itself through the muddy water, should transform into a big-eyed, big-mouthed predator hopping about on land!

SPRING–SUMMER 1987

19 March 1987

Peter and I doubled up on our teaching at the University of Florida so we could begin fieldwork early this year. Since there won't be any meadow treefrog tadpoles until after the start of the rainy season, I'll begin with harlequin frogs and their fly parasites. Years ago Alan Pounds and I had found parasitized frogs only during the dry season, so the timing should be right. I probably have until late May to learn more about how the flies select their hosts and whether the frogs have any way of discouraging female flies from laying tiny maggots on them.

Today I search for harlequin frogs in the reserve. An intense search nets me only two males and one female, all extremely emaciated but without maggots. The ground is dry and the stream barely has any flowing water.

23 March 1987

Confident there'll be harlequin frogs at the Río Lagarto, I hike down and spend the day back "home." It's as peaceful and beautiful as before but easier to navigate because the water level is the lowest I've ever seen it. Much of Costa Rica, including Monteverde and vicinity, has experienced warm, dry conditions this year because of a strong El Niño weather pattern. The stream banks are dry, and moss covering the boulders is gray and crusty. Nonetheless, the harlequin frogs are more abundant than ever. I find 308 individuals in one of my study sites, 403 in the other. But not a single frog is parasitized by fly maggots. Could it be *too* dry? Since Alan and I had found almost all attacked frogs in the wettest spots, aggregated around waterfalls, we had concluded that the maggots need to pupate in moist habitats. Perhaps since the water level is so low this year, it's just too dry for the flies. I'm relieved to know that the frogs are fine but disappointed that I can't continue the fly study. I suspect the reason so many frogs are visible is that they've left their retreats to seek out what moist sites still exist, close to the water's edge.

6 April 1987

The kids are in bed, I've just washed the dishes, and now I'm getting my backpack ready for tomorrow's fieldwork. As the wind howls and the rain pounds on my roof, there's a loud knock at the door. There stands Wolf Guindon, field coordinator for the Monteverde Cloud Forest Reserve, shivering beneath the water pouring off his green plastic rain poncho. With his infectious grin, Wolf blurts out, "Marty, the golden toads are out! You've got to come see them!"

I've never seen these elusive toads. Now is my chance. Wolf says that the toads appeared within forty-eight hours after the first real rain in twenty-two days. Surely they're ready to breed. "I'll meet you tomorrow morning at the station at eight o'clock," I promise. I can hardly contain my excitement. I'm finally going to see golden toads.

As Wolf retreats into the rain he turns, waves, and shouts, "Marty, you're not going to believe it!"

I'm almost as excited to spend the day with Wolf as I am to see the toads. Born and raised a Quaker in Alabama and later one of those jailed for refusing to register for the military draft, Wolf is one of Monteverde's original settlers. He is also Helena's father. One of the founders of the cloud forest reserve, and certainly the person who's logged the greatest number of hours exploring its terrain, Wolf is without doubt the person who knows the most about golden toads.

GOLDEN TOADS are the most spectacularly colored of all toads, just as dramatic as the distantly related golden frog of real and legendary fame. Males range in color from uniform golden orange to red-orange. Females, in contrast, are mottled black, yellow, and scarlet. Golden toads live in the elfin forest near the continental divide only in this one mountain range, the Cordillera de Tilarán. The elfin forest, so named because the trees are stunted from constant buffeting by strong winds, is a magical setting of drifting mist, tangled tree roots, gnarled tree trunks and branches, and leaves constantly dripping with water. Shrouded in clouds and fog, the tree branches support dense carpets of bromeliads, orchids, liverworts, begonias, ferns, and mosses.

Golden toads are considered to be vulnerable to extinction because their distribution is small and restricted. Although the species was originally described in 1966, few studies have been undertaken on the golden toad's biology, in large part due to the briefness of their annual appearance. The toads live underground inside networks of tree roots year-round except for a few days or weeks during the transition period between the dry and wet seasons, in April and May—a time when most academic biologists are teaching. During this time, the toads emerge to engage in a frenzy of mating activity and to lay eggs in the tiny rain pools that form at the bases of trees.

7 April 1987

Standing in the heavy mist, still with the grin of anticipation on his face, Wolf is waiting for me at 8:00 A.M. sharp. We begin our hour-and-a-half uphill trek along a meandering path through constant drizzle and deep mud, first hiking through cloud forest and then through the gnarled elfin forest. Visibility is nil. The forest is dark and dank. I shiver beneath long underwear, wool sweater, down vest, and weatherproof jacket. I try to keep pace with Wolf (which would be an impossible task even for an experienced cross-country runner, which I'm not), all the while thinking to myself, "This is *miserable!*"

As I round a bend, I slide to a sudden halt. In front of me is one of the most incredible sights I've ever seen. Congregated in and around the small pools at the bases of stunted trees sit over a hundred dazzlingly bright orange toads, poised like statues—jewels scattered about the dim understory.

I forget that I'm cold and wet. Quietly leaning against a moss-covered tree trunk, I watch as a male twitches ever so slightly, inducing his nearest neighbor to pivot 180 degrees and pounce on him. The victim utters a soft "release" call that functions to tell the aggressor that he has made a mistake and is attempting to mate with another male. The aggressor dismounts, and both resume their statuelike poses. I can feel the tension in the air. Each male toad is waiting for the chance to mate as soon as a female appears. I whisper to Wolf that this sight is the ultimate for a field amphibian biologist. Timing is perfect. Males are still waiting for the females to emerge. I'll

Two male golden toads, poised like statues at a breeding pool in the elfin forest.

hike up and watch the toads every day they're out. Wolf offers to accompany me and help with observations.

8 April 1987

Golden toads are labeled "explosive breeders," meaning that all the females lay eggs during a short period of time—over a couple of days or weeks at most. Males of explosive breeders not only call to attract females, they also actively search for females that haven't yet approached the mating aggregations. Often males act aggressively toward one another, jostling their neighbors and displacing one another from favored sites and even from females. In contrast, the harlequin frogs at the Río Lagarto are the epitome of "prolonged breeders"—species in which different females reach the egg-laying stage at widely different times over a period of many weeks or months. Although competition for mates may be just as intense among males of prolonged breeders as among males of explosive breeders, aggression is much less overt. Chance may play a leading role in which male is in the right place at the right time when a receptive female wanders by.

In contrast, in explosive breeders, certain males perpetually seem to be more successful than others. What influences success? One factor might be size. In some cases, pairing may be random, which means small and large males may have an equal chance of mating with a female of any size. In other instances, though, large males may have a consistent advantage, obtaining the most matings with females of any size. In still other situations, a sorting process occurs: large females mate with large males and small females with small males. But how do the different-sized frogs get sorted out? Most likely either the females choose from among males of different sizes, or else males compete aggressively for females with the bigger males winning the choice females—larger ones, which produce more eggs.

Last night I planned my preliminary study. First, to address the question of which male golden toads end up with the most matings, Wolf and I will measure all males and females at each of several breeding pools and identify the pattern of mating. Then I'll sit on the ground and watch, hoping to blend in with the mud and mist in order to see females actively choosing certain males over others, or else males jostling or displacing each other for access to females.

WOLF AND I spend all day in the forest taking measurements. Females have emerged from underground. We find six pairs laying eggs in a tiny pool, about a half meter in diameter, almost hidden under a tangle of tree roots. Nine other pairs hide under plants a few meters away. Near the same pool, we see a large orange blob with legs flailing in all directions: a writhing mass of toad flesh. Closer examination reveals three males, each struggling to gain access to the female in the middle. Forty-two brilliant orange splotches poised around the pool are unmated males, alert to any movement and ready to pounce. Another fifty-seven unmated males are scattered nearby. In total we find 133 toads in the neighborhood of this kitchen sink–sized pool.

It looks as though large males might have the advantage. Unmated males away from the pool average 45.5 millimeters, whereas unmated males waiting at the prime spots at pool's edge average 48.0 millimeters. Mated males are the largest, averaging 51.0 millimeters.

14 April 1987

Wolf and I have been measuring toads at pools for quite a few days now, and every time we find the same trend. Mated males are the largest, unmated males at the pool are intermediate, and the smallest males are scattered about some distance from the pool. The breeding pools are all similar: small water-filled depressions that form at the bases of trees when strong winds rock the trunks back and forth and loosen the root masses. Each breeding pool seems overcrowded with up to twenty pairs of toads simultaneously laying eggs.

Today I spend several hours glued to the muddy ground, watching toads in action. Unmated males at the pool remain motionless until a slight movement by one individual starts a chain reaction of twitches across the whole group, resulting in pounces and release calls. During one twenty-five-minute time period, I watch a male-female pair engaged in egg laying get molested by twelve different unmated males, each attempting to dislodge the mating male. None of the aggressors is successful. Unmated males away from the pool generally don't attempt to enter the breeding site, but they pounce on each other and attempt to dislodge mated males from incoming pairs as these hop toward the water. Again, none succeeds in displacing the mated male. I see only two unmated females, and both are quickly pounced on by males.

20 April 1987

Breeding seems to be over. I found the last female four days ago, and gradually the males have returned to their underground retreats. Every day the ground is drier and the pools contain less water. Today's observations are discouraging. Most of the pools have dried completely, leaving behind desiccated eggs already covered with mold. Unfortunately, the dry weather conditions of El Niño are still affecting this part of Costa Rica.

5 May 1987

The shady understory of the elfin forest once again sparkles with electric orange splotches. Male golden toads are back, the day following the first good rain since the breeding bout in April. Sadly, none of the pools I studied has tadpoles. Apparently none of the offspring from April has survived. Females have not yet appeared for the second round. Perhaps they're waiting for more rain.

17 May 1987

Finally, rain and heavy mist have filled the pools. Females have resurfaced, and the mating frenzy has begun anew. I'll continue to take measurements and observe behavior, but I'll also pull out the plastic cups again and do an experiment with golden toad tadpoles.

NOT ONLY ARE golden toads highly unusual in their spectacular color as adults, but their eggs are also quite different. While most toads lay many thousands of small eggs, golden toads lay only about two hundred to four hundred large eggs full of yolk. Why are they so different? The other day while watching a pair of golden toads deposit eggs in a tiny rain pool, I began thinking about the contrasts in the sorts of places where eggs are deposited. The other common toads here, marine and evergreen toads, lay their eggs in relatively large, permanent bodies of water that are virtual organic soups of algae and other plant matter that tadpoles eat. Considering that golden toads lay their eggs shortly after the tiny elfin-forest pools form, there isn't much time for algae to accumulate. And because many golden toad females lay their eggs in the same pool, thousands of tadpoles may compete for what little food exists. Might the large yolk-filled eggs of

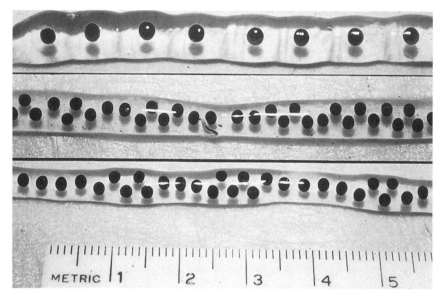

Egg strings from three species of toads at Monteverde. Note the size difference between golden toad eggs (*top*) and the smaller marine toad and evergreen toad eggs.

Rob watching toad tadpoles swim about in their cups.

golden toads provide backup food, enabling the tadpoles to complete transformation in their impoverished environments?

To answer this question, I set up an experiment with newly hatched tadpoles of golden toads, marine toads, and evergreen toads. I put each hatchling, fifty per species, into its own plastic cup, where it will grow and develop: 150 cups arranged on the floor in a room inaccessible to Rob. Half the tadpoles (twenty-five per species) will be fed as much as they can eat of a mixture of tadpole chow and powdered fish food. The other seventy-five tadpoles won't be fed at all. Over the next month I'll record growth, development, and survival for each of the 150 individuals.

22 May 1987

In the elfin forest, many pools have eggs that are about ready to hatch. Egg laying seems to be over, however, as the females and most of the males have disappeared once more. If the mist and drizzle continue this time, the tadpoles in their forest pools might develop and transform.

I've pieced together a preliminary picture of the golden toad's reproductive biology. Males emerge first and exhibit one of two behaviors in attempting to acquire a mate. Some congregate at pools. Others hang out in the woods away from the pools. After a few days the females emerge from underground. There seems to be no female choice involved in pairing; and in fact as soon as a male spies a female, he rapidly hops over and climbs aboard. The female, carrying the male piggyback, seeks out a secluded spot under vegetation where the pair remains for eight to ten hours. Presumably during this time the female ovulates her eggs. Eventually the pair leaves the safety of the vegetation and heads toward a pool. Along the way the pair runs a gauntlet of unmated males, each of which attempts to displace the piggybacking male by actively trying to push, kick, or pry him off. Finally arriving at the pool, the pair still isn't home free. A ring of intermediate-sized males lies in wait. Balls of writhing toad bodies suggest that competition for females is intense. It's no wonder. At any given time, the pool and its surroundings hold from three to over twenty times as many males as females. Large males seem to be the most successful in mating. Although smaller individuals clasp unmated females just as eagerly, apparently their chances of holding on to their prizes are low. Their time will come. With another year's worth of growth, they may become fathers yet.

20 June 1987

Karen is very concerned about the marine and evergreen toad tadpoles that are not getting fed. They still swim around their cups, but they aren't growing. On the other hand, the unfed golden toad tadpoles are growing and developing. All the tadpoles that are being fed are large and many have well-developed hind legs already.

Rainy season has finally begun, and meadow treefrogs have been laying their eggs wherever they can find water. After "playing biologist," Karen left some of my extra bowls outside. Overnight they filled with rainwater and little black and white eggs. Much to her delight, she now has her own *cabezones* to raise.

2 July 1987

Miraculously, we've made it through the entire toad tadpole experiment without a child-related mishap. The agreement was that the kids could play quietly in the room as long as I was working there but would not go near the cups without supervision. I was especially afraid that Karen might sneak some food to the unfed toad tadpoles. Or that Rob's rubber ball might hit one plastic cup, knock it into the next, and so initiate a classic domino effect of toppling cups and stranded tadpoles.

The results of the experiment are intriguing. All tadpoles that I fed, of all three toad species, transformed successfully into little toadlets. Not surprisingly, none of the unfed marine or evergreen tadpoles survived. In contrast, every one of the food-deprived golden toad tadpoles metamorphosed successfully into a healthy-looking toadlet by metabolizing its huge belly full of yolk. Amazingly, the food-deprived tadpoles transformed even faster, though at a smaller body size, than the fed tadpoles. It seems that if external food is not available, in real life golden toad tadpoles will metabolize their yolk as quickly as possible, transform at a small size, and leave the pool for better hunting on land. If food is available to the tadpoles, they'll eat, bulk up, and develop more slowly. Thus, the large sizes of golden toad eggs appear to provide flexibility in their unpredictable environment.

I PLAN TO write a proposal to the National Geographic Society for funding so that I can continue to work with the golden toads for another two years. This has not been a good year for the toads with respect to recruiting new individuals into the population. During April nine of the ten pools where I found eggs had dried up completely before the eggs had even hatched, and all the hatchlings from the tenth pool dried up later. From May's breeding bout, half the pools containing eggs dried up before the tadpoles were a week old, and only twenty-nine tadpoles survive in the remaining pools. Assuming that each of the 151 females I found during April and May had laid an average of three hundred eggs, then about 45,300 eggs were deposited. Even if all twenty-nine tadpoles transform successfully, certainly that's not sufficient to replace the aging adults that will die over the coming ten months. The toads will need better luck next year.

SPRING–SUMMER 1988

2 May 1988

The proposal to the National Geographic Society was successful. I'm back, this time with a research grant to study the reproductive behavior of golden toads.

Anxious to see what's going on, I spend a few hours with Wolf today in the reserve. Last year the toads first emerged in April, so Wolf has been checking for toads and monitoring the condition of the breeding sites for the past month. No toads yet. Wolf says that the forest is about as dry as he has ever seen it, and that those few pools that did form dried within forty-eight hours. The leaves on the ground crunch under our feet, in stark contrast to last year's soggy ground. We don't see many dink frogs or tree-frogs, probably because it's so dry. They may be hiding out wherever they can find a moist retreat.

21 May 1988

Finally the long dry spell is over. We've gotten buckets of rain in the last few days. One afternoon after tromping through the rain and mud for five hours, I finally see in front of me the first reddish orange male sitting like a rubber bathtub toy next to a pool of water. Eagerly I rush to pick him up and measure him, then stop and decide just to admire him. I don't need to know his exact body length. As I continue down the path, I tell myself that surely his compatriots will soon arrive.

5 June 1988

We just suffered through two weeks of cold, rainy weather, just like the storm that brought out the toads last year. But no toads. Not even the lone male that I found last month. The forest seems sterile and depressing without the bright orange splashes of color I've come to associate with this weather. I don't understand what's happening. Why haven't we found at least a few hopeful males, checking out the pools in anticipation for the big time? Is the temperature too cold? Too warm? It's already past the time the toads have always emerged before.

18 June 1988

Ten, twenty, thirty, forty, fifty, sixty, seventy, eighty, ninety, one hundred, ten, twenty, thirty, forty, fifty, sixty, seventy, eighty, ninety, two hundred, ten . . . For the past hour I've been sitting in the rain counting eggs that meadow treefrogs deposited in my experimental beige bowls around the edge of a small pond. If the golden toads never emerge, at least maybe I can complete a different project. My attention-diverting experiment is designed to test whether female meadow treefrogs choose some sites over others in which to lay their eggs.

First, I predicted that more eggs would be deposited in bowls with deep water than in bowls with shallow water. Since deeper puddles are less likely to dry up than are shallower ones, tadpoles are more likely to meta-morphose successfully. So if females can perceive the difference, deeper puddles should be more popular egg-laying sites. Several days ago, after

Plastic bowls set out in pairs around a pond, an experiment to determine if meadow treefrogs make wise choices about where to lay their eggs.

sunset I placed bowls in pairs around the edge of a pond, one bowl with deep water and the other with shallow water. The next morning I recorded in which bowls the frogs had deposited their eggs, and I counted the number of eggs in each bowl. As expected, thousands of eggs were deposited in the bowls with deep water. There were hardly any eggs in the shallow bowls.

The following night I tested the prediction that fewer eggs would be deposited in bowls that already contain meadow treefrog tadpoles than in bowls that lack tadpoles. Because meadow treefrogs are cannibalistic, a female should avoid laying eggs in a site that already has hungry tadpoles. I set out bowls in pairs (one bowl of each pair with tadpoles, the other without) and then recorded how many eggs had been deposited in each bowl the following morning. Again, as predicted, thousands of eggs were deposited in the bowls lacking tadpoles, versus very few eggs in the bowls with tadpoles.

Finally, last night I gave the frogs a choice between two "bad" situations—shallow water without tadpoles versus deep water with tadpoles. I predicted that females would deposit eggs randomly and thus the number of eggs deposited per bowl would not differ substantially between the two conditions. Hallelujah! Earlier, on the first two nights of experiments, the frogs not only cooperated in using the plastic bowls, they actually preferred them to the natural pond. Last night when the bowls presented only the two "bad" choices, most females laid their eggs in the pond instead of the bowls. The few bowls that acquired eggs showed no difference in the number of eggs between the two experimental conditions. All three of my predictions have been supported, suggesting that female meadow treefrogs indeed make "wise" choices regarding where to lay their eggs.

6 July 1988

A few days ago I spent six hours searching for harlequin frogs in my former study site along the Río Lagarto. I couldn't find even one. Last year I'd found over seven hundred individuals along the same stretch of stream, sitting on boulders and on the ground at the edge of the forest. During my year-long study in 1982–83, the frogs were always out and active, dry season or wet season, hot or cold, sunshine or rain. What's happened? Have I done something? Maybe I inadvertently transmitted a virus to both the golden toads and the harlequin frogs and they've all died? Maybe my boots were contaminated with a lethal fungus or bacterium that I introduced into both habitats? Maybe it wasn't my doing at all. Could the drought have caused massive mortality? Could it have been pollution from the Arenal Volcano eighteen kilometers away, which has been erupting violently in recent years, spewing out noxious chemicals? Or maybe a local outbreak of a particularly nasty parasite that attacks and kills frogs?

31 July 1988

A feeling of golden toad catastrophe nags at me more and more. Over the past three months, Wolf and I have made innumerable four-hour round trips to the toads' known breeding sites. We were there in weather only a golden toad could love: windy, cold, wet, and miserable. Yet the only record is the one I made in mid-May. With every passing day, we've gotten more and more discouraged. Nine toads were sighted at a pool about five kilometers southeast of the main breeding area. Wolf checked the pool a week later and found no adults, eggs, or tadpoles. It seems that golden toads have just skipped breeding this year.

Wolf laments that this year is the first time since the reserve was established in 1972 that the toads haven't been out breeding en masse in April or May. He personally has seen them every year. Likewise, visitors to the reserve report having seen hundreds of golden toads each year in the past. But not this year. Contraband golden toads are advertised for sale in the clandestine European pet trade for $500 apiece. Perhaps a team of mercenary collectors has vacuumed the forest and sucked up the toads. But when could they have done this? Somebody would have seen them. And, anyway, there's no way every last golden toad could have been snatched up and smuggled out.

Perhaps it can be blamed on this spring's unusually dry weather. Because the soil was so dry, the depressions around tree roots that normally fill with water from mist during the transition between dry and wet season instead held no water at all until the real rains began in late May. With the abrupt switch to daily downpours, the pools overflowed every day and thus were unsuitable for the toads. I'm thinking that the window of opportunity between dry and wet season, when the toads normally breed, simply didn't exist this year. Somehow the toads may have "known" that conditions were never appropriate for breeding, and they're simply underground. But what about the harlequin frogs? Why aren't they out as usual?

SPRING 1989

5 April 1989

I'm on top of the world in my little rented cabin, one of the highest dwellings in Monteverde at an elevation of 1,560 meters, surrounded by trees and birds. For the next two months, I'll study golden toads while Peter holds down the fort in Gainesville. Swallow-tailed kites soar above me, resplendent quetzals feed at nearby fruit trees, and three wattled bellbirds *bonk* incessantly from all sides. The cabin has two rooms: a downstairs that doubles as living room and kitchen, and an upstairs sleeping loft. A two-burner electric stove and a little wood stove keep me nourished and warm. Taped to the wall next to my bed is a message, hastily scrawled by Karen five minutes before my departure: "Momy. I hop you hav a nis time in Costaryca. I will mis you. I hop yor goldin tods come out. Love, Karen."

I've gotten into a blissful routine here, beginning with the wake-up call at about 5:00 every morning. My alarm clock is a resident troop of howler monkeys that begins their day by vigorously advertising their territory. I stoke up the wood stove, make myself coffee, toast a piece of bread, put a cassette in the tape player, and settle into two luxurious hours of pleasure reading. I've already finished the books I brought: *Eva Luna*, *Gorillas in the Mist*, and *In the Rainforest*. Now I'm working on the library of books in the cabin—a wide selection ranging from adventures of anthropologists in South America to the history of the Spanish conquest in the New World.

By 7:30 I'm decked out in rubber boots, field pants and shirt, and rain gear. I hike up to the elfin forest and until midafternoon I search for golden toads. About 5:00 I return to my cabin, and after a cold shower I start up the stove again, make myself a cup of hot herb tea, and fix myself a simple supper. I spend two to three hours working on my lectures for the course in vertebrate reproductive behavior I plan to give in Tucumán, Argentina, next year. By 9:00 I hit the pillow. Eight hours of sleep on a regular basis! Yes, life is good. Peter and the kids are precious to me, but I must admit I'm enjoying the freedom to set my own schedule and be responsible only for myself. I haven't had such independence since my year in Santa Cecilia. That was over seventeen years ago.

THIS AFTERNOON as I emerge from the cloud forest, I witness the courtship flight of several male quetzals over the pasture in front of me: a dramatic and graceful spiraling through the sky, after which they nose-dive back into the forest with their magnificent tail plumes trailing behind. Resplendent quetzals are one of the most spectacular of all Central American birds, top on the list of "must-sees" for most bird-watchers who come to Monteverde. Their common name comes from *quetzalli,* an Aztec word meaning "precious or beautiful," no doubt in reference to the male's almost meter-long emerald green tail feathers. Males have matching shimmering green heads, backs, and wings and a deep red breast. Although females are colored similarly, they lack the iridescent brilliance and the long tail plumes.

The Monteverde Cloud Forest Reserve and the community itself have become a mecca for ecotourists, especially bird-watchers. In addition to resplendent quetzals, visitors to the area are almost sure to augment their bird life lists with three-wattled bellbirds, and if they're lucky, with a bare-necked umbrellabird or a black guan.

To accommodate the influx of ecotourists, Monteverde has changed dramatically since the days I first worked here in 1979. Now there are buses and taxicabs that shuttle visitors from their hotels to the cloud forest. Hotels and restaurants have sprouted along the road, from Santa Elena nearly to the highest reaches of Monteverde. Wisely, the number of visitors permitted in the reserve at any one time is regulated for the sake of the trails, the vegetation, and the wildlife. In 1985 about seven thousand people visited the reserve. Last year about fifteen thousand visitors signed the register and walked the cloud forest paths. The numbers are expected to rise in the future.

Opinions vary concerning the changes in Monteverde. Some of the original settlers yearn for their former isolation, others feel that "Green Mountain" and the cloud forest they've protected are meant to be shared with others. Although some ignore the intruding strangers, many benefit economically from the tourists. As long as I can remember, some residents have wanted to pave the road up from the highway. The majority, however, argue that if the road were paved, Monteverde would be overrun in no time. So the bumpy dirt road that leads into the clouds still is not paved.

20 April 1989

I keep expecting to see golden toads. It's been raining and the depressions around tree roots are full of water. Just in case the toads had decided to emerge early, Wolf checked the breeding sites throughout March. No toads. Where are they? And where are the other frogs? Today as I walk through the forest, I realize that the dink frogs that used to hop out of my way with every step are now missing. And last night as I crossed the bridge over the Río Guacimal in Monteverde, I noticed an eerie silence. No calling glass frogs. There are still no harlequin frogs at the Río Lagarto. Something is very wrong.

5 May 1989

Frank Hensley, one of my graduate students, just finished up the semester at the University of Florida and arrived here a week ago to help on the golden toad project. He's relieved that the toads haven't emerged yet, as he didn't want to miss the excitement. If there's only one breeding bout this year, perhaps all the females will participate. What an orgy that would be!

This is Frank's first experience in the tropics, and he responds with as much enthusiasm as I did my first trip to Santa Cecilia. Everything is new and exciting. I'm having almost as much fun introducing him to the cloud forest as he's having being introduced to it: katydids imitating munched-on leaves, anole lizards bobbing red and yellow dewlaps at each other, howler monkeys throwing branches (and other objects) down on us, a pair of quetzals preparing a nest in a hollow tree, "hot lips" shrubs displaying their pair of bright red bracts framing the "teeth" of small white flowers. Frank says he feels in the middle of a gigantic greenhouse, surrounded by orchids, begonias, flowering bromeliads, exotic ferns, and giant philodendrons. The cloud forest still feels like a gigantic greenhouse to me, too, even after all these years.

SPEAKING OF howler monkeys . . . having drunk too much herb tea last evening, this morning I wake up about 3:00 and stumble groggily to my rustic outdoor flushless bathroom facility. Just as I collapse onto the wooden seat, without warning a deafening roar erupts from the large tree overhead, scaring the bejeezus out of me. Good thing I'm already in the outhouse! When my pounding heart starts to slow down, I realize that I've startled awake the troop of howlers that had chosen the tree as their sleeping quarters for the night.

10 May 1989

This afternoon Frank brings me a message that Peter called from Florida. I'm supposed to call him back this evening. It's urgent. I worry for the next three hours that something has happened. An accident? An illness? Who is it: Peter, one of the kids, my folks?

At the appointed time I walk down to the community phone and make the call. Peter's voice at the other end sounds strained as he reports the bad news. Yesterday he had his "annual" checkup (which he'd neglected for three years) for his congenital heart defect, a small leak through the ventricular septum. The tricuspid valve has become deformed, and his heart is enlarging. The cardiologist has scheduled open-heart surgery for 25 May. I'll have to wrap things up here in the next few days and return to Gainesville.

My own heart pounds as I hurry back up the hill toward Frank's house to break the news that he'll be in charge. My mind leaps from one thought to another. *Peter:* Soon to have open-heart surgery, he must be frightened. And he must be thinking "What if I don't pull through it?" *Karen and Rob:* How are they handling the situation and what do they know about it? *Frank:* His first time in the tropics, and his major professor not only deserts him, but also dumps the responsibility of a failing research project into his lap.

Frank seems apprehensive but agrees to stay and continue looking for the toads. When they emerge to breed, he'll know exactly how to take the census and record the observations of behavior. And there are plenty of biologist friends here who can help if he needs it.

15 May 1989

I spend my last day packing. Frank searches for golden toads and reports back that *he found a male!* Curiously, it was sitting about three meters from where I found the only one from last year. Maybe this is the beginning. I just pray that, unlike last year, the lone toad will have company. Frank is thrilled. He has finally seen what he came to Monteverde for.

FRANK'S SEARCH for toads after I left was futile. They never appeared. For the second year in a row, we saw no breeding aggregations. There was only the one lone male each year. Despite intensive searches of pools, we found no eggs or tadpoles. No visitors to the reserve reported toad sightings.

Feeling terribly guilty that I'd spent all the funds from the National Geographic Society with nothing to show, I called the director of research as soon as I returned to Gainesville. I optimistically told him that perhaps the toads have simply remained underground for the past two years waiting for better weather. Then I admitted that another possibility is that warmer temperatures and dry conditions may have caused massive die-offs, not only of golden toads and harlequin frogs, but of many other species of amphibians in the reserve and surrounding area. Realistically, I argued that at this point we just don't know. Fortunately, he was sympathetic and reassured me that the society understands the vagaries of field-work. "You're not alone. We've given researchers thousands of dollars to attach radio collars to wild cats so they can track the animals and watch their behavior. And they never even see a cat the whole season, much less attach any radios!"

Next year Peter, the kids, and I will spend our sabbatical year in Argentina. Wolf will survey the elfin forest from March to June. As soon as   and if—male golden toads emerge en masse, he'll call me and I'll hop on a plane to Costa Rica.

8

Mama Llamas and Toothy Escuerzos

WHILE PETER recuperated in the hospital from open-heart surgery, I read aloud to him about Argentina in preparation for our sabbatical year in the northwest of the country. We learned about history, recent politics, geographic diversity, and customs. One description portrayed Argentina as "a nation of Italians who speak Spanish and think they're British." Other authors referred to Argentina as a "neo-Europe," in reference to the country's abundant European immigrant population. As we found out later, neither description is true. Argentina is a tremendously diverse country. The northwestern part resembles Bolivia, in landscape and culture, at least as much as it resembles the central and southern, more European, parts.

The Spanish explorer Juan Díaz de Solís was the first European to set foot on what is now Argentine soil, in 1516. He and other early Spaniards came in search of silver and gold but found none. Spain ruled the region for the next three hundred years until 1816, when the provinces declared independence from Spain. The leader in the fight for independence was General José de San Martín, whom Argentines consider their greatest national hero. Only later, in 1860, did the country take on the name Argentina, from the Latin word for "silver," *argentum*.

KAREN, AT seven years old, had just finished first grade and Rob was 4½ years old when we left Florida for our sabbatical year in Argentina. Karen's first-grade teacher was confident that whatever Karen missed by not going through the second grade in the Gainesville school system would be more than compensated for by experiences gained in Argentina. Her one suggestion was that Karen practice writing English by keeping a daily journal. Peter and I were not to correct her spelling, but to let her sound out the words. And we were not to coach her about what to write. If we had stayed in the States, Rob wouldn't have been old enough to begin kindergarten in the fall, but in Argentina a child begins at four years of age. Thus, before leaving Florida we enrolled both kids in a private bilingual school in the suburbs of San Miguel de Tucumán.

13 July 1989

Seven weeks after Peter's operation, we pack our sixteen suitcases and boxes (mostly scientific equipment and supplies, including a computer, printer, fax machine, and microscope, but also clothes for growing kids, stuffed animals, Legos, and books) into a rented van, drive to Miami, and there pay the exorbitant price of $1,166.40 in overweight charges. Our flights to Santa Cruz, Bolivia, and then to Salta, Argentina, though delayed, are uneventful. Miraculously all our luggage arrives with us, and as the price for passing it through customs, the officers request only a few novelties from our supplies: three counters, a stopwatch, several rolls of flagging tape, and a waterproof notebook. Our friend Monique and another colleague meet us on the other side of customs and drive us south to San Miguel de Tucumán (Tucumán for short). Karen and Rob are thrilled when the car breaks down twice, allowing opportunities to explore. All four of us sleep the last hour of the trip and are awakened at 10:30 P.M. by the announcement "Wake up, here's your new home." We dump the luggage in the living room and collapse into bed, thirty-five hours after leaving Gainesville.

16 July 1989

Anxious to try the famous Argentine beef, I order what I assume to be the smallest steak on the menu: filet mignon. The waiter brings me a huge oval platter with a charcoal-broiled steak hanging off both ends. I object and say there must have been a mistake, this couldn't be filet mignon. He responds that yes, this is what I ordered. Nearly three centimeters thick, the steak is one of the most tender and flavorful I've ever eaten. The steak, lettuce and tomato salad, and a huge mound of French fries add up to the equivalent of $1.50, contrasting sharply with the six-ounce can of tuna fish we bought for $3 at the supermarket yesterday.

After our satisfying dinner, we go to the home of herpetologist Raymond Laurent, our host at the Miguel Lillo Institute, where Peter and I will be working. Monique, who is Dr. Laurent's stepdaughter and also a herpetologist, takes us to the backyard patio, where about twenty-five guests, graduate students and faculty from the institute, stand up. We proceed around the patio and are introduced to everyone Argentine style, kissing on the right cheek. This quantity of kissing is too much for Rob. He objects and soon hides behind me, much to the amusement of the Argentines, whose kids grow up on this form of greeting. Peter gets a break, as men and women kiss, women and women kiss, but men and men generally shake hands. Following introductions, we enjoy a surprise chocolate cake in celebration of Peter's birthday.

I am warned by my new colleagues not to wander out at night around town looking for frogs by flashlight, as I might get picked up by the police for suspicious behavior. Everyone is still nervous about personal safety because of the "Dirty War," a reign of terror during which an estimated thirty thousand people disappeared. *Los desaparecidos* (the disappeared ones) were imprisoned without a trial, tortured, and presumably killed, though many victims have never been found. The Dirty War is still very fresh in people's memories, having ended only six years ago. Of the ten students and faculty involved in this conversation, all but one had colleagues or relatives who disappeared—academics who'd been accused of being "subversives."

The Dirty War began in 1976 with a military coup that overthrew President Isabel Perón. Formerly the vice president, Isabel became president when her husband Juan Perón died in 1974. [As an aside, Juan Perón's first term as president of Argentina began in 1946. His second wife, "Evita," died in 1952. He was overthrown in 1955 and fled to Spain, where he remained in exile through a series of civilian presidents and military dictatorships, until 1973 when he returned to Argentina with a third wife and was once again elected president.] Juan Perón's death left the country in a chaos of soaring inflation and widespread terrorism by both right- and left-wing extremists. Isabel proved inept at handling the crisis, prompting the military coup. Following the takeover, the country's new president, General Jorge Videla, initiated a campaign to eliminate corruption and end terrorism. In reality the campaign (the Dirty War), which involved paramilitary death squads and the military itself, was brutal state-sponsored violence to end opposition to the regime. The Dirty War continued through several changes of leadership until 1983, when widespread political and economic unrest forced the military leaders to call for free elections. Disappearances did not stop overnight, however. Listening to this recent history, I understand why I shouldn't roam the roadside ditches searching for frogs at night.

The get-together continues until early evening, when again the four of us make the rounds of the patio and kiss everyone good-bye, except for the men, who shake hands. Rob cooperates this time, but once in the car announces that he doesn't like all the women kissing him. We warn him he'd better get used to this Argentine custom. And that if he returns to the country in another twelve years, he might actually enjoy it!

6 August 1989

These first few weeks in Tucumán have been hectic: getting the kids registered and ready for school; settling into the rented house; buying a used car; dealing with money changers, bankers, and policemen (to get our residency certificates); shopping for household items; going to the field several times; and socializing. At least we don't have a telephone. The house has been on a waiting list for three years, but it often takes ten years to get a line.

We've finally gotten the kids' school schedules worked out. Karen goes to school all day. During the morning, classes are held in Spanish, then in the afternoon the teachers go over the material a second time in English. Rob's kindergarten is held only in the afternoon, so we've enrolled him in a nursery school for the mornings. The school bus picks up Rob at the nursery school and delivers him to the elementary school in time for him to have lunch with Karen. Both kids seem happy in their situations, although Karen complains that the teachers at school "talk English funny."

We're finding that certain aspects of life here will take time to get used to, for example:

- No shopping between 12:30 and 4:30 or 5:00 P.M.—all businesses are closed for siesta.
- Dinner hour is 10:00–12:00 P.M.—whether in someone's home or a restaurant.
- Electricity outages three hours every day—due to drought and a malfunctioning nuclear power plant.
- Extreme and highly visible air pollution—dust from dirt streets and ash from burning sugarcane fields.
- Irrationality of prices—Rob's nursery school costs only $3.13 per month, but his official smocks cost $22.50 each.

- Inflation—a box of the kids' favorite chocolate cookies today costs three times what it did last week.
- Strangers coming to the front gate and clapping for attention—selling lemons or asking for bus fare home, food, clothing, or money.

ANOTHER CUSTOM to get used to is maté, a strong tea made from the maté plant, a South American member of the holly genus. Very high in caffeine and related stimulants, maté is the national drink of Argentina but is also consumed in Paraguay, Bolivia, Uruguay, southern Brazil, and southern Chile. Drinking maté is an important social ritual, often described as a magical way of strengthening camaraderie and bonding within the group of participants. Dried leaves and stems of the maté plant, or yerba maté, are spooned into a hollow gourd. The gourd is then filled with hot water, and the tea is sipped through a communal metal straw. As each person finishes sipping, he or she returns it to the originator, who pours more boiling water into the gourd and passes the apparatus on to the next person. Each time I burn my lips on the hot metal straw or my palate on the hot water spurting from the straw, I wonder if Argentines have developed callused lips and palates from years of imbibing boiling water. Perhaps I'm just doing something wrong.

Most Argentines never stray far from their maté gourd, metal straw, and thermos of hot water. A typical day at the office begins with a maté-drinking session, everyone sitting around sucking and chatting. After a couple hours of work there's a maté break, and then perhaps another one before lunch. Everyone leaves the office for lunch around 12:30 or 1:00 P.M. and returns between 4:00 to 5:00 P.M. The first activity is another maté-drinking session, followed by work. After another maté session, everyone finishes up the day's chores, then goes home for more maté about 8:00 or 9:00 P.M.

How can Argentines sleep after so much caffeine? Perhaps their bodies become desensitized, since maté drinking begins at a tender age. After the first week of nursery school, Rob informed us that the three- and four-year-olds in his class have a cookie and maté snack every afternoon.

SEVERAL DAYS ago two graduate students, Félix and Gaby, introduced me to the dry chaco habitat of the province of Salta, six hours' drive north of San Miguel de Tucumán. The chaco consists of dry, hot scrubby thorn forests and thickets full of cacti and other spiny plants. We see flocks of forty to fifty green parrots, lots of lizards, and a few snakes.

Félix and Gaby are assistants on a study of the tegu, a large lizard that reaches a meter in length. Unfortunately for the lizards, their skin is beautiful: small, shiny scales, brown or black with crossbars of white, cream, yellow, or peach. Each year more than a million tegu skins are exported from Argentina to various countries, including the United States, where they are made into exotic leather accessories such as belts, shoes, purses, and cowboy boots. The export value of tegu skins is worth millions of dollars to Argentina every year, and tegu hunting represents a significant source of income for rural people. At $4, the price received for just one tegu skin is about the same as a day's wages for a farmhand. Biologists and conservationists are concerned about whether tegu populations can survive this intense harvesting, and the long-term goal of this study is to ensure the continued existence of tegus.

As we walk across the crusty ocher mud of a dried-up pond, Félix and Gaby assure me that if I can't locate a field site closer to Tucumán, this would be the perfect place for my planned study on the interactions between predaceous tadpoles and the tadpoles they eat. After I squander a roll of film photographing cacti and the parched landscape, Félix tells me that he no longer can afford to take pictures. A roll of film and processing costs $10, and his salary as assistant on the tegu project pays $19.50 per month. If he is lucky enough to be awarded a fellowship for the coming year (there are only thirty available for all fields of biology in the entire country), it will pay only $40 per month. Every time the government changes hands, the national funding agency places a different emphasis on research. One year an ecologist may have funding, but the next year the agency no longer funds ecology. Biochemistry or physiology may be preferred. Research programs are constantly being interrupted, for both students and faculty, by the ongoing financial crisis.

13 August 1989

"Run!" I shout to Karen, who is already running as fast as her little legs can carry her away from a spitting mama llama chasing her at full speed. Peter, who has been photographing llamas, is also running at full speed to get between the two. I'm sitting in the car, with one foot on the gas pedal because our old Peugeot has serious ignition problems. Rob watches with awe from the backseat.

It all starts when Karen leaves the car to get a closer look at the llamas in the altiplano (high plains) area during our weekend trip in the mountains west of Tucumán. Her door is permanently jammed, so she climbs out the window and ambles toward a fluffy brown-and-white baby llama, about thirty meters away. Soon its overprotective mama charges full speed toward Karen, spitting white foamy saliva.

Terrified, Karen outruns the mama llama to the car and climbs back in through the window. Peter jumps into the front passenger seat and slams the door. I still have my foot on the gas pedal and my head turned toward Karen in the backseat. When I face forward again, the mama llama's spit-covered nozzle is about six centimeters from my wide-open mouth. I then realize the advantage of manual windows. Our car has very laid-back automatic windows, and it seems an eternity from the time I hit the button until the window is closed and the mama llama's head is *outside* the car. Here's Karen's version of the incident from her journal:

> August 13, 1989. Today was gust wonderfol. It was grat! We went on a long trip to the mountens. We went to Amaicha del Valle wich is a inden vileg. But the most icsiting thing was that on our way back we saw some llamas! And I have never seen llamas! And when we saw them my Dad stoped the car and got out to take some pichers. But I was so cereas that I climed out of the car and went out. And I saw a mama llama and it's baby! And I was so cereas that I went rilly close and the mama probly thot that I was trying to get her baby becus the mama llama ran just as fast as she could. And so did I! But my Dad saw me and held his armes out to cach me. And then as fast as I could I got in to the car! And then the same llama wich had chast me came rite up to the car but the windo was open so it stuck it's head in the windo and snifed my Mom!!!!! But it did not hurt enyone at all. It was so cyoot. It was rill fuzzy. And it had a silly little tale!

17 September 1989

I'm in Canterbury, England, for a week at the First World Congress of Herpetology. Nearly fourteen hundred people representing sixty different countries are attending the meeting. On the first day of the congress, I told friends about my second consecutive lost field season with the golden toads in Costa Rica. Perhaps because golden toads are so well loved as one of the showiest of all amphibians, word spread quickly. Soon strangers as well as acquaintances from many countries shared with me their own recent experiences of failing to find their study animals. A theme soon surfaces. Many populations of amphibians that had previously seemed healthy are now declining or have disappeared entirely. A note of serious concern soon buzzes throughout the congress, with numerous investigators openly sharing their stories and their worries. In hallways, dorm rooms, cafeterias, and pubs, we speculate about the possible causes.

We agree that some declines are clearly the result of habitat destruction, but causes for other declines are not clear. Speculation runs rampant. Perhaps extreme temperatures or drought, due to global warming, are responsible. Many investigators, however, echo the fears I had a few months ago in Monteverde: that they themselves may have been directly or indirectly responsible for the declines. Perhaps we're inadvertently transferring pathogens of some type to amphibians. Could it be a virus? Bacteria? Fungus? Parasites? Others, however, continue to argue that widespread environmental contamination is the more likely culprit—acid rain, heavy metals, or airborne pollutants.

We hope that these informal discussions, though depressing, will lead to coordinated attempts to identify the causes so that we can stop the declines. We're all very worried about losing amphibians. The worry is not only about losing our research livelihood, or fears of what might happen because of their crucial role in the ecosystem (imagine the insect plagues without amphibian predators!), but also because we really care about amphibians. These animals were around long before the first dinosaurs roamed the earth. Although dinosaurs went extinct about 65 million years ago, amphibians are still with us after more than 350 million years. All of us are wondering, though, if we are witnessing the beginning of their end.

20 October 1989

"No!" I screech as I flail my arms while running to the yellow plastic bowls full of tadpoles neatly arranged on the grass in my backyard in Tucumán. A yellow, black, brown, and white kiskadee, a flycatcher relative, has just helped itself to one of my research tadpoles. The bird flies away, but I know it will return. So I vow to turn the kiskadee's depredations to my advantage.

As a spin-off of my work in Monteverde with meadow treefrog tadpoles and aquatic insect predators, I begin a similar experiment with kiskadees as predators of tadpoles. Are four-legged tadpoles, during that awkward teenage phase, more likely to be eaten by birds than are their younger puddle-mates? My first trial is a failure, as recorded in Karen's journal.

> October 20, 1989. In the morning I helped with a icsperement! About a cinde of bird that eats tadpools. They'r called kiskadees. And so we poot some tadpools in a bowl and wached. And I was the first to see the kiskadee! See we would poot a tadpool and a tadpool that's almost a frog in the bowl. See the poynt was that we wanted to see wich one it liked better. But it ate bowth so we don't know wich one it likes better!

LEARNING FROM my mistake, for each of the subsequent trials, I run out and chase away the kiskadee after it eats one tadpole so I can record the identity of the survivor. Most of the birds take a break in between eating successive tadpoles. They wipe their bills on the edge of the plastic bowl and then look around as if to make sure no competitor is lurking in wait to horn in on the bounty. As I'd predicted, nearly all the tadpoles chosen first by the birds are the clumsy four-legged teenagers.

10 November 1989

Since our neighborhood kiskadees are so cooperative, I'll give them more free lunches. Experiments with kiskadees and tadpoles are the perfect project to do with Marcos, a student visiting from the University of Córdoba for two weeks. Marcos is doing a tutorial with me, for credit at his home institution. As part of his learning experience, we designed the experiments together. In contrast to the trials I did with Karen, which considered tadpole age, we'll now focus on the question of what size tadpole the birds prefer.

A few days ago we collected tadpoles from a nearby pond and then divided them into three groups: small, medium, and large. None had four legs, so they hadn't reached the awkward stage yet. We placed various size combinations in plastic bowls, set them out in the backyard, then each day watched from the living-room window. Off and on all day, kiskadees from the neighborhood flew in, perched on the rim of a bowl, peered into the water, grabbed a tadpole, and ate it. Quickly, before giving the bird a chance to eat a second tadpole, we ran out and recorded which tadpoles were left. Nearly always the missing tadpole was the largest in the bowl.

This finding is significant because until now experiments on tadpole vulnerability have almost always involved aquatic insects as predators. These studies have shown that smaller tadpoles are more likely to be eaten than are larger ones, unless the large ones have four legs. Our experiments with the kiskadees, however, imply that large tadpoles aren't home free by any means. They're actually preferred by larger predators such as birds.

24 November 1989

Rainy season will soon begin, and I'm anxious to start my main study of the interactions between tadpole predators and their tadpole prey. Pagaburo, the driver at the Miguel Lillo Institute, has agreed to be my field assistant for the project. Yesterday at my dining-room table, we pored over maps and plotted our first fieldtrip. At 6 feet 5 inches and weighing over

250 pounds, Pagaburo towers over my 5 feet 4 inches, 115-pound frame. Rob is convinced that Pagaburo is a giant.

Pagaburo and I spend today searching for predaceous tadpoles in Santiago del Estero, the province east of Tucumán. Pagaburo, who has assisted many herpetologists in the past, insists that the species we are looking for should be here. But the extremely arid habitat seems inhospitable to me: salt flats and little standing water. We don't find any predaceous tadpoles, but near evening we do find some charming little frogs with huge bronze eyes bugging out from their heads. I put the frogs into plastic bags and stow the bags in the closet of my rustic hotel room so that I can photograph them in the morning.

We're ravenously hungry after the day's fieldwork, so Pagaburo orders us a *parillada mixta* (mixed grill) at the local restaurant. Before coming to Argentina, I had read about the traditional *parillada mixta*, but I wasn't prepared for the variety of tastes and textures that make up this carnivore's feast. We're served a mix of highly spiced sausage (*chorizo*), mild sausage (*salchicha*), blood sausage (*morcilla*), beef kidneys (*riñones*), pancreas (*mollejas*), lower intestine (*chinchulín*), udder (*ubre*), liver (*hígado*), steak, and pieces of chicken. Pagaburo proudly boasts that Argentina is one of the world's leading producers, consumers, and exporters of beef. We stuff ourselves on the *parillada* (I high-grade the sausages, chicken, and steak) and stagger back to the hotel feeling positively bloated.

"I can't sleep!" complains a man from the hotel hallway. He pounds on my door and shouts something I don't understand. I run to the closet and vigorously shake the bags of the now not-so-charming little frogs. This shuts up their raucous *wrank-wrank-wranks*. The man shuffles back to his room and slams the door in disgust. What if the hotel owner evicts me in the middle of the night? I worry awhile, then fall asleep.

An hour later my irate neighbor again storms from his room, charges down the hall, pounds on my door, and shouts obscenities that this time I do understand. I lie in bed longing to strangle my rambunctious roommates, but I'm afraid to move. There's no lock on my door. I pray the man doesn't barge in. Eventually I tiptoe back over to the closet and violently shake the bags. The frogs shut up. Again the man shuffles back to his room, cursing loudly. The guest's sleep and my fear of bodily injury are more important than a few pictures, so I cautiously open my door and release the frogs onto the mud path in front of my room. I tiptoe back to bed. As I fall asleep, I hear my former captives once again building up to their collective fortissimo, but at least they're now out of my hands and farther away from my neighbor's pillow.

5 December 1989

After searching in vain for predaceous tadpoles within a few hours of Tucumán, Pagaburo and I finally give up and drive the six hours north to the dry chaco habitat I visited in August with Félix and Gaby. We cruise the dusty roads and eventually spy several ponds. The owner of the ranch, a woman named Ignacia whose hard life has aged her till she looks positively ancient, welcomes us to search for tadpoles on her land and allows us to camp on the bare dirt in front of her house. Ignacia tells us that the rains began just yesterday, breaking a long, hot dry season. The ponds are less than twenty-four hours old.

Shortly after dark we survey the newly filled ponds and surrounding scrub and find Argentine horned frogs (locally called escuerzos) and llanos frogs, both of which have predaceous tadpoles. Males are calling, but we find no females. By next week, though, we should find tadpoles in the shallow ponds. The frog cacophony also includes mud-nesting frogs, painted-belly monkey frogs, and weeping frogs. In time their offspring will become food for the escuerzo and llanos frog tadpoles.

I THINK ABOUT how different predaceous tadpoles are from most other tadpoles. The latter feed by drawing water into their mouths and then passing the water across a filtering system designed to trap suspended particles. This may happen either by capturing the particles in a fine strainer or by trapping them in mucus. Water then leaves the body through one or two openings called spiracles. Some suspension-feeding tadpoles simply draw in water and feed on whatever bacteria, algae, and other small particles happen to be present. Other species, however, scrape algae from rocks or leaves, and then once the particles are suspended in water inside their mouths, they filter out the food. Still other species take in detritus and small bits of plant and animal matter from the sediment. Again, these bits of food are suspended in water in the tadpole's mouth and then trapped in the filtering system. In stark contrast, escuerzo and llanos frog tadpoles are active predators. They eat aquatic invertebrates and tadpoles.

Because run-of-the-mill tadpoles feed on plant material, they require a large intestinal surface area for the absorption of nutrients. Their intestines are amazingly long and, as anyone who has ever looked at a tadpole's belly knows, the intestine is tightly coiled. They have no place to store food. It simply passes through the long, coiled gut and gets digested along the way. In contrast, because escuerzo and llanos frog tadpoles eat animals, they have a much shorter intestine. Furthermore, escuerzo tadpoles have an enlarged foregut where food can be stored. Llanos frog tadpoles

Predaceous tadpole of the llanos frog, soon to metamorphose into an equally voracious froglet.

(and the two other species of the genus) are unique among known tadpoles in that they have a thick muscular stomach that secretes digestive enzymes. As adults, both species retain their unusual dietary preferences. Whereas most frogs eat insects, these eat other frogs.

All five species of frogs we find tonight have clever ways of coping with the stressful and unpredictable chaco habitat and climate, conditions that most other frogs cannot tolerate. Escuerzos and llanos frogs essentially say the heck with it all and burrow down into the mud once the pond has dried. A frog sheds layers of skin, forming a cocoon around itself that reduces water loss. Once the rains return and the pond holds water, the cocoon absorbs moisture and the frog breaks out from this protective shell.

Painted-belly monkey frogs, closely related to the giant monkey frog from Brazil, spend daylight hours perched on branches exposed to the dry wind and sunlight. They can afford to exhibit this un-frog-like behavior because of their unique ability to waterproof themselves. Their bright leaf-green skin contains glands that secrete a mixture of substances, including a wax. While secreting these substances, a frog uses its front and back legs to smear the goop over its entire body. When the secretions dry, the frog has a shiny waterproof coating that protects it from the wind and

Painted-belly monkey frog sitting in the sun, protected by its waterproofed skin.

sun. In fact, in this state a painted-belly monkey frog loses no more water from its skin than does a desert lizard.

Weeping frogs, named for their mournful call, produce foam nests full of eggs on the surface of the water. The outermost layer of foam dries to a crust. If the pond dries before the eggs hatch, the crust provides temporary protection from the dry air until the next rain.

AND THEN there are the mud-nesting frogs that construct cone-shaped nests at the edges of ponds. Often there is no standing water at the time the nests are made. Using their feet, males push mud into hollow mounds that resemble miniature volcanoes about four or five centimeters high. Then they climb inside and call to attract a female. If all goes well, a female eventually enters the nest. As the eggs are fertilized, they're suspended within a foamy mass. Mud nests containing eggs usually have the top opening covered over with mud. Who caps off the nest—Mom or Dad? The answer to this question has remained a mystery . . . until tonight when

I happen to be in the right place at the right time. I find mating pairs of frogs constructing foam masses in four nests. If I stay quiet enough, and awake long enough, surely I can see which parent closes over the nest, and how he or she does it.

I'm tired, hungry, and getting eaten alive by mosquitoes, but I can address only one of these three complaints since I'm already covered with mosquito repellent and there's nothing I can do about being tired. I run back to the tent and grab a box of lemon creme sandwich cookies I've been saving for the trip home tomorrow. Sitting on the hard ground, amidst swarms of bloodthirsty mosquitoes, I munch my lemon cookies as quietly as possible and focus my weak flashlight to the side of a blob of mud.

As the minutes tick by and nothing happens, I feel like a cat patiently waiting for a mouse to emerge from underneath the sofa. Just like the cat that knows the mouse is there and if it waits long enough the mouse will appear, I know that if I am patient enough the frogs will emerge. After two boring hours of staring at the blob of mud, at 2:05 A.M. two frogs exit the nest. My heart pounds and I hold my breath, afraid to make a sound. One frog hops away. The other, seemingly oblivious to my presence, uses its

Unoccupied nest of a mud-nesting frog.

front feet to push mud from the ground, along the side, up onto the top of the nest, working all around the sides. Ignoring all distractions, the frog keeps at its task. Finally, at 3:02 A.M. I decide that in the interest of finding out what's happening at the other nests, I'd better just catch the frog and identify its gender. It's a female.

Over the next hour I find two other frogs pushing mud up the sides of nests, covering over the entry holes. Both are females. The fourth nest is left uncovered, but a female sits nearby. Perhaps she's taking a breather. Having answered my question, I stumble back to my tent at 4:00 in the morning.

These observations mark the end of my discovery, but others have filled in different pieces of the story. Although the eggs hatch within a few days, the tadpoles stay inside their cell until rains flood the nest and wash the tadpoles into the pond. What happens during a dry spell? The tadpoles can survive inside the nest for at least forty-six days, absorbing their yolk and perhaps gaining some nutrition from the foam. Why don't the tadpoles poison themselves with their own waste products? Most tadpoles produce ammonia, which is extremely toxic unless diluted in water. In contrast, mud-nesting frog tadpoles produce urea, which is much less toxic than ammonia. Thus, buildup of waste within the nest remains below the lethal limit for the tadpoles.

As I drift into sleep, I think about changing environmental conditions and global warming. If the world becomes a warmer, drier place, will only species of frogs with the flexibility of mud-nesting frogs be able to survive? Will other species be able to modify their behavior, physiology, and morphology in time?

13 December 1989

Pagaburo and I return to Ignacia's ranch to find the ponds wriggling with tadpoles, both predator and prey species. Daily rains have saturated the air with humidity, and even after dark we sweat from the heat. Pigs, goats, and cattle wander aimlessly about and dump their wastes in the ponds, inadvertently providing nutrients for the tadpoles.

Since so little information is available, I plan to document what the predaceous tadpoles eat. Using long-handled dip nets, Pagaburo and I slosh through the ponds and collect a sample of tadpoles, which we preserve. After the fieldwork phase is completed, I'll identify the food items. I'm not too thrilled to be wading in this soup of farm animal feces, but Pagaburo seems to be having the time of his life, shouting with glee every time he finds a predaceous tadpole in his net.

I'm also curious whether the predaceous tadpoles eat whatever happens to swim by, or whether they prefer some species over others. To answer this question, Pagaburo and I collect some of each species of tadpole, predaceous and nonpredaceous alike. I'll take them back alive to Tucumán, where I'll offer the predaceous tadpoles a choice of prey and then record their selections.

Since escuerzo and llanos frog tadpoles have very differently shaped heads, I'm expecting that they eat in quite different ways. Escuerzo tadpoles look almost like "normal" tadpoles except for their massive jaw muscles and sharply serrated beaks. In contrast, llanos frog tadpoles have *huge* cavernous mouths but no beaks. Back in Tucumán I'll observe feeding behaviors of the tadpoles to determine the maximum prey sizes each species can handle, and how long it takes each to devour its prey.

26 December 1989

Christmas in Tucumán was fun, but the climate just wasn't right for us Northern Hemisphere types. December in northern Argentina is summer—hot and humid. Sleep was difficult not only for the sticky heat, but also because the tradition here is to start lighting firecrackers Christmas Eve and continue for the next thirty-six hours. Every kid on our block had an abundant supply.

I'M AMAZED at how aggressive my predaceous tadpoles are. They're so un-tadpole-like! An escuerzo tadpole grabs a victim with its sharp beak, and with its massive jaw muscles viciously rips into it and tears out a hunk. It swallows that before tearing off another chunk, consuming the tadpole victim piecemeal. In contrast, llanos frog tadpoles generally engulf prey tadpoles whole. If the victim is too large to be gulped all at once, the llanos frog tadpole works the prey into its gullet by writhing back and forth.

The contrasting feeding behavior in these tadpoles is a good example of "different strokes for different folks." Llanos frog tadpoles can swallow small tadpole victims in less than a second. For larger victims, six or seven minutes are needed. When the prey is more than 38 percent of the predator's weight, the gluttonous predator tries to force the prey down but eventually spits out the now-suffocated victim. Although escuerzo tadpoles also take longer to eat larger prey, the handling time is very different. Because escuerzo tadpoles eat their prey piecemeal, it takes them longer to eat—up to fifty minutes for a fairly large victim as compared to less than eight for llanos frog tadpoles. But escuerzo tadpoles can eat prey that are up to 63 percent their body weight. Clearly, llanos frog tadpoles are more efficient. They have to be. They couldn't afford to spend the time an es-cuerzo does to eat a meal. A llanos frog tadpole encumbered with a prey hanging out of its mouth would itself be especially vulnerable to preda-tion. On the other hand, an escuerzo tadpole presumably can abandon its meal, no matter how large, and flee rapidly if a predator approaches.

Given a choice between a large and small tadpole, the llanos frog tadpoles try the larger one first. Furthermore, when given a choice among three species of tadpoles of the same size—painted-belly monkey frogs, toads, and weeping frogs—they prefer the toad tadpoles. Painted-belly monkey frog tadpoles are eaten only when nothing else is available. Behavior likely explains this pattern. Whereas painted-belly monkey frog tadpoles rarely move, toad tadpoles are in constant motion and thus attract attention to themselves. As soon as a llanos frog tadpole detects movement, it lunges and quickly engulfs its victim.

10 January 1990

Peter is spending several weeks in Chile, so last week I brought Karen with me to the ranch and left Rob with Monique. Today, though, I have both kids with me as Rob begged to come, enticed by Karen's enthusiastic reports from last week. From collecting frogs and tadpoles to sleeping in the tent, they love the adventure.

So far we've found eleven species of frogs breeding in the ponds. In addition to the escuerzo and llanos frog tadpoles, a third species is preda-ceous—one very similar to llanos frogs, with the same humongous mouth. Tonight we find many weeping frogs (*Physalaemus,* or "fisaleemus" in Karen's phonetic spelling) whipping up their foam nests, and Karen finds a pair of painted-belly monkey frogs (*Phyllomedusa,* or "filumadoosas" in Karen's journal) laying eggs:

> January 10, 1990. Today I woke up very early. Because I'm going to mom-my's study sits! This time Robbie came. When we got there we clected tadpoles! After that I went over to the pepls house and I had a long conver-sashen with them! I shoed them my books. And they liked them! And I had sucses peting a baby pig but not the kittens! And I really injoed talking to the pepl! Then diner was retty. When we were finished we got flashlites and went out looking for frogs. Pogobooto found a feemal eskuerso! A feemal! And I found filumadoosas mating! And there were hundreds of fisaleemus! It was a lot of fun! And I also found a hyoog water bug eating a frog haf its sise! And I and Robbie staed up intill 1 oclock. I was so sleepy wen I got in the tent!

Male Argentine common toad calling to attract a mate.

Escuerzo calling to attract a female.

Ignacia, Karen, Rob, and a pair of baby goats.

11 January 1990

Always before I leave the ranch, Ignacia insists that I join her for a huge slice of homemade goat cheese, smothered with the rich honey from her beehive. The cheese is . . . well, homemade goat cheese. The sweetness of the honey is overpowering. And the combination is too much for me. Whenever possible I surreptitiously wrap part of the strongly scented cheese in a napkin and stuff it into my pocket.

Today as Karen and I say good-bye, I wonder how Karen will respond, as I've told her about the wonders of goat cheese. Politely Karen says, "No, thank you. I have a tummyache." She watches me choke down the cheese and honey. I ask her afterward if she really had a tummyache. She replies, "Of course not, Mommy. Why didn't you say you had a tummyache too?"

AFTER RETURNING home this afternoon, Karen and Rob watch me feed small chunks of raw steak to the baby escuerzos that have metamorphosed from the tadpoles we raised. Each frog lunges toward the forceps and greedily grabs its morsel. Karen asks to feed her special frog, and I warn her that the two fanglike teeth on the bottom jaw are already well developed and that if she gives the escuerzo a chance, it will clamp its jaws onto her fingers—this innocent little pet she lovingly raised from a tadpole. She acknowledges the danger and successfully feeds her froglet. As I pick up the next bowl and its hungry occupant, our five-month-old kitten named Socks appears—no doubt attracted by the smell of steak. Socks nonchalantly approaches the bowl and sniffs the baby escuerzo, which immediately raises up high on its front legs, inflates its body by filling its lungs with air, opens its mouth, and hisses loudly at Socks. As Socks jumps backward in fright, Karen and Rob laugh hysterically at the unlikely scenario: a cat frightened by a baby frog. I tell the kids that many adult Argentine people are also deathly afraid of escuerzos. The story goes that if an escuerzo bites a horse, the horse will die. Not so. Although aggressive when defending themselves, the frogs are not venomous.

15 January 1990

"Let's go around the pond one more time," I urge Karen. It's 1:30 A.M., but I need another mating pair of llanos frogs for an experiment. Off we stumble, half asleep.

"Oh my god!" I gasp as I grab Karen's arm and yank her back toward me. She has just stepped on a coiled fer-de-lance. The very venomous snake must have been cold, as it sits there stunned and then slowly uncoils and slithers away. Or maybe it was so startled at being stepped on by a little blond English-speaking girl at 1:30 A.M. in the middle of the Argentine chaco that it simply forgot to bite.

In a trembling voice I suggest, "OK, let's forget the one-more-trip-around-the-pond idea." Karen readily agrees, and we return to the tent and crawl into our sleeping bags. I explain to Karen that the snake she stepped on is very dangerous and could have bitten her. Calmly, she promises to be more careful in the future and quickly falls asleep. I am clearly more shaken than she is, as suggested by her journal entry:

> January 15, 1990. Today I got up very early! Because I'm going to mommy's study sitts! And this is the last time we are going there. I'm so sad. And on our way we saw a fox! It was just byootyfol! It was brown and black and a tiny bit of wite. We saw it very well! When we got there I helped clect tadpoles! It was fun! Then I said hy to the pepl who lived there and shoed them how to jump rope but they coun't do it! Then we ate yummy chicen for diner. Then we looked for frogs. And there were ESCUARSOS! It was the best nite ever! And I and Mommy were the only ons that found laty escuarsos! And I saw a posunis snac but I saw escuarsos calling! And it was just a wonderfol nite!

How could I ever have forgiven myself if the fer-de-lance had bitten Karen? My feelings of guilt are reminiscent of those I had when Karen's skin test for tuberculosis tested positive during our last sabbatical, in Costa Rica. But then I remind myself that nowhere is completely safe. Karen could have a fatal accident falling off the monkey bars at school in Gainesville. A mother's job is not to provide an impervious protective bubble around her child, but rather to teach her child safe ways of dealing with the real world. Now Karen knows about venomous snakes.

To get my mind off the fer-de-lance encounter, I muse about declining amphibians. No declines have yet been reported from Argentina. I feel fortunate that frogs are so abundant here at Ignacia's ranch, yet I worry that someday they may not be. The number of animals I've removed is less than 5 percent of the tadpoles that would die if the pond dried up, which is still likely to happen. Though rationally I know that the effect of my "predation" is minuscule, I feel a twinge of conscience as I ask myself what effect herpetologists have on the animals we study.

25 January 1990

Today we leave for a five-week vacation. During the first hour of driving, Peter explains to the kids that we'll see everything from tropical cloud forest to barren desert to lovely lakes surrounded by cool forests of southern beech trees. As Peter describes the red sandstone mesas and canyons, grasslands, forests, mountain ranges, and scrub vegetation we'll pass through, the kids' attention wanes and they begin squabbling. Peter quickly switches gears and tells them about some of the particular places we'll visit: Ischigualasto Reserve (the world-famous dinosaur site); Peninsula Valdés (we'll see rheas, flamingos, penguins, guanacos, sea lions, and elephant seals); glacier-fed lakes where we'll camp and eat s'mores; Cholita (where Butch Cassidy and the Sundance Kid lived for a few years while hiding out from Pinkerton's agents); Bariloche with its numerous chocolate factories (we can watch them make chocolate—and, yes, we'll buy lots); the island of Chiloé (we'll cross over a high mountain pass into Chile and explore some of that country); and the shrine of La Difunta Correa (we'll explain that one later). By this time the kids are excited and want to visit each place *now*.

11 February 1990

The first two and a half weeks of vacation have been great fun. At Peninsula Valdés we saw the very fossil cliffs that Charles Darwin described:

fossils that played a role in his formulation of the theory of evolution. Of greater interest to the kids, we watched rheas grazing on the open flats, guanacos galloping through the woodlands, sea lions and elephant seals lazing in the sun on the sandy beach, flocks of pink flamingos flying over the beach, and Magellanic penguins and their chicks waddling along the pebbly shore. Truly a nature lover's paradise, Peninsula Valdés will be a high point of the trip for all of us. After leaving the ocean, we crossed through the vast desolate interior of Patagonia. Jagged snow-covered Andes in the distance were a welcome sight. Our destination was Los Alerces National Park, where we planned to camp for a week next to Lago Futa-laufquén, a beautiful glacier-fed lake.

The week at Lago Futalaufquén has been a mix of relaxing times (fishing and reading *The Lion, the Witch and the Wardrobe* to the kids by the campfire) and invigorating activities (strenuous hikes up the mountain to play in the snow, and daily baths in the coldest lake water imaginable). Gourmet dinners cooked over the campfire have included spicy sausages, leg of lamb, and grilled chicken, but the best was a seventy-centimeter trout that Peter caught and grilled over the coals. The salmon-colored flesh was superb.

We took a boat trip along the lake to a magnificent forest of alerce trees, "Southern redwood." The average age of the trees is eight hundred years. One fifty-seven-meter high giant with a diameter of over two meters is estimated to be 2,600 years old. The scientific name, *Fitzroya,* was given to the alerce tree in honor of Robert FitzRoy, the captain of the *Beagle,* which charted the coastline of South America and brought Charles Darwin to the continent a mere 167 years ago, a moment ago in the life-time of these magnificent trees.

Yesterday we drove to a river famous for fly-fishing. No luck snagging any trout, but the surrounding arrayán trees were lovely. Apparently Walt Disney felt the same way. A visiting group from Walt Disney Studios was so impressed by these unusual cinnamon-colored trees that they used them as the inspiration for the scenery in the movie *Bambi*.

27 February 1990

Today we visit the shrine of La Difunta Correa, in the province of San Juan. The Difunta Correa is an unofficial saint and the focus of a popular cult. According to the legend, an outcast pregnant Indian woman died during childbirth while walking alone in the desert. Three days later she and the baby were found, the healthy baby nursing from the dead mother's breasts, which were still flowing with milk. Numerous small shrines to the Difunta Correa are scattered along back roads throughout the country, but this is the main one. Here, in a half-dome shrine right on the hill where the miracle occurred, lies a larger-than-life figure of a supine woman and a nursing baby. Near the figure sits an altar where visitors leave small but precious offerings of thanks, and a table where candles are lit. Larger offerings cover the slopes of the hillside, all arranged by category: a huge pile of empty wine bottles from once-thirsty travelers, hundreds of license plates attached to a wire frame, elaborately painted model houses or models of small stores accompanied with plaques giving thanks to the Difunta Correa, a wall of baby shoes, a model washer and dryer, and a large plastic pig. Of the busloads of pilgrims that arrive during our visit, we seem to be the only visitors who have come merely out of curiosity. Everyone else is here to commune with the Difunta Correa and give thanks for the good she has bestowed upon them. Before leaving, we support the local economy (a long line of booths by the parking lot) by buying bumper stickers, magnets, and plastic-coated wallet cards.

PRICES IN Argentina make no sense. Recently we spent 27,000 australes (almost $6) to have several days' worth of clothes washed at a laundromat, and our night in a very pleasant hotel in the same town cost only 21,000 australes for the four of us. That same day we spent more for two bags of ice and four bottles of mineral water than for our dinner of a large deluxe pizza, beer, cheese sandwich, Coke, and ice cream.

2 March 1990

This afternoon in the car on our last day of the trip, Karen viciously scratches her scalp. Several hours later the rest of us are doing the same. Clearly, we have picked up head lice. Having had no previous experience with these parasites, commonly called "cooties," we stop at a pharmacy, inquire what to do, and buy the recommended remedy. Back in Tucumán, after a quick supper of bread and cheese, we begin the gruesome and time-consuming process of delousing ourselves and each other. First each of us showers and washes his or her hair with a caustic shampoo that stings our raw scalps. Next comes the tedious nit-picking procedure. I take Karen, Peter takes Rob, and we slowly run the fine-toothed comb through the hair hundreds of times, picking out the louse egg cases, or nits. An hour later Peter picks out my nits, then I do the same for him. We'll repeat the procedure daily and hope that by the time school starts five days from now the kids will be louse-free.

ONCE THE nit-picking is done, Peter and I share a bottle of wine, unwind, and reminisce about all we've seen and done in the 9,271 kilometers we've traversed since we left Tucumán on vacation. The diverse landscapes were indeed the highlight for us: wet subtropical cloud forest, semidesert with towering saguaro-like cacti, dry scrub steppe, salt flats, the southern beech forest interspersed with jewel-like lakes, red and gray sandstone mountains, mesas, canyons, wildlife-littered ocean beaches, vast and desolate volcanic expanses with bright green oases from time to time, grassland pampas, spectacular snow-covered Andean peaks, and icy-blue glaciers. Also as we expected, seeing the huge vats of chocolate in Bariloche (and buying lots of the finished product), playing in the snow above our campsite at Lago Futalaufquén, and watching parent penguins and their chicks waddle along the dunes at Península Valdés were highlights for the kids.

Just in the five weeks we've been gone, the exchange rate has soared from 1,700 to 7,000 australes to the dollar, with buying power plummeting daily. President Carlos Menem says, "Bear with us. We're trying to resolve the situation." How much more will people tolerate before widespread riots break out? And if so, will the military intervene once again?

9 March 1990

Pagaburo and I revisit my study site to see what's happening at the ponds. No mud nests and no predaceous tadpoles. A few algae-eating tadpoles swim about in the ponds that still have shallow water. They'd better develop quickly, or it'll be too late. Two ponds have already dried out completely, and hundreds of little tadpole bodies bake on the parched surface. It's hot. Last evening we heard only a few painted-belly monkey frogs chuckling and a few weeping frogs whining. One confused llanos frog sat in a shrinking puddle, all that's left of its former pond. Two morose toads hunkered in the mud of a roadside ditch. Even though rain temporarily lubricated the dusty ground last week, breeding activity has stopped. Now that the rainy season is about over and the ponds' continued existence is unpredictable, it's time for amphibians to rest. Most of the llanos frogs and escuerzos have probably already burrowed under the mud and are forming cocoons. Other species will seek shelter inside rotting logs, at the bottom of rodent burrows, and under cow pies to wait out the long dry spell. Some will die and mummify before the rains return in late November or early December.

While I'm forcing down my goat cheese and honey in the farmhouse, Ignacia notices me looking at a picture on the wall. She asks if I know who the person is. I respond that yes, I recognize Eva Perón. Ignacia whispers,

"Evita," with a faraway look on her face as she gazes at the cracked and faded photo that has probably occupied that same space for more than three decades. Although much of the world saw Eva as a woman devoured by her passion for power, she was and still is loved by the Argentine working class. Eva understood their fears and desires because she was one of them. Ignacia and millions of others keep Evita alive in their memories and her portrait on their walls.

19 April 1990

Since returning from vacation, I've been identifying prey items from the tadpoles I collected during December and January. As soon as Karen and Rob leave for school, I get out the specimens. I work all day and then pack them away before the kids return in late afternoon. I don't want them to know their mother killed tadpoles.

Although a few tadpoles have nothing to reveal, most are crammed with food. By weight, more than half the food eaten by both species consists of the tadpoles of toads, weeping frogs, and mud-nesting frogs. Escuerzo tadpoles had not eaten llanos frog tadpoles, or vice versa, probably because they rarely occur in the same ponds. Escuerzos prefer deeper, more permanent water, whereas llanos frogs prefer shallow ephemeral ponds. Some individuals of both species were cannibalistic, though. In addition, mixed in with tadpole prey were fairy shrimp, tadpole shrimp, small beetles, fly larvae, dragonfly nymphs, and backswimmers. The tadpoles seem to eat any little creature that moves.

Larger and older tadpoles eat more and larger prey. An interesting difference between the two species occurs just before metamorphosis. Like most other tadpoles, escuerzos stop eating during transformation because their guts are undergoing major reorganizational changes. In contrast, because the digestive system of a llanos frog tadpole already is almost like that of the adult, little reorganization occurs. Not only do these tadpoles continue to eat throughout metamorphosis, they eat a lot. One individual had forty-one tadpoles in its distended stomach!

18 May 1990

Today is the last day of my course on vertebrate reproductive behavior at the National University of Tucumán. My tongue and brain tie for being the most exhausted. Speaking and thinking in Spanish all day, every day, for the last two weeks has been a challenge! But it's also been extraordinarily rewarding because of the enthusiastic responses of the students. They really want to learn and are hungry for information. I spent about two-thirds of each day lecturing on fish, amphibians, reptiles, birds, and mammals: frequency and periodicity of breeding, number of offspring produced, age at first reproduction, courtship, and parental care. The rest of each day we had group discussions over assigned papers. I was impressed by how hard the students worked to read these papers in English. Not a slouch in the bunch. Many had no idea such literature exists. There's no stopping them now.

PETER HAS had similar experiences teaching in Latin America. Most students are extraordinarily motivated and thirsty for knowledge. Peter and I ponder the possibility of retiring from our positions at the University of Florida and focusing instead on teaching and mentoring activities in Latin America. It seems that we could really make a difference here. How ironic that I came so close to beginning my teaching career in Latin America, but with trepidation as to whether I'd be happy doing so. Now I think perhaps I'd feel most fulfilled working with students in Latin America.

Times have changed, and circumstances are different. Latin America is now much more accepting of women scientists. Then I had an Ecuadorian fiancé who preferred the idea of a traditional housewife and resented my career. Now I have a husband who's a colleague. Peter understands and solidly supports my research and teaching activities. I've changed too. No longer do I feel I need to prove my worth as a scientist.

16 June 1990

A few days ago the mail brought a depressing handscrawled note from Wolf Guindon in Monteverde. Once again weather conditions in the elfin forest seemed appropriate in April and May, but the golden toads never appeared. Rain pools formed at the bases of the elfin forest trees, the ground was saturated, and the canopy overhead incessantly dripped moisture. The forest seemed barren without the familiar bright orange splotches of color glowing through the mist.

HERE IN the dry season of Argentina, the former ponds on Ignacia's ranch are now cracked mud hollows and the surrounding ground is a parched desert. Leaves have turned brown and fallen from the spindly branches, exposing naked, wicked thorns that warn passersby not to touch. The only night chirps belong to insects. Is this what a world without frogs would be like?

18 July 1990

Peter and I spend a delightful evening writing a take-off on Judith Viorst's children's story *Alexander and the Terrible, Horrible, No Good, Very Bad Day*. Our version is intended to remind us years in the future, when we look back on our sabbatical year through rose-colored glasses, of day-to-day life here. It all happened, though not really on the same day.

The Crumpsingers and the Terrible, Horrible, No Good, Very Bad Day
or
A Day of Our Lives in Argentina

We woke up scratching sleepily at hundreds of mosquito bites and realized we'd slept through the noise of a plate breaking when the waterlogged mosquito coil drooped down onto it and extinguished itself. It was only 4 A.M. Peter tried to light a new mosquito coil, but the matches wouldn't light.

We could tell right then it was going to be a terrible, horrible, no good, very bad day.

Marty flushed the toilet and it leaked all over her bare feet, and there was a simultaneous rush of odor as the septic tank outside the window flooded an exactly equal amount. Peter staggered into the kitchen to get a drink of water and startled a stray cat, who bolted for the open sliding door and left behind a heavy smell of pee and a trail of strewn garbage. Yes, we could tell it was going to be a terrible, horrible, no good, very bad day.

Just as we drifted off to sleep again, the alarms went off. There was no milk left for the kids or for coffee, and the bakery/milk store nearby was on strike. Halfway through breakfast it started raining, so we gathered up yesterday's laundry from outside and hung wet sheets, towels, and underwear all over the house.

Peter got into the car to go to town to pay the bill for the kids' school (the bill arrived last night with a due date of today). The car had two flat tires so he went to the corner to take the bus, but there was a city bus strike, which he realized after waiting for forty-five minutes. When he finally got to town (thanks to a kindly driver), he went to the bank and stood in the wrong line for an hour and a half and then the right line for thirty minutes but was told he was in the wrong branch of the bank. "I think I'll move to Alaska," he told the banker. When he finally got the bill paid, it was 12:30 P.M. and Tucumán had checked out for the next four hours for siesta.

Meanwhile Marty was answering gate-claps every seven minutes for an interminable string of lemon vendors, small children begging bread, and policemen asking for "contributions." She forgot to save her thirty-page manuscript on the computer and the electricity went out just as she was saying for the thirteenth time, *"No, gracias, ya tenemos suficientes limones"* ("No thanks, we have enough lemons"). When she finally retrieved a semblance of her manuscript, she printed it out but forgot that the Argentine paper was 12 by 8.75 inches instead of 11 by 8.5.

It was a terrible, horrible, no good, very bad day.

As Marty was reprinting her manuscript, a family faintly known to Peter arrived at the door saying they would like to stay with us (for an indeterminate amount of time) but would be no trouble despite the fact that they had two whining toddlers, both with colds.

Peter went to a 2 P.M. parents' meeting at the kids' school, which started two hours late, and listened to twenty women argue for fifty-five minutes about whether the kindergarten kids would prefer cookies every day or cookies alternating with tortillas. "We think we'll move to Alaska," he told the director.

Monique brought over a $300 phone bill, $280 of which was for faxes that never went through, and two faxes from University of Florida graduate students requesting letters of recommendation with deadlines of today. We told her we were having a terrible, horrible, no good, very bad day. Doña Ramona forgot and rinsed the clothes *before* instead of after washing them, but the amount of soap remaining didn't seem any greater than usual. She couldn't re-rinse them because the water went off and ours is the only house on the block that doesn't have a spare water tank on the roof.

The oven door broke, an escuerzo bit Marty's finger, Don Ortiz mowed over Karen's flowers, and the garbagemen didn't pick up our garbage for the fifth day in a row. It was a terrible, horrible, no good, very bad day.

When the kids came home from school at 5:30 P.M., Karen had an invitation to a birthday party tomorrow, Rob had one for a party beginning just as Karen's was ending, and neither party was within walking distance. Karen had lost her gym jacket. Rob had a note saying he had to bring in cookies for class tomorrow; Karen had a note saying that tomorrow was Teacher's Day and it was customary to give the teacher a present. Peter dashed to the supermarket to buy cookies. The lady in front of him got the last box marked 2,000 australes and he had to pay 20,000 australes for the same thing. He told the checkout lady he was having a terrible, horrible, no good, very bad day and she just scowled.

While the houseguests sat idly in the living room, we bathed Rob and found three ticks on him. Marty served the mother of the whining toddlers her dinner of hamburger glop, and as she gently placed the plate in front of her, the "unbreakable" plate shattered into several pieces, oozing glop all across the table. During dinner six little neighborhood boys interrupted us every three minutes asking permission to retrieve their ball from our yard.

After dinner the boys continued their nightly five-hour soccer game outside our gate (because we have the only streetlight on the block, when it works), screaming at the top of their lungs. As all eight of us climbed into our respective beds, the firecrackers started up in earnest on Avenida Aconquija. The faucets dripped (even the one Peter fixed yesterday; the new washer had already crumbled); the toilets ran; the roosters outside crowed prematurely; the neighbors' dogs barked, yapped, and howled; and the local buses (unfortunately they weren't on strike) with holes in their mufflers and shrieking brakes roared up and down the *avenida* half a block away.

As Marty was drifting off to sleep, she reached over to blow her nose for the 198th time that day (thanks to the combination of house mold, dust, and kitty dandruff) on the toilet paper Peter insists she use instead of expensive Kleenex . . . the same toilet paper Karen requested we not buy anymore because "it hurts my crotch."

It has been a terrible, horrible, no good, very bad day.

Monique says some days are like that.

Even in Alaska.

2 August 1990

Home again in Gainesville, we look back on our year in Argentina with fond memories despite the little inconveniences we'd experienced. After all, they were nothing compared to what our Argentine friends dealt with as they tried to cope with the inflation of as much as 10 percent daily. Karen says that Argentina is her favorite country in the world. We're proud that both kids immersed themselves in Argentine culture, made friends, spoke near-perfect Spanish, and in general thrived in their new environment. Though reluctant to leave the freedom associated with a sabbatical year and the special magic of Argentina, Peter and I are looking forward to returning to the school year. I'll be teaching my graduate course in amphibian biology, and I'm looking forward to incorporating new lectures on adaptations of amphibians to stressful environments, predaceous tadpoles, and worldwide amphibian population declines.

THE MAXUS
EXPERIENCE

9

OON AFTER returning from Tucumán to Gainesville, Peter and I decided to act on the idea that had sprung to mind in Argentina of
going on "permanent sabbatical." We resigned from our professor-
ships in May 1992 and moved to Flagstaff, Arizona. Our new career
goals: to focus our energies on research, education, and training in Latin
America but always in collaboration with Latin Americans. Over the two
previous decades, we'd met many enthusiastic and highly capable students
and young professionals eager to play lead roles in the conservation research
and policies of their own countries yet aware that they'd need more training first. We hoped to provide them with some of the intellectual tools
they'd need, through courses, workshops, advising, and simply working
together in the field.

Our first year in Flagstaff, Peter and I began working with EcoCiencia
(Ecuadorian Foundation for Ecological Studies), a nongovernmental
organization based in Quito, Ecuador. Supported in part by international
conservation organizations and conservation-and-development projects,
EcoCiencia engages in research applied to conservation, environmental
policies, and environmental education. Many of its projects stress sustain-
able uses of natural resources in such a way that human needs are met but
at the same time the biological diversity of Ecuador is conserved. Other
projects focus on cataloging that biological diversity itself and on monitor-

ing changes in assemblages of animals through time. During my first year associated with EcoCiencia, I taught a workshop on surveying amphibians and reptiles, then carried out a preliminary inventory. I also designed research to study the impact of a newly constructed road on amphibians and reptiles in the Yasuní National Park. In the process I experienced firsthand the power of an oil company.

SPRING 1993

30 April 1993

I walk into the conference room at EcoCiencia to find fourteen students awaiting the beginning of my week-long course, "Field Methods for Surveying Amphibians and Reptiles." Over the past several years, herpetologists have increasingly realized that we lack data on year-to-year variability in population sizes of amphibians. To evaluate real declines in the future, we must initiate long-term field studies now so that changes can be tracked. This course will provide the students with the knowledge and skills they'll need to monitor populations through time and to undertake inventory studies. We spend the day on introductory lectures. By midafternoon my tongue has loosened up and the students seem to be following my less-than-perfect Spanish. Tomorrow we take a bus to Santa Cecilia.

In 1977 Ildefonso Muñoz and his family were evicted from Santa Cecilia. They did not legally own their land, the army wanted to expand, so Ilde lost out. He and Blanca moved to Lago Agrio. Since then the military has not allowed civilians into the area, and it has been impossible for me to continue my frog studies there. When asked where I would like to give this course, immediately I thought of Santa Cecilia because of the exceptional diversity of amphibians and reptiles that I had known twenty years earlier. Knowing that the director of research at EcoCiencia, Rocío, is married to a high-ranking officer in the Ecuadorian military, I asked if her husband could wangle permission for us to hold the course at the Santa Cecilia base. He pulled the proper strings.

3 May 1993

Unbelievably altered, the road to Santa Cecilia is now lined with thatched houses, parcels of *yuca* and *plátano,* and soccer fields instead of rain forest. Colonization within the upper Amazon Basin has spread like a cancer. The army camp is five times its former size and includes modern homes for the officers, a large recreational building, and comfortable office buildings outfitted with computers. Even more of the surrounding vegetation has been cut, and the compound resembles a carefully manicured park. Smooth rocks, hauled up from the Río Aguarico and painted white, line the paths between buildings—no doubt some officer's idea of a chore to keep the conscripts out of trouble.

Yesterday I awoke early, and before any students were up, I strolled down the path toward the Río Aguarico to see what was left of Muñozlandia. Memories of Mario sprang up for the first time in many years. I wondered where he is and what he's doing now. I recalled the Asthmatic Monster, the jeering rat, the Quechua wedding, falling through the floor of the shower stall, and my close call with the bushmaster. Most of all, I thought about the day to day fieldwork and how exciting it had been back then—finding poison dart frogs carrying tadpoles, watching cat-eyed snakes eat leaf frog eggs, picking up frogs I had never seen before and suspecting they were new species, and listening to the cacophony of ten species of frogs calling from a swamp.

At the bottom of the hill, the path led only to the river. Muñozlandia was now a thick tangle of second-growth vegetation. I wondered how many other traces of humanity were buried beneath jungle vegetation in the Amazon Basin. Perhaps entire civilizations. Even though the immediate surroundings looked totally unfamiliar, the air felt the same as I had remembered—heavy, hot, and humid. And the river was still there. The jungle may have devoured the physical structure of Muñozlandia, but the spirit of Ilde's compound lived on. Yes, it was good to be back.

EACH DAY is broken into a combination of lectures, lab work, and fieldwork. Lectures cover the classification and natural history of amphibians and reptiles, sampling considerations, research design, and data analysis. Lab work involves learning the distinguishing characteristics for identifying frog, lizard, and snake species. In the field we practice sampling techniques.

I emphasize to the students that the field techniques appropriate for a given study depend on the specific questions being asked. If the investigator wants to know what species occur in an area so that he or she can recommend effective conservation guidelines, the appropriate technique is an inventory, a list of species. Inventories are generally carried out by searching for animals in all appropriate microhabitats during the day and at night. On the other hand, if the goal is to determine the status of certain species at a given site to look for changes in population size, then one should use techniques appropriate for monitoring, such as repeated transects or quadrats in microhabitats where those species occur.

A transect is a preestablished line laid out in the habitat. I usually make mine a hundred meters long and tie a strip of colored plastic flagging tape at ten-meter intervals. The field personnel walk slowly and record each animal observed within one meter on each side of the transect line. I like to have two persons work a transect so each can take a side. Depending on the purpose of the study, the investigator might wish to record sex, size, age class, reproductive condition, and behavior of each animal encountered. Transects can be run on a regular basis to track changes in the composition and relative abundance of animals.

For quadrat sampling, the investigator samples a number of square parcels (quadrats) on the ground. These squares may be of any size, depending on how many people are available to search each quadrat and how large the target animals are. For amphibians and reptiles, I find that squares of five by five meters work well if four people are searching. We measure off each side and tie a length of cord between the endpoints. Each person takes a different side of the quadrat and, working toward the center, sifts through the leaf litter and peers under rocks and rolls logs searching for amphibians and reptiles. We place each animal encountered in a plastic container so that it's not recorded more than once. Once the whole area is searched, we record data for each individual. Finally, after replacing the leaf litter and cover objects, we release the animals back into the quadrat. Then on to the next spot.

Quadrat data tell us what species are present and the relative abundance of each. Also, this technique provides data on density (number of individuals per unit area) because the assumption is that we've recorded all animals present. Transects don't really provide good density data because it's hard to keep the width searched at precisely two meters along the entire one hundred meters of the transect. Furthermore, many animals will be missed because they're not exposed. An advantage of transects, however, is that they disturb the habitat minimally while quadrat sampling is fairly destructive.

5 May 1993

Our hopes of finding lots of frogs after today's hard rain are dashed when the Colonel tells us he's sending all his men out to search the forest for *"guerrillas del norte"* (guerrillas from Colombia) who just kidnapped two North Americans working in nearby Bermejo. For security reasons, we aren't allowed outside. The conscripts are inexperienced and nervous, and the Colonel can't risk any accidental injuries. Disappointed, we return to the classroom. Partway through the lecture, a lieutenant barges in to verify that all of us are accounted for. He emphasizes that the situation is serious. A military policeman has been wounded in the forest between Santa Cecilia and Lago Agrio while attempting to capture the kidnappers. Tomorrow a helicopter search is planned and we won't be able to leave the base all day, our last day here. We're surrounded by nearly a hundred well-armed Ecuadorian soldiers, essentially held hostage by a handful of Colombian guerrillas.

Tonight I'm confronted by my nemesis from former Santa Cecilia days—chicken foot soup. Through a surface layer of golden globs of chicken fat rests the scaly detached foot of an aged chicken. As in former days, I avoid all contact with the foot, slurp the broth, and work my way around the fat globules. After a few minutes, I look around the table and notice that everyone else has chicken foot in hand and is determinedly gnawing the tiny slivers of meat from the tarsal bones. John and I had always assumed the foot was just a garnish. This time peer pressure forces me to emulate my students. I make a pretense of eating the foot but can't bring myself to touch my teeth to it. I place it back in the bowl where it slides through the rejected fat globules and resumes its position on the bottom. Self-consciously, I wait for the army draftee to come and clear the bowls from the table. I generally pride myself in fitting in with the culture, but I've disappointed myself this time.

6 May 1993

We awake to the whirs of helicopters landing nearby, and soon afterward the air search begins. The sixty men from the base who spent last night combing the forest are still out. Midmorning the helicopters return because of low visibility and heavy rain. The rain continues throughout the day and into evening, and still the soldiers haven't returned. I plead for permission to take the students out tonight to gather up the stakes, thermometers, and rain gauges we left set up along several transects. Grudgingly, the head officer left in camp allows us one hour, and he insists on sending a bored conscript along with us. So much for sneaking in a full night of fieldwork on our last evening in Santa Cecilia.

Although some of the frogs and toads that were abundant in the 1970s are still common, I'm struck by numerous changes. Twenty-one years ago, small yellow treefrogs were extremely abundant in the water-filled ditches along road edges. Now they seem to have disappeared, even though there's more of the disturbed habitat they'd preferred. And we're finding very few of the dink frogs that used to perch everywhere in disturbed areas, peeping and chirping regardless of the weather. Has environmental contamination snuffed out even those species that used to thrive cohabiting with humans? Other species that we once found predictably in undisturbed forest are now scarce. I wish I could have shown the students the defensive display of an egg-brooding horned treefrog, but we never found one. Very little of their forest home remains intact.

During our three days of inventory work, running transects, and quadrat sampling, we found twenty-two species of frogs, six species of snakes, and five species of lizards. These would be impressive numbers for three days in most places in the world, but are only a small fraction of what actually occurs (or at least occurred twenty-five years ago) at Santa Cecilia.

Despite the guerrilla-induced restrictions, the students are glad to have experienced Santa Cecilia. Where else could they have seen a fer-de-lance, rainbow boa, cat-eyed snake, roughskin anole, jaguar leaf frog, bleating narrowmouth toad, and brilliant-thighed poison dart frog within seventy-two hours? I too am thankful for the opportunity to be here for a few days, although it's sad to see that populations of amphibians have declined. I wonder if there is any correlation between mode of reproduction—my dissertation subject long ago—and current population health. Maybe someday John Simmons, my former field assistant, and I can re-census our study sites at Santa Cecilia.

Many-colored bush anole, one of the more spectacular lizards at Santa Cecilia.

Amazon Basin white-lipped frog. Males vigorously kick their legs during the egg-laying and fertilization process, whipping up air, water, mucus, sperm, and eggs into a frothy mass.

7 May 1993

Sunrise reveals a clear morning, and the helicopters resume their search. Save for two students and myself, everyone boards the bus for the return to Quito. Ana María, Armando, and I pile into a separate car with Edison, the driver from EcoCiencia.

Our destination is the northwestern edge of the Yasuní National Park. Largest of all the national parks in Ecuador, the Yasuní Park was established in 1979, less than two years after we did our floral and faunal survey at the eastern edge. Now Maxus Energy has an oil concession that overlaps with part of the park. Laborers are working feverishly to build a road through the forest to the oil fields. We'll inventory amphibians and reptiles in the area being mapped for the road. A few trees have been cut to make a path, but no real forest destruction has occurred yet. In addition to providing a list of the species present, the preliminary survey will help us evaluate our experimental design for a proposed three-year study of the impact of the road on amphibians and reptiles. Ours is just one part of a proposal that has been submitted to Maxus to be considered for funding. Others from EcoCiencia will survey the impact of the road on primates, other mammals, and birds. Several other Ecuadorian nongovernmental organizations have also submitted proposals to Maxus for impact studies. EcoCiencia has a reputation of being the most objective, thorough, and "scientific" of the organizations, which might frighten a giant privately owned oil company afraid of bad publicity. We'll see what happens. Maxus has promised to make its decision by the middle of this month on which proposal(s) to fund.

Prior to entering the area of Maxus exploitation, all visitors must attend an orientation session at the company's headquarters in Minga. Ana María, Armando, I, and about thirty men who are being initiated as Maxus laborers watch a propaganda video extolling the virtues of Maxus and guaranteeing that its activities will hurt neither the environment nor the indigenous peoples. Warnings are issued throughout the video: Do not litter the forest or rivers, and do not have any contact with the Indian women. After the video, we get our pictures taken for ID badges, our fingers pricked for blood tests, and our arms injected with yellow fever vaccinations.

Our next stop is Coca. Living conditions in town have improved since I was first here in 1977, except that every few days the dirt streets are hosed down with oil to combat the gritty dust. Coca now boasts a population of about three thousand residents plus tourists. We have lunch at a restaurant that obviously caters to the latter, with its menu of wild game: tapir, caiman, peccary, and capybara. Here we are, conservation biologists, confronted by a menu that exploits animals we know to be declining, just to satisfy tourists' demand for the "unusual." Should we leave and go to another restaurant? Though our consciences tell us not to patronize this place, our brains and stomachs tell us to stay because this is by far the most sanitary-looking restaurant in town. We stay and order fried chicken. Edison returns to Quito, and the students and I travel by motorized dugout to Pompeya. Pompeya is the staging point for the huge Maxus project and forest home for a multinational crew of about eight hundred engineers and construction workers from the United States, Canada, Ecuador, Brazil, Colombia, and Chile.

In Pompeya we meet one of the supervisors for environmental control, a heavyset, gruff German-Ecuadorian by the name of Mike. Midway through our explanation of the mission, he bellows, "No way will Maxus help you!" We show him a letter from his supervisor in Quito stating that Maxus will provide us with food and logistics during our preliminary survey. He backs off a little but only a little. According to Mike, unless we do a chemical study (his specialty) our science is useless. He says that Maxus has no interest in the impact of the road on amphibians and reptiles. To cap it all off, he sneers at us, "So, I have to give you everything: food, lodging, and for the women a man and for the man a woman!"

Mike puts us up in a visitors' portable trailer, and there we stew over the insults. Later in the afternoon we meet one of the Ecuadorian superintendents from the road construction company, Compañia Andrade Gutierrez. A pleasant guy, Ricardo assures us that "all can be resolved in this world." He offers to let us use the radio to contact Fernando, the biologist from EcoCiencia who is working with the topographers in the area where we're headed. Fernando's job is to give technical advice to the topographers in order that the road take the route that will do the least damage to sensitive plants, animals, and habitats.

After numerous attempts we finally contact Fernando, who promises to arrange for a dugout to meet us at Kilometer 32 tomorrow and take us across the Río Tiputini. He will borrow two tents, and he assures us there is enough extra food at the camp for the three of us. "Just don't mention it to Mike," he says.

8 May 1993

Ricardo drives us as far as a four-wheel drive vehicle can negotiate along the new road, to Kilometer 14. There we climb atop a huge tractor (locally called "the Dinosaur") being used to construct the road. The road will eventually extend over a hundred kilometers south of Coca, right through the Yasuní National Park and the Huaorani Reserve. The Dinosaur will take us to the farthest point where trees have been felled and the ground has been bulldozed—to the Tiputini River. We'll stay overnight at the Tiputini surveyors' camp, and the next day hike another eight kilometers on a narrow path through primary forest to the point where the topographers are working. There we'll do our survey.

The plan breaks down, however. After nine kilometers of slogging through mud and puddles of water, the tractor operator refuses to continue for fear of getting the Dinosaur stuck. We're on our own, nine kilometers left to walk through the orange-brown mud on the freshly bulldozed road, each of us with a day pack as well as a very heavy backpack that includes sleeping bag and pad, clothes, and field gear. The mud is determined to swallow my rubber boots, and I walk out of them several times, red-stockinged feet sinking deep into the goo. Our bodies are dehydrated from the hot tropical sun, and our clothes are drenched with sweat. None of us has any water left. My spirits sink as I witness the habitat destruction surrounding me. Mangled tree trunks litter the ground. Upturned root masses reach toward the sky. After six hours we see what looks like the Río

Bulldozed swath through the forest in preparation for a major road to the oil fields in the Huaorani Reserve.

Tiputini ahead but fear it might be a mirage. Closer, we spot the dugout and Fernando. As we cross the river, Fernando promises us cold Cokes on the other side.

At the Tiputini camp, José, an intermediary between the oil company and the local Indians, tells us about current problems. The Quechuas have declared a *paro* (standstill). All work on the road must stop. They are angry about the intrusion of the road into their forest home, and if the road is to be built, their demands must be met: a large supply of food, gasoline for their outboard motors, and a school building and teacher for their kids. José warns that the *paro* may hold us all hostage at this camp for a while.

9 May 1993

Seven Quechuas enter camp early this morning and admonish the crew not to work again today. José explains that Ana María, Armando, and I want to hike the eight kilometers to the end of the path where the topographers are working, in search of amphibians and reptiles. After considerable discussion among themselves, the Quechuas agree that we can proceed to the Piraña camp at Kilometer 41 since we work neither for Maxus nor for the road construction company.

The narrow path takes us through virtually undisturbed, lush forest. We weave around towering trees, palms, and a labyrinth of dense tangles of vines, a forest that reminds me of the panoramic murals of Mesozoic forest behind dinosaur exhibits in museums. Sunlight shining through the luxuriant green vegetation is nearly blinding. Partway along the trail the Quechuas overtake us, on their way to hunt monkeys and to warn the men at Kilometer 41 that the *paro* is still in effect.

Basic and primitive, Piraña houses about forty men, who sleep in tents on raised wooden platforms, protected by palm thatched roofs. A large tarp protects the cook's working area and the wooden tables and benches that serve as the dining area. Three shower stalls with hoses connected to the rainwater tank have skimpy pieces of black plastic that function as doors. Serving the entire camp, three crudely constructed one-hole outhouses sit in a row a ways from the sleeping quarters.

While we're eating a filling lunch of boiled potatoes, rice and beans, bow-tie noodles and onions, and canned sardines, the seven Quechuas appear. Their hunt has been successful. Three dead adult monkeys and a baby that fell with its mother are tied with vines to long sticks, each carried by two men. They drop their heavy loads, demand and receive lunch. After eating they threaten to return with lots of men if they hear chain saws or see any topographers working in the forest. They say that if they

Ana María and I share a small tent under a thatched roof at the Piraña camp.

205

Trio of showers at the Piraña camp.

have to return, they'll confiscate the chain saws and all the topographers' equipment.

Camp is quiet all afternoon, filled with forty bored men. After dinner Ana María, Armando, and I begin our survey. In addition to three snakes and many frogs, we see a large spider that has in the center of its two-centimeter-diameter abdomen a pattern that looks just like the Batman logo in reverse: a yellow bat shape on a golden-brown background. I photograph the "Batman spider" in hopes that someday a spider expert can identify it for me.

10 May 1993

This afternoon an out-of-breath, sweaty messenger arrives with news that angry Quechuas broke into the Tiputini camp and sliced through some of the tents with knives. They threatened to come here tomorrow to do the same. The news stimulates a lengthy discussion among the workers about what will happen once they pass into the Huaorani Reserve, only twenty kilometers farther south. Huaoranis are expected to react more violently than the Quechuas. Most of the workers say they will quit. They won't enter Huaorani territory for fear of getting speared.

Two hostile splinter groups of Huaorani still live a nomadic existence, resisting all contact with outsiders, even other Huaoranis. Just five years ago one of these clans, the Tagaeri, speared and killed a Capuchin missionary who had attempted to make friendly contact. Despite periodic reports of hostility and violence by the Huaorani, the Indians' domain is about to be invaded by men drawn by oil fever.

The crude oil reserves in this part of Ecuador are estimated at more than 200 million barrels, worth $2 billion in projected revenues. Sadly, Ecuador depends on oil for nearly half of its revenues. None of this wealth will be shared with the Huaorani because, under Ecuadorian law, the government retains all subsurface mineral rights. The government has outlawed any attempt by the Huaorani or any other indigenous group to impede the oil extraction process. But will the Huaorani, the only Indian tribe in the Amazon Basin that has never been conquered, obey the laws of outsiders?

In talking with the topographers, we realize they too have moral doubts about opening up the forest. One worker laments that because Maxus has a lot at stake, they'll find a way to push the road through Huaorani territory into the oil fields no matter what. He speculates that Maxus will do it with bribery, by dropping gifts from helicopters: baseball caps, knives and machetes, T-shirts, and flashlights. Another man expresses his concern about habitat destruction here in the Yasuní National Park, an area the United Nations has declared a biosphere reserve because of its extraordinary diversity of plants and animals. Also destroyed will be part of the Huaorani

Contaminated pond and vegetation from an oil spill south of Lago Agrio.

protectorate—land promised to them so they could live in peace and isolation. Despite what the Maxus propaganda baldly asserts, Huaorani culture will surely be eroded, disease will spread, and the wild game the Huaorani rely on for protein will move farther back into the forest away from the road traffic, chain saws, and seismic explosions. A Brazilian worker, speaking in Portuguese but clearly understood by all the Spanish speakers, points out that although colonization will technically be outlawed inside the Huaorani territory, people have already carved out farms along the road south from Coca heading toward the protectorate. Many of these colonists are Quechua and Shuar, traditional enemies of the Huaorani, and already violent confrontations have occurred. In addition to social and cultural destruction, many thousands of gallons of crude oil doubtlessly will be spilled on Huaorani lands.

11 May 1993

Again no work today. The men are tense and nervous. Midafternoon, fifteen workers from our camp return from the Tiputini camp empty-handed. The Quechuas won't allow them to transport the gasoline and food supplies they need. They hiked sixteen kilometers in the mud and heat for naught. We have almost no food left. Manuel, head of camp here, decides that everyone except four men who will stay to guard the tents and equipment must leave for the Tiputini camp tomorrow morning. Our inventory will be cut short by two days. Ana María, Armando, and I are frustrated but acknowledge that in the larger scheme of life here, the three of us are quite insignificant. Last week we were essentially held hostage by Colombian guerrillas, now it's the Quechuas.

This afternoon we watch the cook fill a pot of water from the river. He dumps in two packets of powdered orange drink mix and sets it aside for our dinner. So now we know what we've been drinking: an unboiled soup rich in tiny beasties. I also now suspect that this concoction is responsible for the nearly constant rumbling in my intestines. Over the past twenty-five years of fieldwork in the tropics, I've had many run-ins with the beasties in local water. What tropical field biologist hasn't? But today's experience is one of the most ludicrous.

At about 4:00 P.M. I feel it coming. I jam my flip-flops onto my feet and dash a hundred meters through the forest to the outhouse. Fortunately, all three doors are open. I enter the nearest one and find army ants swarming over the floor, walls, and seat. I rush to the second. Army ants. And the third has even more ants. No choice. I slam the door and desperately sweep the ants off the wooden seat. Doubled over, squashing the enraged army ants that are biting my bare feet, I'm thinking, "This is *not* fun!" Eventually I stagger back to my tent. After swallowing an Imodium, I collapse onto my sleeping bag. My intestines are still churning. The tent is sweltering and buzzing with mosquitoes. This is *still* not fun.

By dark my gut has settled down, thanks to the wonders of Imodium. On this last night surveying for amphibians and reptiles, we find a caiman. During our limited time here, we've found forty species: twenty-four frogs and toads, seven lizards, eight snakes, and the one caiman. Almost all these species also occur at Santa Cecilia. Just in these few days, we've seen three kinds of monkeys, many macaws and parrots, a herd of peccaries, and even the tail end of a jaguar. It's sad to think about the changes to come to this forest. Supposedly the forest will be returned to the Quechua and Huaorani, but it—and they—will be forever altered by the intrusive road, pipeline, and traffic associated with oil extraction and pipeline maintenance.

When we return to camp we learn that, fortunately for the workers and for us, the Quechuas never showed up.

12 May 1993

Our hike back to the Tiputini camp nets us a stunning metallic red species of poison dart frog that none of us has seen before. We have the whole day now to wait for something to happen. I head toward the forest to look for frogs but am told that the Quechuas have surrounded the camp with crossed spears. They want us in one place. Instead, I teach Ana María how to play gin rummy with a deck of cards we make from waterproof paper from my field notebook.

Late afternoon a helicopter lands and five Maxus higher-ups climb out, looking very self-important. They explain to the Quechuas that everything has been resolved in Quito. All the Quechuas' demands will be met: food, gasoline, even the school and a teacher. The Quechuas add one more demand: that in the morning Maxus take every member of the Quechua entourage back to his or her home, by dugout. Many of them had walked for more than a day to get here. We radio to EcoCiencia and arrange for Edison to meet us in the village of Pindo tomorrow, which we'll reach by hitching a ride in the dugout along with a group of Quechuas from the *paro*.

13 May 1993

At 6:00 A.M. we step into a dugout with about twenty Quechuas. We're a motley crew: three pale faces staggering under the weight of ungainly muddy backpacks, one teenage girl with a whining baby monkey clinging to her arm, an elderly man with a long spear, a woman with a small baby attached to her breast, and about seventeen young to middle-aged men, many of them armed with rifles. Our 3½-hour dugout trip along the gently flowing Río Tiputini is beautiful, first in thick fog until the sun burns off the mist. During the trip I reflect on how gracious the men at the Piraña camp were to us, intruders into their forest home. I think about their openness and honesty as they admitted their doubts in opening up the forest and their fears of the Huaorani. Edison meets us and we drive to Coca. Back in our fried chicken restaurant, the first sip of cold beer teases my taste buds. I begin to guzzle. How I look forward to a hot shower in Quito. And a flush toilet. And a sink so I can wash my hands before flossing my teeth.

15 May 1993

On my last day in Quito, I meet with Mike's supervisor and describe the obstacles Mike had created. Naturally the supervisor defends his employee, but he assures me that Maxus does want impact work done and that almost surely EcoCiencia will get at least part of the contract to do the study. I emphasize the need to gather the baseline data in the forest *before* the chain saw crew begins. The study needs to begin *soon*. As though spurning my pleas on purpose, the supervisor tells me that review of the proposals will be delayed until 20 June.

We discuss the Indian problem. He says that a massive "education" program is being planned, which will inform the Indians about the oil wells and the road and will offer jobs. When I ask about the Huaoranis who refuse contact with outsiders and spear anyone who enters their territory, he confidently responds, "With time Maxus will solve that problem too." In a patronizing tone, he tells me that until he has assurances that all is safe, he will not allow Ana María or me to go into Huaorani territory because Huaoranis raid other villages for women and then rape and enslave them. I foresee the inevitable. He'll stall on making a decision about the proposal until after the road has already been pushed into Huaorani territory another twenty kilometers. It'll be too late for anyone to do the impact study in the Yasuní National Park, and he'll declare it's not safe for biologists, especially women, to carry out impact work in the Huaorani Reserve.

SUMMER 1993

15 June 1993

One month after returning to Flagstaff, I've packed my bags again for a return trip to Ecuador, this time with Peter and the kids. We drag ourselves out of bed at 3:30 A.M., gulp down some orange juice and toast, and the four of us are off to the airport. The kids (now eight and eleven years old) are excited about going to Ecuador. Both have forgotten most of the Spanish they learned in Argentina, but they promise to relearn it quickly.

18 June 1993

While Peter stays in Quito with the kids and works on revising reports for EcoCiencia, I visit a field site near the coast with Gloria, a student from the Catholic University. Gloria wants to study reproductive behavior of stubfoot frogs, closely related to the harlequin frogs I studied in Costa Rica. Before we leave Quito, Gloria's adviser tells me of several sites where he saw dense populations of stubfoot frogs ten years ago. Now the sites are frog ghost towns. He can't find a single stubfoot frog.

After an all night bus ride to Guayaquil, we take another bus to La Troncal and from there hail a taxi. The cabdriver is not pleased with the muddy, crater-pocked road that seems to lead nowhere. Eventually we reach the end of the line, at Manta Real, a tiny hamlet of twenty houses. The cabdriver promises to return for us the day after tomorrow at 2:30 in the afternoon. We give him a large tip to improve his memory.

21 June 1993

Most everyone in Manta Real works at the nearby sugarcane plantation. High in the mountains sits an illegal still where *aguardiente*, sugarcane alcohol, is made. The brew is poured into large rubber pouches, loaded onto mules, and transported to Manta Real and La Troncal for bottling. While working in the woods, we've encountered several men, teetering from sampling the goods they carry, leading mules packed with rubber pouches. Each is curious and wants to know where we're from and what we're doing on our hands and knees in the mud.

We explain that we're searching for frogs. One wizened, toothless old man tells us he doesn't see as many frogs as he used to. Listening carefully to our description of the stubfoot frog, he nods that yes, he knows it, but that he hasn't seen any for several years. He offers us a swig of *aguardiente* from his mud-splattered whiskey bottle. We politely decline.

For a modest price, one of the local families shares their meals with us—usually soup, huge mounds of rice and potatoes, and small portions of beef gristle. A corner of the kitchen is blocked off as a *cuy* (guinea pig) dwelling and nursery. Over thirty guinea pigs of all sizes, ages, and colors squeal incessantly. Last night when we expressed interest in the *cuy* (actually I picked up a fluffy white-and-brown juvenile and was petting it), the wife insisted on roasting two for dinner. While eating the legs with the little claws still intact, I thought about the two pet guinea pigs named Wilbur and Gub-Gub that Peter and I once had, our surrogate children before they were displaced by Karen. I later commented to Gloria that my idea of eating *cuy* would be to have someone else remove the tiny muscles from the bones and then roast the meat slivers. That way I could enjoy the delicate flavor without thinking of Wilbur and Gub-Gub.

Guinea pigs are native to Peru, Ecuador, and Colombia and in fact were domesticated by native peoples for food long before the arrival of the Spanish in the 1500s. They are still a staple feature of the diet for many families in South America who keep *cuy* colonies as a ready source of protein. As Peter and I discovered, the animals are easy to care for and to breed. In preparation for cooking, guinea pigs are scalded, but not skinned, and then usually are roasted. In some areas they are stewed in the same way that rabbits are stewed.

Early this morning—our last day in Manta Real—just as we are about to give up, we find four stubfoot frogs in a swamp at the road's edge. Each is yellow with a unique pattern of small black spots. Gloria becomes almost giddy at the prospect of a productive study site. An additional three hours of searching yields no more, however. Discouraged, we return to Manta Real and pack up. Two-thirty rolls around, but there's no sign of our taxi. Our panic increases over the next hour, and we fear the cabdriver has abandoned us. He eventually shows up at 3:30, complaining that the road is even worse than three days ago and thus the trip will cost us more.

22 June 1993

Edison drives Peter, Karen, Rob, me, and two students to the end of the road leading to Sierra Azul (Blue Mountain), a large private reserve set in beautiful montane forest to the southeast of Quito, near Baeza. There, two workers from the reserve meet us with four rather bony horses and mules. We load our luggage and mount. Peter and Rob ride on one horse, Karen and I straddle a mule, and each student has a beast. Maybe it's me, maybe it's the mule, but we don't hit it off. The mule seems to have a mind of her own that resists any suggestions from her rider. Early on she separates from the others and takes a parallel path. Suddenly a thick branch of bamboo looms across the trail at neck height. I pull back on the reins to avoid decapitation, but she obstinately plods ahead. Karen and I crash into the branch and tumble off into soft mud.

The Río Aragón, a fairly wide and fast-flowing river, snakes its way through the forest, throwing coils back and forth between the end of the road and Sierra Azul so frequently that during our two-hour ride we cross the river twenty-seven times. Each time our mule stumbles, I warn Karen we're about to plunge into the water. It never happens, although once we sink up to our thighs as the mule swims a little too enthusiastically through swift current. By the time we arrive at camp, Peter and I are bow-legged and have had enough riding. Despite the heavy mist, Karen and Rob think the trip was great fun and beg to ride awhile longer in the pasture. Karen pleads to have her own horse when we return to Flagstaff.

Although thirty hybrid llama alpacas are raised for wool in one area of the finca and several large cattle pastures are in use elsewhere, most of the land is undisturbed cloud forest. Ornithologists have reported that the bird life is extremely abundant and diverse here, as are mammals, including mountain tapir, puma, and spectacled bear. The owners of Sierra Azul, a North American construction engineer and his Ecuadorian wife, are devoted conservationists who recognize the value of their land. They are currently building comfortable cabins to promote ecotourism and encourage scientific research. I have offered to inventory the frogs, photograph all the species, and make a guidebook for visitors to Sierra Azul. The two students associated with EcoCiencia who have come with us will carry out thesis projects here on aquatic insects and flame flower trees. Peter has come to help them design their studies.

24 June 1993

After a hearty breakfast of rice, potatoes, avocados, hot dogs, and fried eggs, I spend a few hours photographing the frogs I collected yesterday. Peter casts his line into the river and catches twelve stunted trout in short order. Karen and Rob have great fun getting soaked in the heavy mist, chasing baby chickens, playing with a little orange kitten they name Tangerine, falling into the river while trying to catch a fish by hand, and riding horses in the pasture.

Today's five-hour hike through rain yields some interesting finds: a green dink frog covered with fleshy spines, peculiar slow-moving warty black toads, and poison dart frogs with tadpoles on their backs. Giant seventy-centimeter-long earthworms slithering in the mud are too good to resist, and we photograph each other trying to hang on to the slippery creatures. Karen and Rob are real troopers throughout the hike. They never complain when the mud swallows their rubber boots and they have to be pulled back out. Nor when their umbrellas turn inside out and they get soaked trying to turn them outside out. They delight in being covered with mud from neck to toe, and Karen doesn't even complain about mud in her hair. The return to camp is a bit traumatic, however, as we must take freezing showers to extract the multiple layers of mud and worm slime from our skin.

Tonight we find another species of dink frog, bringing our total to eleven species of frogs in less than three days of fieldwork. I'm surprised, though, at how few frog individuals we see here considering that the forest is so wet and undisturbed. In response to my asking the workers if they've noticed whether frogs have been declining here over the past ten years, they admit they haven't paid any attention to frogs. Unfortunately, this is the problem herpetologists have encountered trying to make a case for the plight for frogs, especially in the tropics. We have so few background data on frog abundances from ten, twenty, thirty years ago that in many cases it's impossible to document declines.

25 June 1993

The four of us have accumulated an impressive mound of wet, filthy clothes caked with mud. We stuff sodden jeans, sweatshirts, T-shirts, socks, and underwear into a large garbage bag, which we tie onto a mule alongside our luggage. Karen insists on sitting in the saddle so she can "steer," and I'm relegated to the mule's bony butt. We take off in a heavy mist, Karen thrilled to be riding again. All goes well until soon after the last of the twenty-seven river crossings. While plodding up a steep incline, our mule stumbles and I slide off the back end into a mud puddle. That's enough. I decide to continue on my own two feet. Karen, pleased to have the mule to herself, trots off and leaves me behind.

Rocío calls us at home this evening to report that Maxus has abruptly changed the format for proposals. They gave two days to revise ours, so she and the director of EcoCiencia worked on it day and night in order to resubmit it by the deadline. The new decision date will be 15 July. Clearly, Maxus does not intend to facilitate conservation research in the Yasuní National Park.

28 June 1993

Our next adventure began yesterday with a bus ride and two taxi rides to the La Planada Reserve, high in the montane rain forest of southwestern Colombia. Peter and I will join other faculty in teaching an ecology course to fifteen students from Colombia, Ecuador, and Venezuela.

We spend today getting settled in and exploring the lush forest. Much of La Planada is a plateau—as implied by the Spanish word *plano,* meaning "flat"—sitting at about eighteen hundred meters above sea level. With about five thousand millimeters of annual precipitation, the reserve is in one of the wettest areas in South America.

This evening I take some of the students out on a "frog walk." None has ever walked forest trails at night looking for frogs. They all agree that the forest is a different world then, with unfamiliar sights, sounds, and smells. During our walk, we see metallic green beetles congregated on a bush as though in conference, a sleeping hummingbird, and several male glass frogs attending eggs. Tinkling calls of dink frogs surround us and compete with the katydids for air space. The swooshing of bat wings flying past our heads makes one student uneasy. When I pick up a pair of copulating walkingsticks, the interrupted couple responds on cue and sprays a powerfully foul odor in defense. The wet vegetation and soil exude richly organic smells that reflect the abundant and diverse life of the cloud forest.

6 July 1993

Peter and I have an early morning field project with the class. Carla, one of Peter's former graduate students who is studying birds at the reserve, invites the kids to join her for a check of her mist nets. As the kids set off, bundled in warm clothes and raincoats, Peter and I sigh with relief knowing we can concentrate our attention on the students.

The project we assign to the students is to wander around in the vicinity of the visitors' station and think up questions on natural history. Each student will formulate four or five such questions and then develop each into a hands-on exercise that could be done with schoolchildren or other visitors to La Planada. Most of the students' questions focus on insects, plants, and birds. Is there greater diversity of insect life under rocks or logs? What colors do insects prefer? What types of plants grow beneath the crowns of different types of trees? What sorts of differences do you find in the leaf litter of secondary versus primary forest? When birds eat different fruits, do they destroy the seeds of some but not others? Do birds eat any kind of fruits, or does a given species eat only certain fruits? We're all impressed with the creative exercises the students devise based on their questions.

By late morning the kids return, a bit wet but excited about their adventure. Rob chatters at full speed about how much fun it was to see Carla's fingers get bitten as she extracted angry birds from the net. He seems hyper, but it isn't until later that I find out why. To warm their insides, Carla had offered them coffee. Being the more sensible of the two, Karen declined. Rob tried it and loved it because Carla had laced the coffee with a strong dose of sugar. He downed three cups.

In preparation for a class project tonight, I need to survey the stream for male glass frogs attending egg clutches. The kids come along to help out. They soon grow tired of not finding any frogs or eggs and decide to build a fort at the edge of the stream. I leave them with strict orders not to go into the water, and I continue upstream. When I return thirty minutes later, I shudder to find them perched on a pile of logs (their "fort") over a two-meter-high waterfall. But, they didn't go *in* the water.

After dinner I take the students out to observe parental care behavior of male glass frogs. Over the past week I've noticed that the frogs sit closer to their eggs after a day of less-than-usual rain. Of the ten guarding males I've been watching, all have single clutches except for one individual that has four on his large ginger leaf. Judging from the stages of the embryos, these seem to represent clutches from four different days, and therefore eggs from four different females. Why was this stud so much more successful in fertilizing clutches than other males along the stream? Perhaps he called more persistently. Perhaps his call was more attractive to females. Or perhaps his leaf was more attractive than those of other males—more humid or more sheltered with overhanging vegetation. I discuss these possibilities with the students and encourage anyone interested to pursue the question as an independent project.

20 July 1993

After leaving La Planada, we returned to Quito, where we spent several days attending meetings at EcoCiencia—and doing laundry. There was still no word from Maxus about the proposal, though it was past their most recently declared decision date.

WE'RE NOW in the Andean town of Loja in southern Ecuador, where Peter and I will give a short course on ecology and conservation to a group of foresters, university students, and Peace Corps volunteers. The course is sponsored by a local conservation organization, Arcoiris (Rainbow). Rodrigo, a director of Arcoiris, takes us to Podocarpus National Park for an exhilarating five-hour hike through clouds and heavy mist. Semiprotected by rain ponchos and umbrellas, we climb up steep trails, hiking first through lush cloud forest loaded with hummingbird-pollinated plants, orchids, and bromeliads, next through gnarled elfin forest, then through a beautiful shrubby *páramo* (high-elevation treeless plain) studded with knee-high plants, and last to grassy *páramo* at an elevation of thirty-two hundred meters. When we finally reach the top, strong winds nearly blow Rob and Karen off the ground and back down into the elfin forest. A few dink frogs are calling, but nothing like I would have expected. A search on hands and knees for frogs inside the clumps of bunch grass and between the leaves of bromeliads nets only insects and spiders. Rodrigo tells me that eight to ten years ago he used to see and hear lots of frogs on this hike.

24 July 1993

Podocarpus National Park is considered one of the richest protected areas in the world in terms of biodiversity. A botanist recently estimated that the park contains between three to four thousand species of vascular plants (plants with tissues that transport water and nutrients through a system of roots, stems, and leaves). Inventories of birds reveal at least 540 species, representing over 35 percent of the list for all of Ecuador. Although the park includes only about 140,000 hectares, it encompasses a wide range of habitat, from rain forest at less than nine hundred meters elevation to high *páramo* at over thirty-four hundred meters. To date no one has made an inventory of the amphibians. Perhaps someday I can return and make one.

Today we take all twenty-two students up to the *páramo*. It seems like a different place today. There is little mist, allowing spectacular panoramic views over the surrounding tropical alpine landscape and the dense forest below. Still no frogs.

26 July 1993

At 4:45 A.M. we taxi from Loja to the airport and fly back to Quito. At the EcoCiencia office I receive the disappointing, though not unexpected, news that Maxus has awarded the entire environmental impact contract to another local organization. All of us are convinced that the entire proposal process was a scam. It's now too late for anyone to begin a valid impact study in the Yasuní National Park. A swath through the forest has already been bulldozed for the road. Besides being disappointed about not getting the contract, I'm also leaving the country feeling uneasy about the fate of Ecuadorian frogs. Everywhere I've been this trip—from the montane forest southeast of Quito, to the Pacific coast, to the southern Andes—frogs seem to be declining and disappearing.

IN THE YEARS since my preliminary survey in the northwestern edge of the Yasuní National Park, Maxus has indeed succeeded in bribing the Huaorani. Maxus helicopters have dropped clothing and trinkets from helicopters, Maxus has funded school buildings and teachers, and Maxus has offered the Huaorani men menial jobs. Only time will tell how drastically the Huaoranis' lives have been altered. Crude oil has been spilled from ruptured pipeline onto Huaorani lands and into their rivers. How much more will be spilled over the next decade is anyone's guess.

10

REMEMBERING
AYAHUASCA

IN THE SUMMER of 1995, Peter and I began advising on an EcoCiencia-sponsored conservation project in Ecuador. We were to design inventory and monitoring studies and at the same time train Ecuadorian biologists to carry out the fieldwork. The project involved the buffer zone of Cotacachi-Cayapas Ecological Reserve, in the tropical lowlands of Esmeraldas Province in the northwest of the country.

We decided we'd have to undertake this project without Karen and Rob along for three reasons, all related to the fact that we'd be in the lowlands. First, the kids would be miserable exposed to the heat, humidity, mosquitoes, and chiggers; Peter and I have developed coping mechanisms over the years. Second, because of the threat of venomous snakes, the kids wouldn't have the freedom to which they've been accustomed while visiting high elevation sites such as Monteverde, La Planada, and Sierra Azul. Third, the incidence of malaria and other diseases is very high in the area. Peter and I took anti-malarial pills, but we didn't want to subject the kids to these because of possible long-term side effects. Instead, Karen and Rob visited my parents in Fort Collins, Colorado.

SUMMER 1995

6 June 1995

Travel by river is the only way to reach the African-Ecuadorian and Chachi Indian communities on the Río Cayapas in Esmeraldas Province. Peter, Rocío, two field biologists who will work on the project (Pato and Rubén), and I fly to the town of Esmeraldas. We then drive to the logging town of Borbón, where the project's boatman, Cholo, will take us up the Río Cayapas in a dugout equipped with an outboard motor. After a prolonged lunch of freshwater crayfish, we load the dugout and head upriver toward the African-Ecuadorian community of San Miguel. The riverbank is lined with seemingly impenetrable dense vegetation except around the scattered palm-thatched Chachi Indian houses or compact African-Ecuadorian villages that pop up every now and then. Flashes of color dart in and out of the vegetation, and turtles lazily bask on logs. After a while the sun sets, and we are left in darkness and rain with an estimated two hours left to go. I can see nothing. I know Cholo can see no more than I can. Incredibly, he seems to know every bend in the river and avoids every randomly floating log.

After dumping our wet backpacks and supplies at the community house in San Miguel, we meet with about thirty residents to explain the purpose of our visit. EcoCiencia has been awarded funds to study the impact of human activities on the forest. We want the local people to be involved in the monitoring projects from the start and to participate in choosing the specific questions to be addressed. Peter and I will run a workshop during which residents will generate and then vote on the questions they consider most urgent and interesting. We explain that we'll design the monitoring project around these questions and that the project will encompass both the African-Ecuadorian community of San Miguel and the nearby Chachi Indian community of Loma Linda. At this point the president of San Miguel stands, clears his throat, and in a commanding voice declares that they will not go to Loma Linda and likewise the Chachis will refuse to come to San Miguel for a joint workshop. Rocío quickly offers to hold two different all-day workshops for the two communities that are only five minutes apart by dugout.

Our plan to integrate these two communities into one study is clearly challenged by cultural differences and mutual discomfort between the groups. The blacks in northwestern Ecuador (locally called *morenos*) are descendants of escaped or shipwrecked slaves brought over from Africa beginning in the 1500s. The Chachis are descended from Indians who were displaced from Andean regions four centuries ago either by other groups of Indians or by the Spanish. Because neither culture feels comfortable with the other, they remain largely separate social and political entities.

7 June 1995

Our all-day workshop held at the school in San Miguel attracts twenty-five participants, or about 80 percent of the adults in the community, and includes the president and vice president of the village. The meeting begins on an inauspicious note with an antagonistic park guard, who is quite unpopular in the community, demanding that if we work in San Miguel, EcoCiencia should provide funds to build a new, much-needed schoolhouse. We emphasize that we cannot provide funds from the research component of the organization, but that we will be happy to help the community apply for funds from another source. As the park guard blusters on, the president loses his patience and, much to our relief, declares that we will *first* have the workshop and afterward discuss the request for help with the school.

After introductions we ask the participants if they wish to conserve the forest in which they've lived for centuries so that their grandchildren can enjoy the same benefits they've had—solace, beauty, lumber, and food. They all shout, *"Yes!"* enthusiastically. We then ask them how they'll be able to decide which of the many alternative ways of using their natural resources would best achieve their goal of conserving the forest for their grandchildren. They agree that they need to set up guidelines, and to choose guidelines they must recognize the consequences of alternative uses of their forest's resources. We point out that the only way to get an idea of the consequences of different alternatives is to do studies. This requires that meaningful questions be asked. And this will be the focus of the workshop: practice in framing questions.

We assign each pair of participants a fifty-by-fifty-centimeter patch of the schoolyard and give them fifteen minutes to generate questions about what they see in this mini-landscape. Afterward, they proudly present their questions to the entire group, and we enthusiastically praise the insightful ones. Next we discuss how to frame questions so that these will lead most easily to answers and eventually to conservation guidelines. The community members quickly grasp this fundamental thinking process.

We return to the schoolyard and divide the participants into teams, with the charge of proposing the real-life questions they'd like to have answered about their impact on the forest. Finally we convene the entire group, discuss and refine the questions, and the community members vote. Their choices, a compromise between their independent questions and the themes we feel qualified to address, converge on the dichotomy between forest and *chacras* (their slash-and-burn garden plots) and on birds, small edible mammals, and bats. Does planting coffee in *chacras* increase the rate of overall crop damage by parrots and other birds? How do density and diversity of birds, bats, and small edible mammals vary among *chacra,* secondary forest, and primary forest? The participants want to study small mammals, mostly wild rats that bear little resemblance to the rats we associate with cities, garbage, and laboratories, because they rely heavily on these animals as a source of protein. They want to study bats for two reasons: mostly because they don't like them and want to know where they are so they can avoid them, but also because one person points out that many bats eat obnoxious insects, others pollinate plants, and some disperse seeds. All through the workshop, we emphasize that this is *their* project and that we will communicate continually with them by giving informal presentations of the results. The community will participate directly in the research itself, through several individuals whom EcoCiencia has already trained to be field assistants.

The president of San Miguel, a tall, handsome jet-black man named Heladio, is wearing a white T-shirt, its front displaying a design of two green fried eggs and its back a pinkish brown cooked ham. It suddenly hits me that I'm staring at the theme of Dr. Seuss's book *Green Eggs and Ham!* I ask Heladio if he knows the book. He says no, so I describe it and promise to bring a copy in Spanish for his children when I return in November. He grins skeptically and says he'll be waiting.

After dinner several of us meet with community officials and the unpopular park guard to draft an outline for the proposal to request funding for a new schoolhouse. The contribution from the community will be labor; they estimate it will take twelve people four months to build a new school. Thirty-six children attend the school, taught by one teacher who handles grades first through sixth. The government provides one teacher to rural schools, but if the community wants a second, it must pay. The residents of San Miguel would like to acquire a second teacher, but they lack the funds.

9 June 1995

A five-minute dugout trip down the Río Cayapas brings us to Loma Linda (Pretty Hill). While waiting at the schoolhouse for participants to assemble, one of the Chachis fluent in Spanish, Miguel, tells us about the recent local outbreak of malaria. Six people are currently very sick with it;

others have milder cases. All are miserable with the recurring bouts of chills and fever accompanied by headache, muscular pain, and nausea. There is no local doctor.

My first impressions are of the vast differences between the people of Loma Linda and San Miguel. Coppery brown versus black skin. Long straight hair versus short curly hair. Short versus tall. Faded and loose-fitting clothes versus brightly colored and more revealing clothing. Most Chachis are quiet and reserved, whereas the *morenos* are generally outgoing, loud, and friendly. Construction of the houses is different. Chachis build a thatched roof over a bamboo platform raised on stilts, without walls or doors; the *morenos* also use bamboo and thatch but construct walls and doors for privacy. Houses in Loma Linda are widely scattered along both riverbanks, whereas most of the homes in San Miguel are concentrated in a central area.

We introduce ourselves and then ask the same of the eighteen participants. Unlike the African-Ecuadorians, the Chachis are reticent and most refuse to speak. We proceed to the discussion of generating questions, with Miguel translating into the local language, Cha'palaachi, because many participants don't understand Spanish. When we ask for questions, they stare at their feet. During the quadrat exercise, I work with the three women of the group. They are shy and nod in agreement with my suggestions but say nothing. Perhaps they don't understand my Spanish. Or perhaps they speak no Spanish at all. Midmorning the director of the school takes us aside and informs us that women are not full participants in this sort of activity. They came out of curiosity but don't want to be directly involved. He says we need to be aware of their "place" and respect it. The ten minute candy break is a hit, but there's a definite hierarchy and an uneven distribution of resources. The interpersonal dynamics are intriguing. Miguel, who feels himself the important link between his people and the outside world, stuffs his pocket full of hard candies after handing everyone else two pieces each. The school director, occupant of an esteemed position in the community, hoards all the extra chocolates on his desk and openly munches them throughout the discussion without offering any to others.

Only four people, all men, return for the afternoon session. Like the participants in San Miguel, they are interested in the relationships between animals and their *chacras,* and where they can find the highest density of small edible mammals. By the end of the workshop, we have nudged them to choose basically the same research questions that the participants from San Miguel generated. We learn that most of the *chacras* contain naturally regenerating stands of *rampira,* the palmetto-like plant (also called the

Chachi children at Loma Linda.

Moreno children at San Miguel.

Open-air Chachi house at Loma Linda.

Cluster of houses at San Miguel.

Panama hat plant) Chachi women use for weaving mats and baskets. The men hesitatingly tell us that most of the women clean away the vegetation from around their plants and that they would be interested to learn what they could do to improve the size and density of their plants. They seem pleased when we offer to get a project started on *rampira* as well.

THIS EVENING back in San Miguel, the local marimba band comes to the community house. Nearly everyone from the village shows up for the party. The marimba, made locally from bamboo and an extremely hard and durable palm wood called chontaduro, is beautiful. The players are superb, as are the vocalists. The dancing is wild and everyone participates. I feel like an awkward dolt amidst all the locals. I just don't have the rhythm. They are so sexy and vibrant when they dance. So alive. The president, Heladio, decides to take it upon himself to teach me how to dance like San Migueleños. Though I'm clumsy, I must admit this is exhilarating.

11 June 1995

Before returning by dugout to Borbón, we meet with the five men who wish to work as field assistants on the project: three from San Miguel (one is half *moreno* and half Chachi) and two from Loma Linda. We ask them to think of this as one project with a single design. Ideally the five men from the two communities should work together as a team. The three men from San Miguel solemnly nod their heads in agreement. The two Chachis stare at the table, expressionless.

12 June 1995

We wait for several hours by the side of the road for a bus to Esmeraldas, surrounded by our backpacks, duffel bags, canvas carry-ons, and black plastic garbage bags filled with sleeping bags and boots. Finally, after nearly thirty buses chug on by, not wanting to deal with our daunting mound of luggage, an open-air bus, or *chivo,* stops for us. There's no standing room left inside the *chivo,* packed with passengers, chickens, and produce, and looking just like the colorful pottery replicas sold in import shops. We pile our luggage on top of the crates, bags, and woven baskets already precariously balanced on the sloping back end of the bus, and then we climb on top of the cargo, joining other people already perched there. Wedged in between Peter and a young boy holding a cackling rooster upside down, I have nothing to hold on to, to give me even a false sense of security. A pig underneath us squeals most of the trip, protesting the weight of people and cargo it supports. The road is riddled with potholes and blind curves, yet the driver chugs merrily along. Occasionally a passenger pounds on the side of the bus and yells for the driver to stop so that fallen cargo can be retrieved. Although one elderly woman crosses herself repeatedly throughout the trip, most of the passengers seem to enjoy this rattly ride. When the *chivo* rumbles to a halt at the airport, we gingerly descend, thankful to be on our feet once more. As we check in for our flight to Quito, Rocío suddenly realizes she left her backpack with money, receipts, and camera on top of the *chivo*. Panicked, she commandeers a taxi and races after the *chivo*, which fortunately cannot exceed thirty mph and thus is easy to overtake. She returns, backpack in hand, just as we board the plane.

28 June 1995

After spending the last two weeks writing reports and advising on another field project, Peter and I are ready to return to Phoenix, where we'll meet the kids' flight from Denver and then take the bus back to Flagstaff. It's been an intensive but fun month—a field adventure unlike any that either of us has experienced before, because of the unique cultural component.

WINTER 1995

30 November 1995

Hallelujah! My luggage just arrived at the Quito airport, having missed my plane because of delays in Dallas. I've been here for thirty-six hours without a change of clothes. Peter is home with the kids, as this is my turn to advise on the EcoCiencia monitoring projects. Tomorrow I will go to San Miguel and Loma Linda with Pato, Rubén, and a third student, María, who will work with the Chachi women on a study of the Panama hat plant.

3 December 1995

Yesterday we drove to Borbón and found Cholo. The dugout ride to San Miguel was just as pleasant (first half) and as frightening (second half) as the one in June, the second half being in total darkness again. Miraculously, Cholo again avoided the floating logs and other obstacles in the river.

We spend today hiking around San Miguel and Loma Linda, from one family's *chacra* to the next, looking for ideal sites for the bird, bat, and rat monitoring. At one *chacra* a little *moreno* boy motions for us to enter his thatched house. An elderly man, propped up with pillows, lies on a ragged mauve blanket on the floor. Struggling to talk, he tells us that he has had severe stomach pains for over two years, and they are getting worse. He tells us he went to Guayaquil several times to a *brujo* (witch doctor) who promises to cure him if he pays an exorbitant amount of money. He desperately wants to return to the *brujo*, but he doesn't have the money. He says the medical doctor in Borbón just gave him pills for parasites and gas. But the pills haven't worked. Can we help him?

We feel helpless. Pato gives him a pep talk about being optimistic; Maria suggests an herb tea her grandmother uses for stomach pain. I suggest that he revisit the doctor in Borbón. Tilting his head away from us, he mumbles he doesn't have the strength for the long boat trip.

Afterward I reflect on my own negative reaction to the man's desire to return to the *brujo* and my suggestion that he return to the medical doctor instead. I live in a culture that believes that when you're sick, you see an expert trained in medicine. We leave spiritual health to ministers, priests, and rabbis. Many people in the world, however, rely on traditional healers, such as *brujos,* who view the physical body and the spirit as inseparable. They believe that good health can be attained only if the physical and spiritual components are in equilibrium. In order to achieve this balance, the healer must communicate with supernatural forces. Often the source of the problem is perceived to be either a person who has cast a spell or an evil spirit, and thus the healer works to excise the negative influence. Often traditional healers have profound abilities to cure illness because their patients have complete faith and confidence in their powers. I realize now that this sick man might indeed be helped most by the *brujo.*

As we climb out of the dugout back in San Miguel, Heladio, wearing his green eggs and ham T-shirt, strolls up to me and asks if I've brought the book *Green Eggs and Ham.* Together we go to the community house. From my luggage I extract the Spanish translation I found in Flagstaff. Heladio is overjoyed that the picture on the cover matches his T-shirt. Pato reads it aloud to Heladio and Cholo, both of whom chuckle throughout. Dr. Seuss is just as clever in Spanish as he is in English.

4 December 1995

Heladio proudly gives me a large yellow-orange pineapple from his *chacra* as a thank-you gift. He says his sons, ages ten, eight, and five, have read and reread the book already. With a wide grin, he asks me to take his picture holding the book alongside the fried green eggs on his shirt.

Chachi woman in her home, weaving a basket from the Panama hat plant, *rampira*, as her daughter looks on.

Maria has devised a questionnaire for each of ten basket weavers from Loma Linda. She and I spend the day talking with the women, asking questions: How often do you clear the weeds from the ground around your *rampira* plants? Do you prefer plants that grow in the sun or shade? Do you prefer the dark green or light green plants? Miguel accompanies us and acts as interpreter because few of the women speak Spanish. Maria and I are beginning to learn some Cha'palaachi: *pishcu* (birds), *iyu* (rat), *pichuhua* (*rampira*). One basket weaver looks about fourteen years old. Her baskets are lovely, with intricate designs of scorpions, frogs, and monkeys woven into the sides. During the interview we learn she is actually twenty-five. Afterward when I exclaim to Miguel how young she looks, he responds that although she has been married for ten years, she still has not gotten pregnant. Laughing, he explains that kids make Chachi women age quickly.

Dinner tonight is a first for me but is an important part of the diet both for the African-Ecuadorians and Chachis: wild rat. Rat traps are deadfalls, constructed out of heavy logs held up at one end by a cord. Bait is placed on the ground under the raised log along with a stick tied to the cord. When a rat comes to take the bait, it trips the cord and the log smashes it. Because rats are such an important component of their diet, hunters rotate their traps every few weeks among different areas to avoid overhunting

Cholo gleefully gnawing on the skull of a cooked wild rat.

their prey. One of Cholo's traps produced today, so he fixes rat for dinner and offers me some. Similar to chicken, the flavor is quite good, due largely to the spicy curry sauce in which it was boiled. The hind leg I am given is tough, though perhaps this particular rat is an old one. Cholo himself complains of its toughness. Still, he takes great pleasure in gnawing on the skull, sucking out the tiny tidbits of meat.

9 December 1995

The last four days have been productive. In addition to revising the experimental design, we've mist-netted bats, checked traps for rats, and surveyed birds. One night we caught thirty bats of nine species. We clamped an ear tag with an identification number on to each bat and then released them so that Pato and Rubén can keep track of individuals throughout the study. Our field assistants indicated they would have preferred to kill the bats. One morning we saw seventy-three birds of twenty-nine species in one *chacra*. Small mammals are less numerous, but we did catch a couple in our live traps. As we ear-tagged the rats and released them, our field assistants nearly cried as they watched their dinners scurry away.

This morning Rubén and I talk with one of the Chachis about ayahuasca, "the vine of the soul." Widely used throughout the Amazon Basin and beyond by many different groups of indigenous peoples, ayahuasca is a hallucinogenic drink made from a woody vine of the genus *Banisteriopsis*. Ingestion of ayahuasca produces vivid, brilliantly colored visions but also causes vertigo, nausea, and vomiting. The circumstances of use vary considerably with different cultures. Some groups use it only during ceremonies such as initiation rituals and funerals. In other cultures only a shaman is permitted to use it to diagnose an illness, divine its cure, or establish the identity of the presumed enemy responsible for causing the illness. In some cultures warriors take it before a hunt, to become braver or to foresee what game they will kill.

After the Chachi leaves, Rubén tells me about his experiences with ayahuasca, and I share my vivid memories from nearly twenty years ago at Santa Cecilia. Ildefonso knew that I wanted to learn about the local culture, so one day he invited me to participate in an ayahuasca session. "You'll never really feel you experienced the Oriente until you drink ayahuasca," he told me. My experience was as follows.

A QUECHUA *brujo* named Isidro arrived in Muñozlandia early in the morning and began the ayahuasca preparation by cutting pieces of *Banisteriopsis* vine about the diameter of my thumb. After shaving off the brown outer layer, he macerated the vine between two large rocks that he periodically rubbed with leaves from the vine. He placed the shredded vine into a pot of cold water and added some leaves of another plant, one that he said would intensify the ayahuasca visions and enhance hearing during the hallucinations. Isidro made a fire on the ground and heated the water. After simmering the brew for several hours, he passed it through a sieve to extract the fiber and stored the thick brown liquid in a large bowl.

Early evening I entered Ildefonso's abandoned thatched hut. Ilde and Isidro were already there, sitting on wooden crates. Isidro motioned for me to sit on the third crate. Ilde explained that when we need to vomit we should do so off the edge of the porch, without feeling guilty or embarrassed. We sat in silence for about ten minutes. The moon was nearly full. Isidro had his eyes closed and slowly rocked back and forth. He opened his eyes, poured a gourdful of ayahuasca, and drank it all. A disgusted expression on his weathered, swarthy face told me it really must taste bad. He spat onto the floor. A few minutes later he handed the full gourd to Ilde, who painfully swallowed a bit of the fluid. After grimacing a few seconds, he swallowed more and eventually handed the empty gourd back to Isidro. What had I gotten myself into? I thought about fleeing out the open door and returning to the sanity of my cabin. But I hesitated too long. Isidro handed me the gourd. I couldn't back out now. I swallowed the first sip and gagged. I had never tasted anything so bitter. The only way to do this was fast, so I guzzled. The three of us continued to sit in silence on our crates. I nervously wondered when something would happen.

Within about thirty minutes I felt dizzy. I knew the ayahuasca had taken effect when suddenly I was acutely aware of everything around me. Geometrical designs on the bamboo walls and floors wove in and out of focus. A large rat ran toward me. I didn't know if it was real or not. In a panicky voice I told Ilde that a rat was crawling over my foot. He shooed it away and I watched it run out the open door. Every time my eyes focused in a different direction, I saw my eyeballs jump as though they were attached to springs. Kaleidoscope patterns in brilliant colors danced about on the palm thatch above me. I closed my eyes and these images coalesced into a white golf ball falling down a long tunnel. Then the ball changed into a chicken egg, still falling down, until it became a round navel orange and disappeared. The monotonous drone of Ilde's generator was intrusive and annoying, and the incessantly chirping crickets were deafening. Several frogs called back and forth to each other. I visualized the notes as a series of spiraling cadenzas inked onto an orchestral score. My eyes followed every note. A crumpled blanket by the door became a sheep's head with large eyes and buck teeth. I fearfully watched the head for movement.

After a while I lost track of time and was seriously nauseated. I staggered to the porch, fell onto the bamboo floor, and vomited over the edge. I was sure I was dying. Just as I finished Ilde drunkenly wove past me, flopped onto the porch, and emptied his guts. Saying he couldn't sit up any longer, Isidro sprawled onto the floor. We alternated between hallucinations and violent heaving for a while before our brains and intestines stabilized a bit.

CALL ME A slow learner, or a masochist, but when Ilde asked if I wanted to join him for another ayahuasca experience five days later I agreed. Ilde explained that this would be different because this Quechua *brujo,* Francisco, made a more concentrated fluid and we wouldn't drink as much. Francisco promised that the visions would be more vivid with the more concentrated fluid, and the intestinal distress would be less.

Ilde, Francisco, and I sat on the same wooden crates in the abandoned thatched hut. Francisco poured thick brown liquid into a shot glass and blew the smoke from his homemade cigar into the ayahuasca. As I raised the glass, my lips burned from the fumes. My entire intestinal tract screamed in revolt as the ayahuasca traveled downward. Quickly Francisco handed me a slice of lemon to cut the bitter taste.

In my first vision I walked into a small thatched hut. A Quechua woman lay on a bamboo mat, moaning and groaning in the final stages of labor. I touched her sweaty forehead and then I became the woman. As my uterus contracted, I gasped with pain. I was alone. Then another contraction— more intense this time. I pushed and I groaned. Relief followed as I watched the baby emerge from between my legs.

Next, through dense forest the orange, glowing eyes of a howler monkey pierced through me, perceiving my every thought. Slowly the woolly shape transformed into the grotesque head of a wrinkle-faced bat. Its black beady eyes were less threatening than the howler's fiery eyes. A hairy tarantula ambled across the bat's face, climbed into its left ear, and disappeared. Giant insects and spiders appeared in the trees: conga ants, black beetles, and tarantulas. I looked over and saw Ilde playing with a large hairy tarantula. Then it turned into a rat. Dizzy and nauseated, I continued to watch creatures transform into unrelated forms. I vomited only a little.

After the hallucinations stopped, Francisco interpreted our visions for us. His Spanish was rudimentary and his voice crackled. I couldn't follow much of what he said, but I did understand that he couldn't interpret my birth vision. He said he had never given ayahuasca to a woman before.

SEVERAL HOURS after swapping ayahuasca stories, Rubén, Pato, María, and I board the motorized dugout and head toward Borbón. Soon, however, we're drifting in circles, with Angel, the boatman, stubbornly trying to revive his dead motor. Eventually another dugout comes by, looking like the nautical equivalent of a *chivo*, loaded with bags of rice, cackling chickens, bunches of *plátanos*, and crates of produce. Thanks to large sums of money, we convince the boatman to take us and all our backpacks to Borbón. Each of us sits on a gunnysack of rice, our luggage balanced on our laps. Feeling a little guilty, we leave Angel still trying to revive his dead motor. Many hours later we arrive in Borbón fairly wet after a slow trip of riding close to the water in the overweight dugout. Before we have unloaded, Angel arrives, struts up to us, grins with satisfaction, and announces that he fixed the motor.

17 December 1995

After a week of advising in Quito, I finally have a day to myself before returning to Flagstaff tomorrow. I begin the day by walking to a nearby park. There I bask on a sunny bench for a while and write Christmas cards.

Half a dozen cards later, I wander through the crowds of young lovers, picnicking families, well-dressed tourists, urchins stuffing their faces with cotton candy, hungover indigents staggering in search of more booze, and vendors spreading their wares on rickety tables. Perhaps I can purchase the obligatory "Sorry I left you but I'm back again" presents for the kids and stock up on Christmas gifts for friends and relatives. Last year everyone got crafts from Chile, so this is the year for Ecuadorian gifts. I stroll from table to table, unimpressed with the quality of the merchandise: crudely carved wooden spoons, hastily knitted baby sweaters and caps, unevenly woven wallets and wall hangings, and lopsided straw baskets. These items are sadly inferior to their artistic counterparts sold in the expensive tourist shops. The middleman gouges a huge profit for himself, but does an effective winnowing job. Street vendors hawk shoelaces, sunglasses, plastic hair clips, cigarette lighters, soap dishes, and key chains.

I wander over to where painters are setting up their canvases. The images range from mundane still-life scenes (fruit on tables, glasses on tables, and fruit and glasses combinations on tables) to bizarre depictions of violence, each splashed with copious quantities of vibrant red paint. One large canvas catches my eye. It's a composite of three images, each bordered by a brown frame, all set against a pale yellow background. One image is an ancient-looking gnarled tree, another a slightly cupped infant's hand, and the largest of the three is a frog, clearly an artist's rendition of a stubfoot frog. Painted in shades of dark green, cream, and black, the frog is perched atop a craggy cliff above the clouds, next to a lone droopy fern. The frog is sitting in a nearly vertical position, with its head pointing up toward snow-covered mountain peaks. The expression of determination on the frog's face is what I find fascinating. To me it's saying, "Even if I'm the last one left, I will persevere." Did the painter know of declining populations of stubfoot frogs?

I continue on, looking at other paintings, then find myself returning to take another long look at the determined frog. The painter catches my eye and I quickly walk on. Ten minutes later I gravitate back to the painting. Something about the frog has mesmerized me. Again the man notices me, and this time I ask the price. He says, "140,000 sucres, but for you 120,000." That translates into about $42. I explain that the price is more than I can afford, and anyway all I really like is the frog. I tell him that I'm a biologist and that I like the way he portrayed this frog.

Suddenly the man picks up a knife and offers to cut out the frog and sell me just that portion for 80,000 sucres ($28). Aghast, I ask him how he could possibly destroy his painting. He says it doesn't matter, he'll just sell each portion separately. As we sit in the grass together and he slices apart his canvas, I ask him if he's aware that populations of amphibians are declining worldwide. He gives me a blank stare and mumbles something about the chilly temperatures and the wind and how he hopes it will warm up soon. Pleased with my acquisition, I roll up my prize and carry it back to my hotel room, where I unroll it and continue to admire the frog's determined gaze.

THOUGH WE'VE had ups and downs with the monitoring projects, the EcoCiencia biologists and their local field assistants have accumulated a wealth of information over the past two years, information that is now being analyzed and written up. All of the EcoCiencia participants have experienced the joy of discovery associated with asking questions and answering them through fieldwork. And we hope that all have learned how to think within the context of conservation biology.

Since our work in San Miguel, I've heard that the residents decided to encourage ecotourism. They've constructed guest cabins, complete with orthopedic mattresses and mosquito netting. They lead overnight camping trips in the forest and even offer wild rat for dinner. I wonder how soon their culture will be irreparably corrupted.

11

TADPOLE TOTERS

I N MAY 1994, just before Karen's twelfth birthday, my whole world threatened to shatter when a biopsy revealed breast cancer. My initial reactions ranged from a desperate yearning to live long enough to watch my kids grow into adults, to the realization that I might no longer be able to look forward to devoting more time to fieldwork with Peter in the tropics after the kids fledged. The shatter lines began to disappear, though, as surgery, followed by six weeks of daily radiation, resulted in a positive prognosis. Maybe cancer wouldn't rob me of my dreams after all.

Though somewhat weakened by radiation therapy, I was itching to return to the field. Peter sensed my need and suggested I accompany him on his collaborative predator/prey project at the Chinchilla National Reserve in semidesert north of Santiago, Chile. My mother flew to Flagstaff in October and stayed with the kids for three weeks. The upshot of this vacation trip for me was that I initiated a research project on Darwin's frogs.

Our first night in Santiago, Peter suggested I try *caldillo de congrio,* one of Chile's national dishes. While we sipped excellent white wine, he explained that *congrio* was conger eel. I felt my stomach churn but didn't let on. A huge piece of boiled eel, onions, and potatoes provided the substance to the thick soup, and it was indeed delicious. I didn't find any Chilean seafood that I did not like, but *calamares* (small squid) were one of my favorites, prepared in various ways—fried in oil and garlic; stuffed with bits of ham, onions, tomato, bread crumbs, and Parmesan cheese; cooked in their own ink; or simmered in a sauce of onions, garlic, tomatoes, red wine, and herbs.

I DIDN'T JUST eat, however. To earn my keep, I gave a talk on parental care in amphibians for students and faculty at the University of Chile. Afterward Alberto Veloso, one of Chile's foremost herpetologists, invited me to his laboratory. We lamented that very little is known about Darwin's frog, a species with a unique form of parental care in which fathers carry the offspring in their vocal sacs. (A vocal sac is the throat pouch that fills with air and functions as a resonating chamber when a frog calls.) Within an hour we had enthusiastically agreed to collaborate on a study, and we began to outline a proposal to the National Geographic Society. I warned Alberto that I wasn't sure how much credibility I had left with the Society thanks to the disappearing act of the golden toads, but we both felt I should try because the subject matter was appropriate to their mission.

Less than 10 percent of all species of frogs and toads care for their offspring after eggs are deposited and fertilized. Of these approximately 250 species, males of only three species in the world transport eggs and/or tadpoles inside their bodies. One of these is a frog from Australia that carries its young in pouches on the side of its body. The other two carry young in their vocal sacs. One of these two is known only from west-central Chile in a region that has been converted to pine plantations and urban sprawl. No individuals have been found during the past decade, and the species is feared extinct. The third species, Darwin's frog, occurs in southern Chile and Argentina.

Darwin's frogs are named in honor of Charles Darwin, who collected one in 1835 while visiting the coast of Chile during his voyage on the *Beagle*. Darwin sent his specimen back to Europe, and in 1841 two French zoologists named the frog. It wasn't until 1872, when a new series of specimens was examined, that biologists realized that male Darwin's frogs brood their young in their vocal sacs.

These charming frogs are green or brown, with appendages of skin protruding from the tips of their snouts, giving a rather Pinocchio-like appearance. They deposit and fertilize their eggs on land. The female leaves the male to watch over the eggs, and after about twenty days the male engulfs the wriggling embryos that are nearly ready to hatch. The eggs slide through two slits in the throat that lead into the vocal sac, which will serve as an incubator. Soon after reaching the vocal sac, the eggs hatch into small black tadpoles. There they develop and grow. After about fifty days, they transform into tiny frogs. Following transformation the froglets crawl back through the slits and into Dad's mouth. He obliges by opening his mouth, and his offspring hop out onto land to experience the pleasures and perils of freedom.

CHILE PROBABLY got its name from an Indian word, *chilli,* meaning "where the land ends," an appropriate epithet considering its geography. Lying between the Andes Mountains and the Pacific Ocean like a long thin ribbon, Chile displays an impressive moisture gradient from north to south. The northern desert region includes the Atacama Desert, one of the driest places on earth, virtually devoid of vegetation except alongside the rivers flowing down from the Andes. This desolate landscape grades into scrubby cactus-laden semidesert farther south. Chile's heavily populated middle region, known as the Central Valley, is blessed with rich soil that supports abundant crops, vineyards, and orchards. The Lake Country, the southernmost part of the Central Valley, boasts spectacular lakes, forests, and snow-covered volcanoes. From Puerto Montt south, the coastal region breaks up into a plethora of islands, beginning with the island of Chiloé, which is

Male Darwin's frog proudly showing off his Pinocchio snout.

followed by the Archipelago. The Chilean part of Tierra del Fuego sits just above the southernmost tip of South America, Cape Horn. The Archipelago is a sparsely populated, windswept area drenched by torrential rains falling on mountains, glaciers, and forests. Darwin's frogs live in the southern half of the Central Valley, Chiloé, and the Archipelago, some of the most spectacular of all Chilean scenery and the wettest climate in temperate South America.

Long before the Spaniards arrived, various groups of Indians grew crops, fished, and hunted game from the far north of what is now Chile to the far south. In the late 1400s, the Incas came as far south as north-central Chile and conquered many of the endemic cultures. The Inca reign was short-lived, however, as the Spaniards conquered the Incan civilization in Peru and Ecuador in the 1530s. Spain then ruled Chile for nearly three hundred years. After Napoléon Bonaparte and his French army occupied Spain in 1808, Chile rebelled against Spain and many years of war ensued. In 1817 General José de San Martín crossed the Andes with an army from Argentina and, together with Bernardo O'Higgins of Chile, won a final victory over the Spanish in 1818 and secured independence for most of Chile. The island of Chiloé, off the southern coast, was the exception. After the rebellion, the last Spanish governor fled to Chiloé, where the islanders held out and supported the Spanish Crown. Chiloé was the last remaining Spanish possession in South America when the garrison finally surrendered in 1826.

FALL 1996

11 September 1996

The National Geographic Society voted to fund our project on Darwin's frogs, so I've come to Chile to initiate the research. Alberto and I plan to visit ten sites in the central and southern parts of the country, all sites having supported dense populations of Darwin's frogs in the past. We hope to determine whether Darwin's frogs should be added to the growing list of declining species, in which case we'll argue for protection, or whether they are holding their own. At each site we'll gather information on population density, sex ratio, and age class structure. We'll also make detailed observations of mating and parental care behaviors.

For the past two days in Santiago, I've been racing around buying supplies, changing dollars to pesos, and renting the truck. Today, however, all activity has screeched to a halt for the commemoration of the bloody 1973 military coup during which President Salvador Allende was overthrown. Offices and stores are closed. Today is a legal holiday.

In 1970 the Nixon administration in the United States watched anxiously as Dr. Allende, the first Marxist ever to be elected democratically as head of state in a Western Hemisphere country, assumed office as president of Chile. Among other radical reforms, Allende's agenda included state control of numerous private enterprises and a massive redistribution of wealth. Rather than experiencing a peaceful transition to socialism as Allende had promised, Chile plunged into three years of social and economic chaos, apparently exacerbated by the U.S. CIA. Chile's citizens were polarized into left- and right-wing factions. Violent demonstrations and strikes ensued as annual inflation soared to 350 percent and food became scarce. Whether due to internal problems or external sabotage, the socialist effort to restructure Chilean society was not working. In September 1973 the military responded with a coup that ousted and killed Allende (the military claims he committed suicide rather than surrender to them) and initiated a dictatorship that lasted until 1989. To rule Chile, the military leaders formed a junta, led by General Augusto Pinochet. During the military dictatorship, the junta restricted freedom of the press, outlawed political parties, restricted civil liberties, abused human rights, and severely suppressed all opposition. Over three thousand people were killed for political reasons; one-third of them are still unaccounted for. Thousands of others fled the country. Chileans experienced an atmosphere of fear and repression they never dreamed possible in their country.

Every year on 11 September, the anniversary of the coup is observed, both by Pinochet supporters and by the opposition. The military throws a massive celebration, with parades and receptions. The day triggers strong emotions and animosity between neighbors. Supporters of Pinochet idolize the former leader as a savior who rescued Chileans from communism. Opponents see him as a ruthless dictator responsible for over sixteen years of state-sponsored murder and repression. The day has turned into an annual excuse to vent frustration over government policies and the quality of life in general. Many demonstrators don't even know what they are fighting against . . . or for.

Alberto and I head for the university to pack up laboratory supplies. But the street in front of the university is blocked off. Dozens of well-armed police swarm the sidewalks. Demonstrating students yell obscenities and wave placards. Unable to get to the university, we return to Alberto's house and watch the day's events on television. Several bombs have exploded in Santiago. Bloody bodies of injured victims are being rushed to hospitals.

16 September 1996

Alberto, his students Eliseo and Marco, and I begin our trip by driving south through the Lake District to Puyehue National Park, a favorite vacation spot due to its beauty and its proximity to snow-covered volcanoes. We set up tents in a deserted campground. No one camps here in the winter. Ironically, although we are camped at Aguas Calientes (Hot Waters, in reference to nearby hot springs), the night is the coldest I've ever experienced in the field. At midnight, after an unsuccessful search for frogs in disturbed habitat, we stagger back into camp on nearly frostbitten feet. Battling with damp wood, we finally get a fire started and guzzle hot coffee.

I pile on so many layers of clothes, including long underwear, wool sweater, and down vest, that I can hardly squeeze into my down mummy bag. But still I shiver all night. At dawn Alberto emerges from his tent, climbs into the truck, and revs the engine. After thirty seconds of wondering where he is going in the middle of nowhere, I realize he isn't going anywhere. I join him and we sit in the cab, hot air blowing on us for the next forty-five minutes before we muster the enthusiasm to battle the damp wood again. As we thaw we talk of frogs, Chilean politics, mutual friends, and plans for the day's fieldwork. I also describe to Alberto the 1979 Night from Hell that Peter and I spent in eastern Ecuador—the other extreme in temperature.

PETER AND I had just survived a two-day drive in our rented VW bug, from Quito to the hard-drinking oil town of Coca. We got an upstairs room at the only open place in town, the Pensión Rossita. Our tiny room, separated from others by cardboard-like walls, was an oven, certainly well over 110° F and seemingly 99.9 percent relative humidity. We dumped our duffel bags and wandered around town, sweating profusely, until we found a forbidding-looking movie theater. Since the theater was constructed of cinderblocks, it had to be cooler inside than our room, we thought, so we bought tickets. Indeed, the climate inside was slightly less stifling. The theater was half filled with other refugees from the heat, including a cohort of young, very drunken army recruits and an active entourage of bats. The movie, a C-grade import from the States, flickered wearily on the screen, its characters often impossible to discern. The sound track mumbled in an incomprehensible nearly subsonic jumble. After an hour or so, a recruit a few seats behind us began heaving all over himself, the chair, and the floor. The odor and the accompanying sound effects drove us back into the suffocating outdoor heat.

There was no running water at Rossita's. When we asked the owner where we could bathe, he directed us to the Coca and Napo Rivers. We checked them out and indeed found the locals bathing, washing clothes, and brushing their teeth in the water. The sight of raw sewage, garbage, and a dead pig floating by, however, convinced us not to cool even our toes. Brainstorm! We bought twelve bottles of carbonated mineral water and a towel, then returned to our room. Fizzy sponge baths followed, but the cooling effects lasted only for about ten minutes in the sultry room.

Too hot to sleep, we played gin rummy until nearly midnight. The single candle added significantly to the heat. Finally we tried the beds. They were about half as wide as normal twin beds, not good for the tossing and turning we knew we'd be doing all night. The mosquitoes were so thick and oblivious to repellent that our only partial defense was to wrap ourselves in the top sheets, which were soon soaked with sweat.

As we began to drift off despite the discomfort, an awesome series of snuffles, snorts, and world-class snores resonated through the paper-thin wall from the adjoining room. We kicked the wall, hard. The horrific noises stopped. We started to snooze. The snoring started anew. We kicked the wall harder, until we nearly punched a hole through the thin plaster. Still the snoring continued, so we finally gave up, made earplugs out of toilet paper, and crawled back under the sheets.

Just as we finally drifted off once more, a new cacophony penetrated the toilet paper in our ears. Two drunks staggered and yelled their way up the stairs. They managed to reach the top and, just our luck, headed toward the room on the other side of us. Instead of entering, though, they swayed back and forth on the balcony outside, reliving loudly and explicitly their night's experiences in one of Coca's numerous bordellos. Even our volcanic neighbor on the other side awoke and began cursing them. Then came more thumps on the stairs. A policeman arrived, not to quiet the drunks, but instead to accuse one of them of having failed to pay for his whore. The ensuing argument, which took place directly in front of our door, lasted some forty-five minutes, until the exasperated policeman pulled his revolver and forced the staggering, unrepentant deadbeat down the stairs. His chastened companion stumbled into the room and, after bouncing off the wall a few times, fell either onto the floor or bed. We couldn't tell which. Soon a duet of impressive snoring bracketed us. Even this, the mosquitoes, and the chorus of barking and howling dogs that erupted each time a drunk passed by on the street could no longer prevent us from dozing. But less than an hour later a new element penetrated the toilet paper in our ears.

"UNO, DOS, TRES, CUATRO! UNO, DOS, TRES, CUATRO!" It was now 4 A.M. and time for the sergeants at the local army post to drill the recruits back and forth on the dirt road in front of Rossita's. This lasted an hour. Just as the "UNO, DOS, TRES, CUATRO!" finally began to fade into the distance, all the town's roosters awoke, not with a quaint cock-a-doodle-do but rather with an ear-shattering caterwaul. The night was over.

17 September 1996

Back to real time in Chile: fighting against a torrential rainstorm, we drive up the steep, deeply rutted dirt road to La Picada. The road finally ends at a run-down two-story building that was once a lavish hotel for the wealthy. The owner, a young guy who hopes to restore the building, offers to let us spread our sleeping bags on the floor. After the past few days of camping in tents, we'll appreciate the protection from the cold, wind, and rain.

With guarded optimism we dump our packs, don our rain gear, and explore our misty surroundings. Snow blankets the ground around the building, suggesting that perhaps we're too early and the frogs are still hibernating. We hike back down the road to a swampy clearing where the snow has melted. Within ten minutes I see a little green frog sitting in shallow water. Gently picking him up, I giggle at the appendage of skin on the tip of his nose, then yell, "I found one!" Alberto and the students come running over, not sure what to expect from me. After all, I've never seen a Darwin's frog till now. Once everyone is convinced my little green frog really is a Darwin's frog, we hug and screech with excitement. By two hours later, no one has found a second, however. Maybe tomorrow will be better. At least we know they're still here.

19 September 1996

After finding no more Darwin's frogs at La Picada, we drive north to the coastal fishing village of Mehuín and eagerly enter a restaurant after having spent several days and nights eating food cooked over our camp stove: hot dog buns filled with scrambled eggs, noodles and tomato sauce, or rice mixed with minced hot dogs. For our first meal back in civilization, we choose locally caught fish dinners. As the waiter ceremoniously approaches with the salad tray, I think to myself, "That's what I've been missing. Fresh mushrooms!" Up close, however, I see that the brown chunks are not mushrooms. Alberto, Eliseo, and Marco smile and mutter, "*Ulte!*" as they pounce on the salad platter. *Ulte* turns out to be a local seaweed. The flavor is bland and not objectionable, but I find the consistency unpleasantly rubbery. My companions are happy to eat my share.

We begin our search with great optimism because Alberto found abundant Darwin's frogs here a few years ago. By 1:00 in the morning, however, we have found none, perhaps due to the now very degraded habitat. Everywhere we've been so far, human impact on the environment is substantial. Darwin's frogs do indeed seem to be in trouble. So far we've found only one individual. Alberto will return to Santiago tomorrow. The students and I will continue our search elsewhere.

25 September 1996

Never mind the disappointment of finding no frogs the last few days, we're just thankful to be alive today. This morning we drove to a small reserve near Contulmo. An elderly park guard, Victor, assured us he knows exactly where we can find Darwin's frogs. "They've been common here for as long as I can remember." Soon after we left Victor's house, we heard a bird scolding angrily. Looking to my left, I saw a chunky brown bird with an orange chest, black-and-white-striped belly, stout beak, and tail sticking straight up in the air. I recognized the bird from Argentina as a chucao (or chucao tapaculo; *tapaculo* is Spanish for "hide your hind end," in reference to the birds' behavior of lifting their tails above their heads). Victor stopped and in a very worried voice declared that we could not go on. He explained that when a chucao sings off to your left, it's a warning to return home and quit work for the day. If we don't heed the chucao's warning, something bad is sure to happen. Victor returned home, but Eliseo, Marco, and I continued to search in vain for frogs.

Eventually we gave up and drove to the nearby town of Angol. After buying groceries, we headed up the dusty gravel mountain road toward Nahuelbuta National Park in the coastal mountain range. But fate—or is it the chucao?—had different plans. Less than halfway up, we skid on the gravel while rounding a curve. Eliseo loses control, we crash into the road bank, and the truck rolls over onto its side. We're shaken, dazed, scratched, and bruised. Within seconds, providentially (perhaps the chucao relented?) a car arrives full of medical professionals returning to Angol: a nurse, a midwife, and two midwife interns. They pry open the door above us and help us out. Eliseo's shoulder hurts by now. The nurse instructs him to lie down, covers him with assorted jackets, and injects a tranquilizer. Meanwhile a truck arrives, packed with five burly men from a construction crew. They roll our pickup back over and head for Angol to send an ambulance. Fifty minutes later an ambulance arrives and everyone departs for Angol, leaving me and one of the midwife interns, Rodrigo, to guard the truck and wait for the police.

An hour later a police car arrives and disgorges five of the biggest Chileans I've ever seen. All are brusque and downright grouchy. I explain all the details I can remember (which don't seem to be enough), they fill out their report, and then one of them forces open the hood of the mangled truck. He pokes around for a moment, declares the truck *"sano"* (healthy), climbs into the driver's seat, and rudely orders Rodrigo and me to get in. As he turns on the ignition, strains of "Lucy in the Sky with Diamonds" blare from the tape deck, the Beatles' song that was playing as we crashed. The stern-faced policeman cracks a smile, softens, and confesses he's a fan of the Beatles. As we drive, he tells me that the road to Nahuelbuta, with more than a hundred curves, is extremely dangerous and is the scene of numerous accidents each year. He says we're lucky to have fared this well.

Eliseo and Marco are waiting at the police station. Eliseo is grinning, with his arm in a makeshift muslin sling. Apparently the doctor forced his shoulder back into place and pronounced him *"sano."*

26 September 1996

This evening Jaime, the head guard for Nahuelbuta, offers to drive us to the park in our mangled truck. All of us are tense during the trip up the mountain. Each curve seems more dangerous than the previous one. Sections of the road with steep drop-offs make us wonder where we'd be now if we'd plunged over the edge. We arrive safely, and after the tension of the past twenty-four hours, we're soon asleep on Jaime's wooden floor. Eliseo and Marco will stay two days. Since Nahuelbuta supposedly has a dense population of Darwin's frogs, I'll stay for two weeks to observe the frogs' behavior.

6 October 1996

This morning I tell Jaime about Victor's chucao superstition. Jaime says it's a commonly believed myth throughout southern Chile, but that some people swear by an antidote. As soon as you hear a chucao scolding over your left shoulder, you quickly respond aloud with *"El canto para mí, las lombrices para ti."* ("The song for me, worms for you.") As I walk to the forest, I promise myself that from now on I will utter these words, just in case.

After several hours of shivering in dense forest, I enter an open area where several trees have fallen. Sunlight shining on a large log beckons me. As the heat penetrates my body, I feel energized. A little bluish green lizard slowly crawls up a nearby log, stops when it reaches a sunny spot, flattens its body, and basks. Before long a large green hummingbird flies over to inspect my red sweatshirt, hovers over me for a few seconds, decides I'm not a rich patch of flowers after all, and buzzes away. A gnarled dead tree sways in the breeze and rubs against a neighboring tree; it creaks and groans as if struggling to tell its story. The lizard now scurries down the log, through the grass to a puddle of water, and begins to satisfy its thirst. A chucao to my left suddenly scolds, and I confidently respond with *"El canto para mí, las lombrices para ti."*

Jaime claims that although Darwin's frogs are abundant here, they are more commonly seen from November to March, when temperatures are warmer. Nonetheless, I stubbornly spend all of each day searching in case a few individuals might poke their pointed snouts above the surface to check out the weather. So far I haven't seen a one. When I'm not depressed about the absence of frogs, I'm enjoying the southern beech forest and the wildflowers bursting open in response to the warming temperatures.

The forest here is beautiful, and so different from anything else I've seen in Latin America. At the lower elevations, broad-leaved deciduous southern beech trees (*Nothofagus*) dominate. I spend most of my time in this forest because supposedly this is where Darwin's frogs are found. On drier sites with less soil, the dominant trees are araucarias, reaching fifty meters in height. Nahuelbuta National Park provides refuge for the largest remaining stand of coastal araucarias in the country. Branches of these coniferous trees are covered with sharp, scaly leaves, creating a decidedly odd appearance. Araucarias are called monkey puzzle trees because the sharp leaves make them extremely difficult to climb.

10 October 1996

The last two weeks have been terribly disappointing. I hiked two hours each way and spent about six hours each day looking in vain for the frogs. Am I crazy? Stupid? Should I have given up days ago? This has been an incredible waste of time, reminiscent of looking in vain for golden toads in Costa Rica and salamanders from forest along the Amazon River. Unconsciously I seem to compete with myself to make each research study better than the one before. With more experience, each new project should succeed in being better crafted and better executed, not the reverse. But, unlike controlled laboratory experiments, fieldwork is often unpredictable and you don't always get results. Tomorrow I will make the ten-hour bus trip back to Santiago with a nearly blank data notebook.

WINTER 1997

2 February 1997

Alberto picks me up at the Santiago airport nearly twenty-four hours after I'd left Flagstaff and informs me that we leave for the south tomorrow because the ferry makes only one trip per week from Quellón, on the south end of the island of Chiloé. We need to be in that small fishing village by midnight tomorrow, or we lose an entire week.

3 February 1997

We divide into two teams to search for Darwin's frogs. Marco and two others will return to some of the sites we visited in the fall. Alberto, his student Eduardo, and I begin our trip to the far south by flying from Santiago to Puerto Montt, then take a bus and ferry to the island of Chiloé, and eventually a taxi to Quellón, arriving in a torrential rainstorm with fifteen minutes to spare before the ferry boarding. The fourth member of our party, a student from Valdivia named César, greets us by announcing that the ferry won't leave until tomorrow because of the dangerous storm. The good news is that he has reserved rooms at a nearby waterfront hotel and we can get a night's sleep. The bad news is that when he bought tickets for the ferry, *La Pincoya*, he was told that all sixty-five seats had already been sold. We'll have to stand or sit on the floor for sixteen hours.

4 February 1997

At noon we board *La Pincoya*, shrouded in dense fog, and watch as the cargo is loaded: food, cement, and feed for livestock and salmon farms. Two hours later we slowly begin our trip southeast from Chiloé to the Archipelago region, a little-explored area consisting of thousands of rocky, windswept islands separated by fjordlike channels, vast areas of nearly impenetrable forest, beautiful glaciers, and crystal-clear lakes. Few people live in this region, no doubt due to the year-round torrential rains and cold temperatures.

The trip begins well as we secure standing room on an outside deck, where we enjoy the exhilarating salty air and watch dolphins cavort in the ocean waves. Chilled after an hour on deck, I wander in to the covered area, where about eighty people are already standing or sitting on the floor. I locate a spot on the floor behind the last row of seats, just large enough to sit cross-legged, wedged in between an elderly woman and a mother holding her two-year-old son. For fear of losing my spot, I stay in my cramped position for the next six hours.

Understandably, the two-year-old is restless from being cooped up in tight quarters. He's an aggressive little tyke, throwing temper tantrums, punching and kicking his mother and occasionally me, and spitting wads of bread at his brother. Cold drafts constantly blow in on us from the ocean and penetrate my down jacket. Then we enter the Gulf of Corcovado (Gulf of the Bucking Bronco). Within fifteen minutes nearly everyone is green and seasick. One woman frantically vacates her precious seat and spends the next hour bent over the rail. Her seat is quickly filled by two little girls. A teenage boy, threading his way through the bodies in the aisle, doesn't make it nearly to the rail. I vow that if I ever make this trip again, I'll take Dramamine.

Eventually we pass through the Gulf of Corcovado and arrive at the island of Melinka. About fifty people disembark, and we are able to grab seats. The rest of the trip is long, but at least the sea is fairly smooth and we can doze.

5 February 1997

Sixteen hours after leaving Quellón, we arrive at our destination: the tiny settlement of Melimoyu. We unroll our sleeping bags on the floor of the community building, unpack boots and field clothes, and wait for the sun to rise.

Eureka! During our first two hours of searching, we find seven Darwin's frogs. I finally have a population to study. One of the frogs is an emerald green male with a greatly expanded vocal sac full of wriggling tadpoles—a truly special sight. We hear and see several males calling, a faint *peeep-peeep-peeep-peeep*. By the end of the day, we've recorded numerous frogs from near houses, at the edge of the playground, and in the field in front of the church as well as in undisturbed forested areas. I'm relieved knowing I can return to Melimoyu next year and carry out field observations of behavior. I'm also content with the thought that there must be Darwin's frogs in other locations in the Archipelago. The frogs may be disappearing in the northern half of their range, but here they seem to be thriving.

We're finding about as many males as females, and about 30 percent of the males are carrying tadpoles. One of the questions I hope to answer is whether brooding males choose different microhabitats than nonbrooding individuals. I'd thought that perhaps they stay in protected, secure crevices or cavities. But observations thus far suggest that brooding males occur in

Southern coast of Chile near Melimoyu.

exactly the same spots as other males, females, and subadults: exposed on moss, leaf litter, bare ground, and grass.

14 February 1997

We spent the past week searching for Darwin's frogs at other sites in the Archipelago. Our mixed success included one more site with frogs, two without. Alberto and the others have returned to Santiago. I'm back in Nahuelbuta National Park for two weeks, where I hope to observe behavior. Since temperatures are warmer than they were back in late September and early October, the frogs should be out and active.

This afternoon a male Darwin's frog, his vocal sac bulging with wriggling tadpoles, hops from nearly underfoot. What a relief to know they're still here! Jaime warns me, though, that this has been an unusually cold and dry year. He hasn't seen any yet this year, whereas usually by mid-February he has seen many.

19 February 1997

Today, five days after seeing the brooding male, I finally find another Darwin's frog. Perhaps not coincidentally, this is a female and she's less than fifteen meters from where I saw the male. I watch her for over an hour as she hops among the fallen brown leaves. She blends in perfectly with her surroundings. About the same size and color as the leaves, she even mimics their shape. Her fleshy nose appendage closely resembles a leaf petiole, the stalk that connects the leaf blade to the stem.

While watching her, I reposition myself on the ground and, in doing so, my fingers brush against something soft. I look down and see that I've frightened a hairy brown tarantula nearly the size of my hand. The creature has reared back in a defensive display, raised its front two pairs of legs into the air, and exposed its wicked-looking fangs. I can't move or I'll frighten the frog. Shifting my eyes from the frog to the tarantula next to my hand and back to the frog, I sweat out the next few minutes. Soon the tarantula perceives that the threat has passed, and it slowly ambles away through the dried leaves to a log a meter away, where it stops and rests.

I know rationally that my fear of tarantulas is unfounded. Like almost all spiders, tarantulas are venomous, but they rarely bite people. When

Although this hairy brown tarantula looks menacing, it's actually timid and benign.

they do, depending on the species, the reaction varies from no worse than a bee sting to considerable pain and swelling. But there are no documented human deaths from tarantula bites. Tarantulas are sit-and-wait predators. When an insect, frog, or lizard gets too close, the tarantula sinks its fangs into the prey and pumps in venom. The venom digests the prey's tissues, allowing the tarantula to suck out a liquid meal. Unable to eat solid food, the tarantula leaves the exoskeleton or bones behind. Some tarantulas take larger prey: birds and small mammals such as bats. Although tarantulas can be large, some the size of dinner plates, they are timid creatures. From a distance I admire its velvet body and reflect on the disservice Hollywood movies have done by portraying tarantulas as giant terrors, bent on destroying humans.

3 March 1997

After two weeks in the park, I found only the two Darwin's frogs. Again I've wasted precious time. In retrospect, I wish I had stayed at Melimoyu. Jaime was right about the drought. I could almost hear the trees gasping for moisture. Perhaps the frogs were hiding out in more moist places underground. Haven't I said this before? Golden toads?

I've been away for five weeks. Several times each day, I've subtracted four hours from the local time and imagined what my family was doing at the time. Peter checking e-mail messages first thing after morning chores; Rob tossing basketballs after school; Karen tootling her clarinet during Sunday youth orchestra rehearsal; all three watching videos on a Friday night. I miss them and I know they miss me. Each time I leave the kids make a bigger fuss. "Mommy, please don't go! If you wanted to have kids, then why don't you stay home with us?" At twelve and almost fifteen years old, they don't understand that adults have dreams, ambitions, and professional needs that don't always overlap 100 percent with their children's interests and desires. The biologist part of me begins to wither if I'm away from fieldwork too long. But now the plane lands. My heart races when I see them—the smiling faces of my loved ones awaiting my return.

WINTER 1998

8 February 1998

This second year of funding from the National Geographic Society will support a combination of large-scale survey work and small-scale observations of behavior. I've given up on Nahuelbuta National Park and instead will do observations at Melimoyu, where I know the frogs are abundant.

First, though, we trek into an isolated Mapuche Indian Reserve near Osorno in the Lake District. The reserve is isolated because the nearest road is only barely passable by the sturdiest of Jeeps and then only during the dry season. Travel within the reserve is by foot or by horse.

After a twelve-hour bus ride from Santiago to Osorno, we (Alberto, César, one of Alberto's students Antonieta, and I) hire a van to take us to the end of a dirt road, one and a half hours away. At that point Antonieta and I and most of the luggage go by Jeep with Luis, our contact with the Mapuches, another forty-five minutes on a trail with steep inclines, deep gullies, and numerous huge boulders. After fording several deep streams and maneuvering around obstacles, Luis stops abruptly and says we'll have to walk the rest of the way while he returns for the others. Eventually we all rendezvous in Trafunco los Bados, an eight-family community, where we set up our tents in a field of grass.

PEDRO DE VALDIVIA, a Spanish conquistador, led an expedition south from Peru into Chile in 1540, opening up the Central Valley to European colonization. The conquistadors, captivated by the spectacular landscape and the pleasant climate, encouraged colonization despite the isolation of being bordered by the hot and nearly sterile Atacama Desert to the north, the Pacific Ocean to the west, the Andes Mountains to the east, and fierce Mapuche Indians to the south.

Mapuches, called Araucanians by the Spaniards, were one of the original groups of Indians in the southern Central Valley of Chile when the Spanish conquistadors arrived. Mapuches had fought off the Incas and retained their independence. And they weren't about to give it up to the invading Spaniards. They desperately fought the Spanish, then the Chileans, for over three centuries. In fact, the long-lasting struggle between Spaniards and Mapuches or closely related groups in Argentina distinguishes Spanish conquest in those two countries from other regions in Latin America. Elsewhere the Spanish generally claimed quick victories over indigenous peoples, killing or subjugating them. What set Mapuches apart from other indigenous groups? In part, it was because once the Mapuche stole horses from the conquistadors, they became expert horsemen. Also, they rapidly learned European-style warfare from the invaders, including the art of fortification, use of trenches and camouflaged pits, and even psychological warfare.

But in the end the Mapuche lost the battle. Soon after their defeat in

November 1881, at almost precisely the same time as the defeat of related groups across the Andes in Argentina, settlers flooded into the region. Eventually the Mapuche were assigned an area of about 475,000 hectares. Over time much of this land has been usurped by outsiders.

9 February 1998

This afternoon we meet with members of Trafunco los Bados to ask permission to work in the reserve. In an emotional and dramatic speech, Luis emphasizes to the group of about twenty-five men, women, and children that for the first time since Spanish arrival in the mid-1500s, Mapuches are being asked by *huincas*—the Mapuche term for outsiders, including non-Mapuche Chileans—for permission to enter their land. They don't have to grant us that permission. The decision is theirs. An ancient looking, grizzled man speaks up. He says he's been around a long time and that he remembers when the reserve was set aside for the Mapuche. At that time officials warned the Indians not to allow any *huincas* onto their land as they would only bring bad luck. He feels ambivalent about our request because he thinks the Mapuche should benefit in some way. Hesitatingly, he says the Mapuche need money. Luis responds that individuals who wish to serve as guides or rent us horses will benefit financially. When the old man seizes the idea and proposes that the community would indeed benefit from a steady stream of tourists who rent horses and guides, I shudder, recalling how tourism has changed Monteverde, Costa Rica.

After another hour of discussion, the community agrees to grant us permission to search for Darwin's frogs on their land. Two young Mapuche men offer to guide us to the forest where Darwin's frogs occur. Several others offer to rent us horses. We quickly break camp, load one horse, and set off riding the other horses, all of us with heavy packs strapped onto our backs. Both Mapuches are friendly to us, even though neither has had much previous contact with *huincas*. Our three-hour ride takes us over boulders and huge tree trunks, through swamps and tangles of tree roots. Every time my horse stumbles, which is often, I wish she were a sure-footed mule instead. We finally arrive without mishap at 8:30 P.M., just before dark.

After setting up the tents, we fix spaghetti and admire the Southern Cross in the clear sky. The air is cool and crisp, and the billions of twinkling stars seem to be tugging at me with a powerful magnetic force. I think about how fortunate I am to be a part of this scene, and how grateful I am to have survived cancer for nearly four years thus far. I reflect on how the experience of the "big C" has enhanced my appreciation of life.

11 February 1998

Yesterday we found several Darwin's frogs. Now we know they occur here, but they aren't very abundant. Or perhaps they simply aren't active because the ground is so dry. It hasn't rained in over two weeks, which is very unusual according to our Mapuche guides. El Niño strikes again. First El Niño weather patterns affected my study of golden toads, now Darwin's frogs.

15 February 1998

Alberto returns to Santiago, and the second trip for the rest of us begins back in Quellón at the southern tip of Chiloé, where we board *La Pincoya* and head for the Archipelago. Again we sit on the cold, ill-kept floor. But this time I'm armed with Dramamine, and what a difference it makes! Antonieta readily accepts my Dramamine, as do several strangers sitting on the floor near me. This trip, though long, is more tolerable, especially as I know we'll find lots of Darwin's frogs at our destination of Melimoyu.

18 February 1998

We're comfortably ensconced at the Melimoyu schoolhouse, where we're sleeping on the classroom floor. Our luxurious accommodations include very cold water showers, flush toilets (one labeled for teachers, one for girls, and one for boys), a wood stove, and a kitchen sink. Fortunately it's summer vacation here, and school won't start up again until the week after we leave. This year the school, elementary level only, expects to have three students. For further education, children must go to boarding school elsewhere or take correspondence courses. Although the school is free, parents must provide wood for the stove as "tuition." A television set and three videos sit in one corner of the classroom. Two videos are children's stories. The third is entitled *Pinochet y Su Chile* (Pinochet and His Chile)—surely an old propaganda film.

Everyone in Melimoyu emigrated from Santiago beginning in 1985, as part of a government project to colonize the Archipelago. Offered transportation, free land, and a generous allowance to construct a house, people left Santiago with the hope of building better lives. Some feel their lot has improved; others are bitter. One couple, Keli and Marco, left their menial office jobs in Santiago in 1985. They came to the south and spent nearly two years as fishing nomads. Eventually they settled at what would become Melimoyu, a community that now supports fifteen families. Their

Gateway to the community of Melimoyu in southern Chile, site of a dense population of Darwin's frogs.

tanned faces glow as they rave about their love for the sea, their days spent fishing, and the rewards of their new lives. During the cold, rainy winter days, they keep their wood stove burning and live off the dried fish and shellfish from the summer's catch. Marco makes improvements on the house; Keli knits.

In contrast, abandoned houses reveal that others have tried to make a life here but haven't been able to adapt to the isolation, lack of steady income, or violent weather. We spoke with one unmarried woman with two children who has been here for ten years, hates it, and is desperately trying to return to Santiago. Although she helps out at the school and sells bread and *empanadas* (meat-filled pastries), her earnings barely feed her family. She resents that the government encouraged colonization of the Archipelago and then provided little follow-up support. I wonder if her children, both born in Melimoyu, would be able to adapt to the fast pace of life in the metropolis of Santiago.

24 February 1998

I'm thrilled and relieved to be in the midst of a sea of Darwin's frogs. César, Antonieta, and I have been watching every frog we find for twenty

Seaweed drying on a railing in Melimoyu. Seaweed is both eaten by locals and exported to Japan.

minutes, recording temperature and humidity at the site, gender and size of the frog, and any notable behavior such as feeding or calling. So far we've watched nearly two hundred different individuals. Again brooding males are found in exactly the same sorts of places as nonbrooding individuals. Paradoxically, they don't seem to hide themselves. I've seen many brooding males catch and swallow insects, so now I know they continue to eat during this stage in their lives. I haven't seen any brooding males call, however. Presumably the wriggling cargo carried in the vocal sac, and perhaps hormonal changes as well, precludes peeping.

Chucaos are common here and, despite the myth, they are delightful birds. They're curious about any novel object, including people. They hop up to within a meter of me and check me out. When I leave my notebook, tape recorder, or hat on the ground, they check those out also. I've seen several calling Darwin's frogs suddenly become quiet in the presence of chucaos. Two chucaos hopping through the leaf litter changed from their usual scolding song to a peep very similar to that of a calling Darwin's frog. Because chucaos eat small frogs, I wonder if the birds could be vocalizing like Darwin's frogs to encourage the frogs to keep calling, thus enabling the chucaos to home in on their prey. I'm definitely more likely to see a chucao nearby when I'm observing a calling male than a noncalling individual.

Although all three species of frogs I've observed extensively in the field are active by day, poison dart frogs and harlequin frogs are toxic; Darwin's frogs are not. Poison dart frogs and harlequin frogs advertise their toxicity with bright colors: black and yellow, orange, red, and blue. They actively move about through the undergrowth or sit fully exposed to potential predators as if to warn, "Don't eat me!" So they're easy to watch. In contrast, because palatable Darwin's frogs rely on blending in with the environment for protection, they're more difficult to watch. Their green and brown colors blend in perfectly with the grass, moss, leaves, and soil. Even a green frog on a brown background is hard to distinguish from a green leaf. A brown frog on a green background likewise resembles a fallen dead leaf. It's no wonder that excellent behavioral field studies have been published on various species of poison dart frogs and harlequin frogs and that virtually nothing is known about the behavior of Darwin's frogs.

OUR FERRY, *La Pincoya*, will be delayed by one day. Extensive forest fires are burning on Melinka and several nearby islands. Colonists are burning in preparation for planting, and several of the fires raged out of control due to the dry conditions brought about by El Niño. Dense smoke has become a health hazard, so people are being evacuated from Melinka and ferried to Puerto Montt.

26 February 1998

Two sets of heavy footsteps run up the front porch of the school. Two sets of fists pound on the front door to advise us that the ferry will be here in one hour, at 8:30 A.M., four hours earlier than expected. Not only have we not begun to pack, we haven't begun to clean up after ourselves. César, Antonieta, and I explode into activity, rolling up sleeping bags and mats, throwing possessions into backpacks, sweeping floors, and cleaning sinks and toilets. At 8:27 we load everything onto our backs, shoulders, hands, and one wheelbarrow and stagger to the beach. We're just in time, as the ferry is already unloading a week's worth of supplies for Melimoyu.

In a cold drizzle, we board *La Pincoya* and begin our long trip north to Quellón. This time we have seats because few people are traveling. As I sink into mine, I think about how isolated Melimoyu is. If we hadn't made this ferry, we would have been stranded a week. The ferry is subsidized by the government, to give a break to the residents of this isolated part of the country. Residents are grateful for the transportation but are frustrated by unforeseen schedule changes such as happened this week: twenty hours late because of ferrying people from Melinka to Puerto Montt, and four hours earlier than the announced delayed arrival time.

As the ferry bounces over the waves, we alternate between sleep and semiconsciousness. The ride is too rough to read and too noisy to think, so we pass the time watching a succession of movies. I'm looking forward to spending two days in Valdivia before taking the bus back to Santiago.

1 March 1998

Saturday afternoon at Valdivia's Plaza de la Republica provides a great opportunity to people-watch. The locals are out in full force. Children run, laugh, and play; young couples hug and kiss by the water fountains; elderly men and women, glued to their park benches, enviously watch the children and lovers. Gangs of little boys terrorize the pigeons. A blind man plays the accordion and accepts coins in a tin cup. A younger man, dressed as a clown and pantomiming, accepts bills in a large red bucket. Others extract pesos from the Saturday crowd by shining shoes, painting faces, or selling balloons. A woman dressed in a bright red blouse and multicolored skirt cradles an infant, keeps an eye on her roving toddler, and strums a guitar. Her hand-painted sign explains that she is from Romania and seeks donations to pay for passage home.

My next stop is the open-air market by the waterfront, which is fascinating once I get used to the fishy smells. The row of wooden stands next to the water is solid seafood: live crabs, at least eight kinds of fish including conger eel and salmon, four types of mussels and clams, two types of dried algae (a light brown one that looks like tough rawhide tied in bundles and a dark brown one, pounded into chunks that resemble blocks of peat), sea urchins, and bright orange sea squirts. A parallel row of stands is allocated to produce: yellow, red, and green apples; bananas; raspberries; three kinds of melons; green and red grapes; tomatoes; cabbage; plums; cucumbers; peaches; potatoes; green beans; lettuce; three kinds of onions; garlic; four types of squash; corn; carrots; green, red, and hot peppers; chives and other herbs; pears; lemons and limes; radishes; beets; and cherries. The colors are dazzling: reds, yellows, greens, oranges, whites, and purples. At either end of the market, vendors sell potted plants and fresh-cut flowers whose spectrum of colors rivals that of the produce. Along the sidewalks, artisans display handmade wooden objects, jewelry, and woven and knitted sweaters, ponchos, jackets, caps, and socks. An Indian woman from Otavalo, Ecuador, dressed in the traditional white blouse, blue skirt, and gold beads around her neck, sits on the sidewalk next to her display of wall hangings, ponchos, and sweaters. To my eye, these are the nicest textiles in this Chilean market. Most of the women vendors are passive. While minding their stands, they nurse babies, wipe toddlers' noses, or knit. In contrast, the men aggressively attempt to outcompete their neighbors by yelling prices of their seafood or produce and bragging that theirs is the freshest and tastiest.

At dusk I indulge in one last seafood dinner before returning to Santiago. While savoring my *congrio,* I think about my data notebook bulging with observations, my most valuable possession back in the hotel room. Finally I have something to show for my efforts and the National Geographic Society support.

4 March 1998

As I begin my long flight back to Flagstaff, I think about the hundreds of resident Darwin's frogs back in Melimoyu: males with distended vocal sacs brooding their young; other males peeping hour after hour hoping to attract a mate; females gobbling tiny insects to provide the energy for another clutch of eggs; subadults struggling to survive and become adults.

So far we've surveyed twelve sites that had supported dense populations of Darwin's frogs within the past two decades. Dense populations remain at only three of these. We've been unable to locate even a single individual at six sites, and at the other three we've seen only one or two frogs. Populations of Darwin's frogs seem to be declining, but why? Three of these sites have experienced severe habitat destruction or modification. The other six, however, are national parks or protected reserves. Although the habitats are basically intact, might the frogs be disturbed by human activity, for example, constant walking on trails and wading in streams? Or are visitors inadvertently polluting the environment? Frogs are also closely associated with humans in Melimoyu, but humans have only been a major part of the landscape there for less than fifteen years. Will these populations also decline in the future?

It's now October 1999. Next month I'll return to Melimoyu to continue watching males brood their tadpoles. It'll be early enough in the season that, with any luck, I should be able to watch males court females. Will I find that chucaos do indeed imitate frog calls to ambush Darwin's frogs? What else will I discover?

Most exciting is that my seventeen-year-old niece, Lauren, will accompany me as my field assistant. Although biology no longer interests my own children, Lauren is thinking seriously about field biology as a career. There's no better way to decide if she really wants to do this than to jump in and get her feet wet. Very wet in this case, as locals from Melimoyu tell me to expect torrential rain, high winds, and cold temperatures in November. Bill Duellman not only passed on to me his own love for fieldwork, he passed on the joy of introducing others to fieldwork.

12

REFLECTIONS

RECENTLY ON a cold winter evening, as I huddled next to my wood stove in Flagstaff and sipped herb tea, I reflected on some of the major changes I've seen and experienced over the past thirty years in Central and South America. On one scale I've matured, both as a scientist and as an aging body. I design stronger field experiments now, but thirty years ago I had more energy to carry them out. On a very different scale, dramatic changes have occurred in the landscape of the Ecuadorian Oriente. When I first visited the Oriente in 1968, we flew to the isolated region of Santa Cecilia by small plane. At that time airplanes were the only transportation other than dugout canoes along the Río Aguarico. Now roads crisscross the rain forest, allowing not only access to the oil fields and pipeline, but also bus transport for colonists and tourists. A third change is in the amphibians themselves. Many species are declining or disappearing entirely. Where once I listened to hundreds of frogs, I now hear only crickets, katydids, and the occasional owl or nightjar.

From Pigtails to Bifocals

Decked out in Vietnam jungle boots and pigtails, I gloried in my first tropical field experience at Santa Cecilia: watching leaf-cutter ants parade through the forest carrying green umbrellas; male Hercules beetles battle with each other; poison dart frogs transport tadpoles piggyback; and ugly duckling tadpoles metamorphose into radiant lime-green froglets. Everything was new and exciting. Every day brought novel discoveries. At twenty-one years of age, I thought I was having the adventure of a lifetime, surveying amphibians and reptiles in the upper Amazon Basin. Now, thirty years later, decked out in tall rubber boots and a soup bowl haircut, I glory in watching Darwin's frogs tote their tadpoles around in their throat pouches. Each field trip is still the adventure of a lifetime. Fieldwork is still a magical search for the golden frog.

While my enthusiasm has not waned, my naïveté has. I no longer assume that frogs will breed when conventional wisdom deems environmental conditions to be appropriate. In fact, I'm no longer surprised when they don't breed at all. I no longer expect that a strong experimental design will lead to a valuable study. The tadpoles might eat each other before they have a chance to compete for the tadpole chow I've offered them, compromising my study of competition. Rains might not come and the pond not fill. The pond might fill, but the frogs never appear. The pond might fill and the frogs lay eggs, but cows subsequently trample and destroy the eggs. The pond might fill, the frogs might lay eggs, the cows keep their distance, but the pond dries up, taking the tadpoles with it. I've learned to be flexible, to change the location or focus of my research in midstream. In 1968 I crawled beneath vegetation without noticing a coiled fer-de-lance, grabbed on to an electric eel from the mud in the dip net, and allowed an egg-brooding horned treefrog to clamp its surprisingly strong jaws onto my finger. Thirty years later I'm more cautious. I even respect the chucao, and I chant as I walk through Southern beech forest, "El canto para mí, las lombrices para ti."

And then there's the negative side to maturing—the aching shoulders after carrying a forty-pound pack; the heart-stopping tension of teetering across a narrow log bridge three meters above a raging stream (I can scarcely believe I used to do that without fear); instead of contacts the bifocals, which during the best of times mean tolerating an irritating line across my field of vision and during the worst of times mean no sight at all when rain pounds against the lenses or fog envelops them. Formerly it was PMS; now it's hot flashes. I huff and puff more as I climb mountains, and I pop more pain reliever for the inevitable aches and pains that follow. Where once I politely spurned offers of help over large fallen logs, now I graciously accept all the help I can get. Especially offers to carry my pack. It's only a matter of time before a young field assistant will ask, "What species is making that chirping sound?" And I'll respond, "What chirping sound?" But aging is an inevitable process that affects us all—rich or poor, brain surgeon or amphibian biologist.

Change in the Ecuadorian Oriente

In 1968 Santa Cecilia was a primitive base camp for Texaco; Muñozlandia was a small compound on the Río Aguarico where a Colombian expatriate, Ildefonso Muñoz, lived with his family; the site of the future oil boomtown of Lago Agrio was undisturbed rain forest; and the Yasuní National Park wasn't even a twinkle in the environment minister's eye. Thirty years later Santa Cecilia is a large Ecuadorian army base with big-screen televisions, computers, and microwave ovens; Muñozlandia has returned to jungle; Lago Agrio (renamed Nueva Loja) boasts a population of thirty thousand and its main street is paved; and the Yasuní National Park, established in 1979 and later designated as a World Biosphere Reserve, has been invaded by men hungry for "black gold."

Virtually all the dramatic changes in the landscape and culture of the Oriente have resulted either directly or indirectly from the discovery of oil. Take, for example, the multiple effects of the roads that were cut through the forest for oil exploration and extraction. Predictably, these roads became conduits for colonization. Ecuador has the highest average population density of any country in South America, so it's not surprising that the moment land is made accessible, it's overrun by people desperate to spread out. Because of the roads, an estimated 1 million hectares of rain forest in the Oriente have been opened to colonization. Land along the roads is free for the working, so colonists swarm in from elsewhere in the Oriente, the coast, the central mountains, and the southern province of Loja (whence the name Nueva Loja). These migrations are often encouraged or even subsidized by the government. I first watched colonists settle along the road between Quito and Lago Agrio, then between Lago Agrio and Coca, and most recently between Coca and Huaorani territory. Many newcomers are unable to adapt to the high heat and humidity of lowland rain forest. Discovering that life isn't as easy as they thought or were promised, they battle mosquitoes carrying malaria, sand flies carrying leishmaniasis, loneliness, and depression. They don't understand the fragile nature of rainforest soil and often import inappropriate agricultural practices from their home landscapes. Many colonists have given up fighting the land. Instead they've taken back-breaking low-paying jobs working for the oil companies: cutting forest in preparation for more roads, drilling oil wells, and cleaning up after oil spills. Many colonists have given up entirely and don't work at all.

Invaded by roads and drained of wildlife by seismic explosions and other disturbances, the rain forest has been grossly violated. Water, air, and land are polluted. Oil exploitation has proceeded virtually without regulation in the rain forest since 1967, creating monumental environmental disasters. From 1972 to 1989 the pipeline ruptured at least twenty-seven times, spilling nearly 17 million gallons of raw crude into the environment. The Texaco pipeline is now all but worn out, and oil is routinely spilled from secondary flow lines. Rivers turn black. But people continue to bathe and swim in the rivers. They experience high rates of respiratory and intestinal illness, skin rashes, and birth defects. Dead fish float in the rivers. Gardens choke and wither.

Indigenous peoples in the Oriente have been strongly affected by the discovery of oil on their land. When I first visited Santa Cecilia, the Cofán nation, though small in numbers, was thriving. Their traditions were scarcely touched by the outside world. Now many of their traditions are lost except for artifacts crafted for tourists. Many live in poverty. The Cofán and other indigenous peoples succumb to diseases brought in by oil workers, road construction crews, and tourists. Their cultures disintegrate as, willingly or unwillingly, they become "Westernized." One by one the native people slink into the newly created lowest class of the oil slum towns and villages dominated by mestizo colonists. Now that the Huaoranis' rainforest home is being exploited for oil, even that proud tribe finds itself being exploited by tour guides and gawking tourists who pay to see "naked savages." Outsiders have brought epidemics, alcohol, and prostitution. Many Huaorani are now addicted to the gifts (bribes) they receive from the oil companies. They feel compelled to work for the oil companies because they need money to buy batteries for their flashlights, gasoline for their outboard motors, and cartridges for their rifles. What will happen to these people in another fifteen years or so when the oil runs out and the oil companies pack up and leave?

Declining Amphibian Populations

My first field experience, at Santa Cecilia, was not unlike that of many tropical field herpetologists back in the late 1960s. Frogs seemed to be everywhere. The difference was that I was surrounded by the most species-rich assemblage of frogs in the world. I was fascinated by the many ways frogs at Santa Cecilia reproduce, so I made their natural history the focus of my early research. Later, unintentionally, I found myself in the midst of the fast-breaking story on declining amphibians, because I happened to be studying two charismatic species, harlequin frogs and golden toads, at the moment that they vanished. How well I remember the moment in September 1989, at the First World Congress of Herpetology in Canterbury, England, when we all stared at each other in shock as we heard story after story of sudden declines in the amphibians we studied. Many of us are now focusing our research efforts on individual declining species, on entire assemblages of amphibians in trouble, and on the causes of worldwide declines.

Thanks to the mass media, the general public is now quite aware of amphibian declines. Nonherpetologists, including those rare individuals who don't even like amphibians, have heard that amphibians may be the proverbial canaries in the coal mine—bio-indicators of the overall health of the environment. By their very nature, most amphibians are exposed to a wide range of environmental conditions. The word *amphibian* is derived from the Greek *amphibios,* meaning "living a double life." Because most amphibians begin life as eggs and larvae in water followed by an adult stage on land, they are potentially more exposed to environmental contaminants, vagaries of the weather, and myriad other stresses than are either completely aquatic or completely terrestrial animals. Furthermore, because amphibians have permeable skin, they are vulnerable to environmental contaminants prevalent in the air, water, and soil.

Although we've learned much in the past decade, we still have no definite answers to explain worldwide declines of amphibians. Declines have been reported from montane and lowland sites, from drenched cloud forests to oases in desert landscapes, from Europe, Australia, Africa, Asia, and North, Central, and South America. In some areas only a single species has been identified as declining; in other areas whole assemblages are affected. Natural population fluctuations no different from those of the past probably explain some observed declines, but they don't explain the simultaneously plummeting numbers worldwide. At present there's no single explanation. Many factors have been implicated, and most likely a combination is responsible for any given decline.*

Habitat destruction, fragmentation, and degradation are the leading causes of loss of biodiversity in general. The same is true for amphibians. Deforestation, not only in the tropics but also throughout the rest of the world, occurs at an alarming rate. Many of the documented population declines of amphibians in Canada, Europe, and the United States are due to disappearing habitat, especially suitable breeding sites. I suspect that habitat modification and destruction have caused significant declines of amphibians from the area around Santa Cecilia. And I fear that many populations of Darwin's frogs in Chile have disappeared because of habitat degradation.

---

* For those interested in a bit more information than I have included here concerning amphibian declines, please see appendix B.

Another factor implicated in declines is abnormal weather patterns—all the aberrations associated with El Niño, global warming, and other phenomena. For example, extreme drought, either in itself or in concert with some other factor, is likely responsible for the decline and probable extinction of certain populations of the harlequin frog and of the golden toad from the mountains of northwestern Costa Rica. It has now been over twelve years since the last breeding bout of golden toads, and not a single individual has been seen since that lone male in 1989. There have been many rumors and outright fabrications, such as marine toads painted bright orange and displayed proudly to gawking tourists. But as far as we know, real golden toads exist only in our memories.

Certain environmental factors are known to cause deformities and death in amphibians. For example, fairly strong evidence suggests that acidified rain is responsible for declines of tiger salamanders in some areas of the Rocky Mountains in Colorado and for declines of natterjack toads in Britain. Acid water decreases fertilization success because the sperm become less active and often disintegrate. Those eggs that are fertilized may develop severe abnormalities. Another detrimental factor is ultraviolet radiation. Due to depletion of the ozone layer, amphibians may be exposed to higher levels of ultraviolet radiation than in the past, just as humans are. Many amphibians, especially those living at colder high elevations, bask in the sun to warm up. They often lay their eggs in shallow water directly exposed to the sun's rays. And tadpoles frequently seek out the shallow areas of a pond, where they bask in water being warmed by the sun. Research has uncovered lethal effects of ultraviolet radiation for amphibians in the Cascade Mountains of Oregon.

Disease has also been implicated in some amphibian declines. Outbreaks of a disease called "red-leg," caused by bacteria, have resulted in massive die-offs of frogs and toads in the United States and Canada. Symptoms of red-leg are hemorrhages on the skin (thus the name red-leg), edema, skin ulceration, and lesions of the eyes. Scientists suggest that high levels of stress may suppress the immune system of amphibians and make them more vulnerable to the bacteria.

The news hot off the press as I write this chapter involves the discovery of a pathogenic fungus associated with mass death of frogs in montane rain forests of Panama in Central America and in Queensland, Australia. The fungus, identified from dead and dying animals, is common in soil and water. Many of the frog victims were particularly infested with the fungus on the belly, the area of water uptake. Because frogs are dependent on their skin both for breathing and for absorbing water, the fungus may damage the skin so badly that the frogs suffocate and dehydrate. Alternatively, the fungus may release a toxic substance that's lethal when absorbed by the frogs. Why all of a sudden would this fungus be killing off frogs? As with red-leg bacteria, perhaps frogs only succumb to the fungus if they have been stressed by some factor such as drought, rising temperatures, or

Ecuadorian painting of the frog with a decidedly determined gaze.

environmental contaminants, which may depress the immune system to the point where there's no natural defense against this pathogen.

WHETHER AMPHIBIANS are facing a loss of breeding habitat or a multitude of increased stresses that lead to greater susceptibility to pathogens, the result is the same. We're losing these fascinating animals. The other day as I walked along the bike path in a Fort Collins city park, I watched a little girl hunched over the edge of a pond. Sneakers buried in the mud, she was poised for action with an aquarium net positioned above a school of wriggling black toad tadpoles. She lunged, splashed herself in the face but caught several tadpoles, and carefully transferred them to a glass jar. As she held up the jar and peered inside, the expression of combined delight and curiosity on that little face was priceless. I wondered to myself whether her own daughter or son will have the opportunity to catch tadpoles in that city park or any other.

Although changes over the past thirty years leave me wondering about the future of amphibians, at the same time I'm heartened that people are now more familiar with these animals. When I first studied poison dart frogs, very few nonbiologists had ever heard of them. These and other tropical frogs are now household images. Who hasn't seen poison dart frogs or red-eyed treefrogs on T-shirts, note cards, calendars, puzzles, and even boxer shorts and ties? Increasing familiarity has led to more positive attitudes toward amphibians. During the 1960s and 1970s, there was a pervasive feeling that amphibians were so abundant that, within reason, human activities didn't much affect populations. We know differently now. Every spring concerned citizens dig artificial ponds for amphibians in areas where natural breeding sites have been destroyed. Children, teenagers, and adults work together and form toad patrols: toads migrating to breeding ponds are collected in buckets and carried across busy roads. Partly because of more stringent regulation and partly for moral reasons, increasing numbers of people who keep exotic amphibians as pets purchase only captive-bred animals, thus reducing the demand on wild populations. I'm hopeful that children will be able to catch tadpoles in city parks for a long time to come.

Epilogue

A ND SO . . . as the embers die and the night grows late, I conclude my story of one field biologist's search for "mystical truth and beauty in nature." Although this story is over, my search is not. The next couple of decades will be busy ones for field herpetologists. We not only have the responsibility of documenting amphibian declines, we have the challenge of identifying the causes and then trying to reverse the situation. As biologists we can carry out our research with minimal impact, suggest solutions, and work with locals and international organizations to implement these solutions. Ultimately, however, it's up to every individual human being to tread more softly. Humans are responsible for much of the loss of biodiversity, but we also represent the future for the conservation of plants and animals.

Although some species of amphibians are declining, others are thriving. There are many lifetimes of studies to be done with species still common, including those yet to be discovered. Much of the New World tropics, from many areas in the Amazon Basin to the mountaintops of the Andes and the Atlantic rain forests of Brazil, has not been thoroughly explored. Every time herpetologists work in isolated areas, we discover species of amphibians new to science. Every year we uncover natural histories we never knew existed: mother frogs that provide eggs for their tadpoles to eat; frogs that swallow their tadpoles and brood them in their stomachs; frogs that eat other frogs and lure them by twitching their toes to simulate moving insects; frogs that remain in the water with their tadpoles and defend them from predators; frogs that specialize on eating snails. What will we discover next? *That* is the question that intrigues field biologists. *That* is why we search for the golden frog in the places we do.

YOUR SEARCH for the golden frog may lead you along a very different trail. No matter what that trail is, may your search be richly rewarding, and may you hold on to the golden frog once you've found it.

Belize

Guatemala

Honduras

El
Salvador

Nicaragua

200 km

Costa
Rica

Panama

CENTRAL AMERICA

Venezuela

Guyana

Suriname

French Guiana

Colombia

Ecuador

Brazil

Peru

Bolivia

Chile

Paraguay

Uruguay

Argentina

500 km

SOUTH AMERICA

Cañas

Monteverde

Puerto Limón

San José

San Vito

OTS station

50 km

Osa
Peninsula

COSTA RICA

Esmeraldas • Borbón
San Miguel
& Loma Linda
Lago Agrio •
⊛
Quito • Baeza •
Sierra Azul Coca •
Nuevo
Rocafuerte
Pastaza •
Guayaquil •
• Manta Real
100 km
Loja •
3
1 Cotacachi-Cayapas Ecological Reserve
2 Yasuní National Park
3 Podocarpus National Park

Ecuador

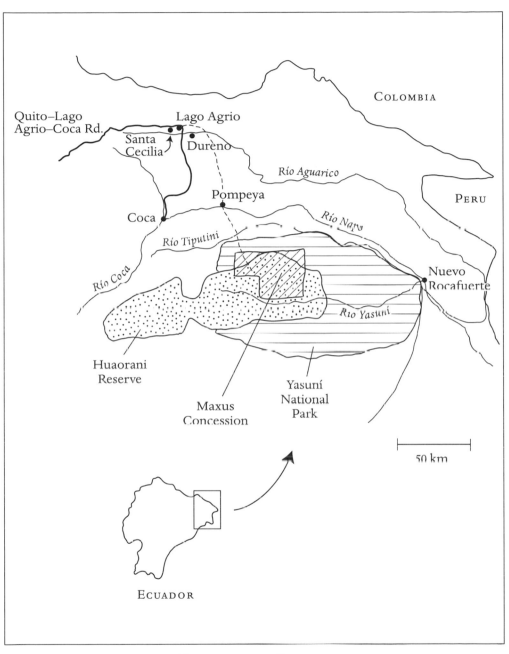

Manaus

Óbidos

Santarém

Belém

Brasília

500 km

BRAZIL

Salta

Ignacia's
ranch

Tucumán

Santiago
del Estero

La Difunta
Correa

Buenos Aires

Bariloche

Peninsula
Valdés

Los Alerces
National Park

500 km

ARGENTINA

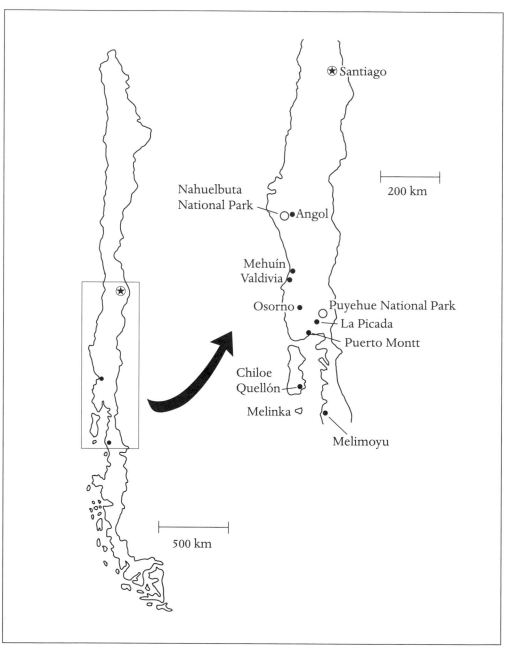

Nahuelbuta
National Park

○ ●Angol

Mehuín
Valdivia ●

Osorno ●

Puyehue National Park
○
● La Picada
● Puerto Montt

Chiloe
Quellón ●

Melinka ◁

Melimoyu ●

⊛ Santiago

├─────┤
200 km

├─────┤
500 km

CHILE

APPENDIX A

COMMON AND SCIENTIFIC NAMES
OF AMPHIBIANS AND REPTILES

mushroom-tongue salamander   *Bolitoglossa* (Plethodontidae)
Nauta mushroom-tongue salamander   *Bolitoglossa altamazonica*
         (Plethodontidae)

tiger salamander   *Ambystoma tigrinum* (Ambystomatidae)

caecilian   order Gymnophiona
Linnaeus' caecilian   *Caecilia tentaculata* (Caeciliidae)

Agua Buena dink frog   *Eleutherodactylus vocator*
         (Leptodactylidae)

Amazon Basin white-lipped frog   *Leptodactylus mystaceus* (Leptodactylidae)
Argentine common toad   *Bufo arenarum* (Bufonidae)
Argentine horned frog   *Ceratophrys cranwelli* (Leptodactylidae)
black-legged poison dart frog   *Phyllobates bicolor* (Dendrobatidae)
bleating narrowmouth toad   *Hamptophryne boliviana* (Microhylidae)
blue-sided leaf frog   *Agalychnis annae* (Hylidae)
brilliant-thighed poison dart frog   *Epipedobates femoralis* (Dendrobatidae)
brownbelly leaf frog   *Phyllomedusa tarsius* (Hylidae)
Cascades frog   *Rana cascadae* (Ranidae)
Colorado river toad   *Bufo alvarius* (Bufonidae)
crested toad   *Bufo typhonius* (Bufonidae)

Darwin's frog	*Rhinoderma darwinii* (Rhinodermatidae)
dink frog	*Eleutherodactylus* (Leptodactylidae)
egg-brooding horned treefrog	*Hemiphractus proboscideus* (Hylidae)
escuerzo	*Ceratophrys cranwelli* (Leptodactylidae)
evergreen toad	*Bufo coniferus* (Bufonidae)
giant monkey frog	*Phyllomedusa bicolor* (Hylidae)
gladiator frog	*Hyla boans* (Hylidae)
glass frog	family Centrolenidae
golden frog	*Atelopus zeteki* (Bufonidae)
golden poison dart frog	*Phyllobates terribilis* (Dendrobatidae)
golden toad	*Bufo periglenes* (Bufonidae)
granular poison dart frog	*Dendrobates granuliferus* (Dendrobatidae)
harlequin frog	*Atelopus varius* (Bufonidae)
harlequin poison dart frog	*Dendrobates histrionicus* (Dendrobatidae)
jaguar leaf frog	*Phyllomedusa palliata* (Hylidae)
Kokoe poison dart frog	*Phyllobates aurotaenia* (Dendrobatidae)
La Palma glass frog	*Hyalinobatrachium colymbiphyllum* (Centrolenidae)
leaf frog	*Phyllomedusa* (Hylidae)
leopard frog	*Rana* (Ranidae)
llanos frog	*Lepidobatrachus llanensis* (Leptodactylidae)
marine toad	*Bufo marinus* (Bufonidae)
meadow treefrog	*Hyla pseudopuma* (Hylidae)
Mexican burrowing frog	*Rhinophrynus dorsalis* (Rhinophrynidae)
mud-nesting frog	*Leptodactylus bufonius* (Leptodactylidae)
Muñoz's glass frog	*Hyalinobatrachium munozorum* (Centrolenidae)
narrowmouth toad	family Microhylidae
natterjack toad	*Bufo calamita* (Bufonidae)
Pacific treefrog	*Hyla regilla* (Hylidae)
painted-belly monkey frog	*Phyllomedusa sauvagei* (Hylidae)
plantation glass frog	*Hyalinobatrachium valerioi* (Centrolenidae)
poison dart frog	family Dendrobatidae
red-eyed treefrog	*Agalychnis callidryas* (Hylidae)
ruby poison dart frog	*Epipedobates parvulus* (Dendrobatidae)
slender-legged treefrog	*Osteocephalus* (Hylidae)
South American bullfrog	*Leptodactylus pentadactylus* (Leptodactylidae)
stubfoot frog	*Atelopus* (Bufonidae)
Surinam toad	*Pipa pipa* (Pipidae)
tiger-striped leaf frog	*Phyllomedusa tomopterna* (Hylidae)
toad	family Bufonidae

treefrog	family Hylidae
weeping frog	*Physalaemus biligonigerus* (Leptodactylidae)
western toad	*Bufo boreas* (Bufonidae)
white-lined leaf frog	*Phyllomedusa vaillanti* (Hylidae)
white-lipped frog	*Leptodactylus* (Leptodactylidae)

REPTILES

ameiva	*Ameiva* (Teiidae)
anole	*Norops* (Polychrotidae)
black tegu	*Tupinambis teguixin* (Teiidae)
copper anole	*Norops cupreus* (Polychrotidae)
dwarf iguana	*Enyalioides* (Hoplocercidae)
gecko	family Gekkonidae
helmeted iguana	*Corytophanes cristatus* (Corytophanidae)
Jesus Christ lizard	*Basiliscus basiliscus* (Corytophanidae)
many-colored bush anole	*Polychrus marmoratus* (Polychrotidae)
roughskin anole	*Norops trachyderma* (Polychrotidae)
tegu	*Tupinambis* (Teiidae)
blunthead tree snake	*Imantodes cenchoa* (Colubridae)
boa constrictor	*Boa constrictor* (Boidae)
bushmaster	*Lachesis muta* (Viperidae)
calico false coral snake	*Oxyrhopus petola* (Colubridae)
cat-eyed snake	*Leptodeira* (Colubridae)
coral snake	*Micrurus* (Elapidae)
emerald tree boa	*Corallus caninus* (Boidae)
fer-de-lance	*Bothrops atrox* (Viperidae)
rainbow boa	*Epicrates cenchria* (Boidae)
snail-eating snake	*Dipsas catesbyi* (Colubridae)
two-striped forest pit viper	*Bothriopsis bilineata* (Viperidae)
vine snake	*Oxybelis* (Colubridae)
viper	family Viperidae
matamata	*Chelus fimbriatus* (Chelidae)
river turtle	*Podocnemis* (Pelomedusidae)
South American yellowfoot tortoise	*Geochelone dendiculata* (Testudinidae)
caiman	*Caiman* (Alligatoridae)
spectacled caiman	*Caiman crocodilus* (Alligatoridae)

APPENDIX B

DECLINING AMPHIBIAN POPULATIONS

MANY CAUSES for amphibian declines have been suggested. Following is additional information and a brief description of a task force that focuses on amphibian declines.

ABNORMAL WEATHER

Each species of amphibian is unique in its tolerance to environmental conditions, including extremes of weather patterns. The fact that some species have wide tolerances and others have narrow tolerances explains why within a given assemblage some species are more adversely affected by unusual weather phenomena than are others. For example, amphibian declines and local extinctions have been reported from two different sites in southeastern Brazil. In each case only some of the species were affected. At one site the cause is thought to be an unusually severe frost, in the other extremely dry winter weather.

Golden toads disappeared during an extremely dry El Niño year. Alan Pounds and I analyzed twenty years' (1970–90) worth of rainfall data for Monteverde and found that July 1986 to June 1987 was the only twelve-month cycle with abnormally low rainfall during all seasons. Rainfall during the mid-late wet season of July–October 1986, the time when ground water is normally replenished, was almost 40 percent below the twenty-year average. The "misty" season of November–December was much less misty than normal, and it was followed by a particularly severe dry season (January–April 1987). The toads had emerged and laid their eggs during the one brief wet period of April 1987. Likewise the transition period between the dry and wet seasons, May and June, was dry. In fact, May 1987 was the driest May ever recorded—64 percent below the twenty-year average. Again the toads had taken advantage of the sole wet period in May to lay their eggs.

Then the wet season rains began late, making June 1987 abnormally dry. The breeding pools vanished. If the level of the water table had plummeted, the toads may not have been able to stay moist in their underground cavities. They may have dried up just as their eggs had a short time earlier. On the other hand, the drought during the El Niño year of 1986–87 may not have been the direct cause of the toads' death. Instead, abnormally dry conditions may have stressed the toads to the point where they succumbed to parasites, fungus, bacterial infections, or environmental contamination. Either way, the toads may all have died—except the one male—before I ever returned in May 1988.

Golden toads and harlequin frogs weren't the only amphibians to disappear from the vicinity of Monteverde during the late 1980s. Alan Pounds and several other investigators reported that half of the fifty species of frogs and toads known from the area disappeared in the late 1980s, likely from the prolonged drought. Of the twenty-five species that disappeared, only five reappeared during 1991–96. Species that are completely independent of water for breeding were affected less than those that lay their eggs in water and have aquatic tadpoles. Furthermore, population declines in the late 1980s weren't limited to amphibians. Populations of some kinds of birds and anole lizards declined also.

Ultraviolet Radiation

Andy Blaustein and his collaborators conducted a field experiment in which they measured the effects of UV-B radiation (wavelengths in the middle of the ultraviolet spectrum, the ones most harmful to living organisms) on hatching success in Pacific treefrogs, Cascades frogs, and western toads in the Cascade Mountains of Oregon. All three species lay their eggs in open water, exposed to sunlight. In the experiment, eggs were placed inside screened enclosures that were either (1) exposed to natural unfiltered sunlight, (2) covered with a piece of plastic acetate that allowed transmission of UV-B radiation, or (3) covered by clear plastic (Mylar) that shielded the eggs from UV-B radiation. When exposed to UV-B radiation, hatching success of treefrog embryos was significantly greater than for the other two species. This result suggests that the treefrog is more resistant to UV-B radiation. In fact, there was no significant difference in hatching success for treefrog eggs exposed to filtered or unfiltered sunlight. In contrast, hatching success of Cascades frog and western toad eggs was lower when exposed to unfiltered sunlight than when shielded from UV-B radiation.

How does UV-B radiation affect embryos? When the DNA (the molecule that encodes an organism's genetic material) of the cell nucleus absorbs energy from rays of ultraviolet radiation, the bonds that hold the molecule together break apart and new structures are formed. These changes can disrupt the normal functioning of cells and may kill them. In many organisms, damage to DNA caused by ultraviolet radiation can be repaired by activation of an enzyme known as photolyase, which eliminates the abnormal structures.

Blaustein and his colleagues examined the ability of Cascades frog, western toad, and Pacific treefrog eggs to repair UV radiation damage to the DNA by measuring levels of the repair enzyme. The Cascades frog and western toad had significantly lower levels of photolyase than did the treefrog, suggesting that they are less able to repair damage to their DNA. Not surprisingly, both Cascades frogs and western toads are declining in the Cascades, where this study was done. Apparently, populations of Pacific treefrogs are not declining.

PARASITIC FUNGUS

The most recently discovered culprit for massive amphibian declines is a parasitic chytrid fungus originally identified from Central America and Australia. How was this fungus identified from two such distant continents? Since 1991 Karen Lips had been monitoring diversity and abundance of frogs at two high elevation sites: one in Costa Rica and the other in Panama. She noticed declines in the Costa Rican site in 1994, including the complete disappearance of three species, reduced abundance of two previously common species, and dead or dying individuals of five species. In 1996–97 she found dead or dying individuals of ten species and reduced abundance and diversity of frogs along streams at her site in Panama. The suddenness of the declines, the fact that most of the affected species are stream dwellers that have aquatic eggs and tadpoles, and the clinical symptoms of the dead and dying individuals suggested to Karen that an epidemic of some pathogen common to both sites might be the culprit. She preserved some of the dead frogs from Panama for later examination by pathologists.

Meanwhile Australian biologists reported what they believed to be a "death wave" of frogs caused by a pathogen in the mountains of Queensland, Australia, in the 1980s and 1990s. They suspected a virus, perhaps transmitted by imported aquarium fish, but were unable at first to identify a pathogen. Eventually the biologists and pathologists from the two continents compared their slides of frog skin and found that their animals had been attacked by the same fungus. This fungus might even have been a factor in the disappearance of golden toads and other frogs from Monteverde, farther north and earlier than either of the declines that Karen reported—part of a death wave in Central America.

Recently the same chytrid fungus has been strongly implicated in die-offs of frogs from Arizona and California. Amphibian biologists around the world are wondering where the killer fungus will turn up next, and what environmental stresses are suppressing the immune systems of their victims. Will the fungus spread like a plague, and are people inadvertently responsible for spreading it?

ENVIRONMENTAL CONTAMINATION?

Frogs with deformed limbs and eyes have been turning up in unusually high numbers in more than two dozen states in the United States and two provinces in Canada. For example, in August 1995 a teacher in Le Sueur, Minnesota, reported to the Minnesota Pollution Control Agency that she and her students had found numerous malformed leopard frogs while studying a farm pond. Imagine the kids' horror when they found frogs with multiple, missing, or twisted legs, and single or misplaced eyes! Some frogs had emaciated and paralyzed back legs; some had clublike feet. Over two hundred more deformed leopard frogs were collected from the wetland during the following several weeks. Soon afterward another teacher reported deformed leopard frogs from a different farm. By the end of September, numerous additional reports of deformed frogs were confirmed. In 1996 the Minnesota Pollution Control Agency received more than 160 reports of abnormal frogs from well over half of the state's counties. A Minnesota biologist who had been studying frogs in the state since 1976 had found virtually no deformities prior to 1996. In 1996 he too began to document abnormalities by the dozens, in eight species.

State and federal scientists have been working together to identify the causes of the unusually high numbers of deformities. In one experiment, scientists brought water from a couple of suspect sites into the laboratory and used the water to raise newly fertilized frog eggs. Within ninety-six hours, a wide range of deformities developed. But local tap water likewise resulted in deformities. Reporters smelled a good story: "Environmental contaminants in the water seem to cause frog deformities in Minnesota!" Their reports caused public alarm. Agencies passed out bottled water to panicked people living near populations of deformed frogs. To date, however, whatever it is in the water—if this is indeed the culprit—hasn't been identified.

One possibility is that the deformities of the frogs found in the farm ponds were caused by parasitic flatworms called trematodes. Experiments carried out on tadpoles in the western United States have shown that trematodes can enter the developing legs of tadpoles and cause stunted and extra legs. If indeed this is the cause for the high numbers of deformities in Minnesota, for example, why trematodes have suddenly become such a problem for amphibians is a question for further investigation.

Exotic Organisms

Weekly World News (April 1990) presented yet another view of the underlying cause of amphibian declines in an article entitled "Space Aliens Stealing Our Frogs!" Below is the article in its entirety:

A UFO researcher says space aliens are wiping out the world's frog population because they eat tadpoles and use the mature creatures for research!

The decline of frogs is a worldwide phenomenon that has repeatedly been blamed on pollution and the destruction of natural habitat.

Walter Caine contends that the environmental explanation is all hogwash.

He further claims to have the evidence to prove that extraterrestrial hunters alone are wiping frogs out. In some areas populations have declined as much 90 percent, scientists report.

"It's the only explanation that makes any sense," said Caine, who founded the California-based research group, Extraterrestrial Today.

"I have hundreds of reports from eyewitnesses who have seen extraterrestrials gathering frogs and tadpoles all over the world.

"I can't vouch for the character and credibility of all these witnesses but I know for a fact that most of them are rock solid.

"Their independent descriptions of saucer-shaped UFOs and slender, large-headed space aliens are uncannily similar. And these people swear they saw the extraterrestrials stealing frogs and eating tadpoles."

Washington sources refused to comment on Caine's theory and report but conceded that America and other governments are investigating UFO activity in regions where frogs grow and breed.

Caine says that's evidence enough to show that world authorities are aware of alien interference in earth ecology.

And he has called on them to take "immediate steps to end the interference before the only frogs we see are in books."

"There isn't a doubt in my mind that space aliens are eating our tadpoles as a delicacy and experimenting with our frogs," said Caine.

"This is a very serious situation."

Space aliens as the culprit is unlikely, but, indeed, exotic organisms are responsible for some declines and even extinctions of populations of amphibians. Introduced bullfrogs and fishes such as trout have caused population declines of resident amphibians in the upper Midwest, Arizona, California, and Canada either by direct predation, competition, or habitat disturbance.

So, WHAT IS being done to understand the nature, extent, and causes for amphibian declines? In 1991 the Species Survival Commission of the International Union for the Conservation of Nature (IUCN) formed a Declining Amphibian Populations Task Force (DAPTF), designed to be a coordinating center for investigators and agencies from all over the world involved in investigating amphibian declines. The task force identifies priorities for research and recommends uniform field methods so that different species and habitats can be compared. Eventually the task force plans to set up a computerized database and establish a global monitoring program. Various regional working groups composed of independent investigators gather data on species at local study sites in an effort to document declines and investigate causes of these declines. Thanks to contributions from interested organizations and individuals, the task force offers limited funding for selected field studies. Symposia and workshops facilitate interactions among scientists, creating opportunities to share and discuss their data. Certainly one of the major contributions of the DAPTF has been coordination of worldwide activities and facilitation of communication among those involved in studying amphibian declines. For more information on the DAPTF or on donations to help support their field studies programs, please contact:

Ron Heyer, DAPTF Chair
Office of Biodiversity Programs, NHB Mail Stop 180
Smithsonian Institution
Washington, DC 20560-0180

BIBLIOGRAPHY AND
SUGGESTED READING

Altig, R. 1979. *Toads Are Nice People*. Columbia and Eldon, MO: Gates House/MANCO.

Beebee, T. J. C. 1996. *Ecology and Conservation of Amphibians*. New York: Chapman & Hall.

Beletsky, L. 1998. *Costa Rica: The Ecotraveller's Wildlife Guide*. San Diego: Academic Press.

Berger, L., R. Speare, P. Daszak, D. E. Green, A. A. Cunningham, C. L. Goggin, R. Slocombe, M. A. Ragan, A. D. Hyatt, K. R. McDonald, H. B. Hines, K. R. Lips, G. Marantelli, and H. Parkes. 1998. Chytridiomycosis causes amphibian mortality associated with population declines in the rain forests of Australia and Central America. *Proceedings of the National Academy of Sciences, USA* 95:9031–9036.

Bernhardson, W., A. Draffen, K. Dydynski, R. Rachowiecki, R. Strauss, and D. Swaney. 1994. *South America on a Shoestring*. Berkeley: Lonely Planet Publications.

Blaustein, A. R., and D. B. Wake. 1995. The puzzle of declining amphibian populations. *Scientific American* 272 (no. 4, April 1995): 56–61.

Bloom, P. 1994. *Brazil 1994*. Redondo Beach, CA: Fielding Worldwide.

Box, B., ed. 1990. *1991 South American Handbook*. New York: Prentice Hall Press.

Carey, C. 1993. Hypothesis concerning the causes of the disappearance of boreal toads from the mountains of Colorado. *Conservation Biology* 7 (2): 355–62.

Caufield, C. 1984. *In the Rainforest*. Chicago: University of Chicago Press.

Cochran, D. M. 1961. *Living Amphibians of the World.* Garden City, NY: Doubleday & Company.

Collins, M., ed. 1990. *The Last Rain Forests: A World Conservation Atlas.* New York: Oxford University Press.

Crump, M. L. 1971. Quantitative analysis of the ecological distribution of a tropical herpetofauna. *Occasional Papers of the Museum of Natural History University of Kansas* 3:1–62.

———. 1974. Reproductive strategies in a tropical anuran community. *Miscellaneous Publications of the Museum of Natural History University of Kansas* 61:1–68.

———. 1977. The many ways to beget a frog. *Natural History* 86 (1): 38–45.

———. 1983. The rainbow connection. *Animal Kingdom* 86 (3): 20–27.

———. 1991. You eat what you are. *Natural History* (February 1991): 46–51.

———. 1996. Parental care among the Amphibia. In *Parental Care: Evolution, Mechanisms, and Adaptive Significance,* edited by J. S. Rosenblatt and C. T. Snowdon, pp. 109–44. Advances in the Study of Behavior, vol. 25. San Diego, CA: Academic Press.

Dobzhansky, T. 1950. Evolution in the tropics. *American Scientist* (spring): 209–22.

Duellman, W. E., and L. Trueb. 1986. *Biology of Amphibians.* New York: McGraw-Hill.

Emmons, L. H. 1997. *Neotropical Rainforest Mammals.* Chicago: University of Chicago Press.

Forsyth, A., and K. Miyata. 1984. *Tropical Nature.* New York: Charles Scribner's Sons.

Gentry, A. H., ed. 1990. *Four Neotropical Rainforests.* New Haven: Yale University Press.

Hilty, S. L., and W. L. Brown. 1986. *A Guide to the Birds of Colombia.* Princeton: Princeton University Press.

Jacobs, M. 1988. *The Tropical Rain Forest.* Berlin: Springer-Verlag.

Janzen, D. H., ed. 1983. *Costa Rican Natural History.* Chicago: University of Chicago Press.

Kandell, J. 1984. *Passage through El Dorado.* New York: Avon Books.

Kane, J. 1995. *Savages.* New York: Alfred A. Knopf.

Kimerling, J. 1991. *Amazon Crude.* National Resources Defense Council.

Kricher, J. 1989. *A Neotropical Companion: An Introduction to the Animals, Plants, and Ecosystems of the New World Tropics.* Princeton: Princeton University Press.

Laurance, W. F., K. R. McDonald, and R. Speare. 1996. Epidemic disease and the catastrophic decline of Australian rain forest frogs. *Conservation Biology* 10:406–13.

Mattison, C. 1987. *Frogs & Toads of the World.* Poole, Great Britain: Blandford Press.

Milton, K. 1994. No pain, no game. *Natural History* (9): 44–51.

Ortiz, A. D. 1997. *Eva Perón.* London: Little, Brown and Company.

Pariser, H. S. 1992. *Adventure Guide to Costa Rica.* Edison, N.J.: Hunter Publishing.

Pearson, D. L., and L. Beletsky. 1999. *Ecuador and Its Galapagos Islands: The Ecotraveller's Wildlife Guide.* San Diego: Academic Press.

Pearson, D. L., and D. W. Middleton. 1997. *The New Key to Ecuador and the Galápagos.* Berkeley: Ulysses Press.

Phillips, K. 1994. *Tracking the Vanishing Frogs: An Ecological Mystery.* New York: St. Martin's Press.

Plotkin, M. J. 1993. *Tales of a Shaman's Apprentice.* New York: Viking.

Pough, F. H., R. M. Andrews, J. E. Cadle, M. L. Crump, A. H. Savitzky, and K. D. Wells. 1998. *Herpetology.* Upper Saddle River, NJ: Prentice Hall.

Pounds, J. A., and M. L. Crump. 1994. Amphibian declines and climate disturbance: the case of the golden toad and the harlequin frog. *Conservation Biology* 8 (1): 72–85.

Pounds, J. A., M.P. L. Fogden, and J. H. Campbell. 1999. Biological response to climate change on a tropical mountain. *Nature* 398 (6728): 611–15.

Pounds, J. A., M.P. L. Fogden, J. M. Savage, and G. C. Gorman. 1997. Tests of null models for amphibian declines on a tropical mountain. *Conservation Biology* 11:1307–22.

Savage, J. M. 1970. On the trail of the golden frog: with Warszewicz and Gabb in Central America. *Proceedings of the California Academy of Sciences* 38 (14): 273–87.

Schreider, H., and F. Schreider. 1970. *Exploring the Amazon.* Washington, DC: National Geographic Society.

Sick, H. 1993. *Birds in Brazil: A Natural History.* Princeton: Princeton University Press.

Smith, R. 1993. *Crisis Under the Canopy: Tourism and Other Problems Facing the Present Day Huaorani.* Quito, Ecuador: Rainforest Information Centre (RIC).

Stebbins, R. C., and N. W. Cohen. 1995. *A Natural History of Amphibians.* Princeton: Princeton University Press.

Stiles, F. G., and A. F. Skutch. 1989. *A Guide to the Birds of Costa Rica.* Ithaca, NY: Comstock Publishing Associates.

Stolzenburg, W. 1997. The naked frog. *Nature Conservancy* (September/October): 24–27.

Wilson, E. O. 1971. *The Insect Societies.* Cambridge: The Belknap Press of Harvard University Press.

———. 1975. *Sociobiology: The New Synthesis.* Cambridge: The Belknap Press of Harvard University Press.

———. 1992. *The Diversity of Life.* Cambridge: Harvard University Press.

INDEX

References to photographs are printed in italics.

African-Ecuadorians (*morenos*), 220–26,
    224, 228–29
aggressive behavior
    anole lizards, territorial defense, 11, 22,
        62, 163
    gladiator frogs, 16
    harlequin frogs, 124, 127–29
    Hercules beetles, 24, 138
    hummingbirds, territorial defense, 68,
        74
    poison dart frogs, territorial defense, 64
Allende, Salvador, 240
Amazons (female warriors), myth, 45
ants
    ant gardens, 112
    army, 31–35, 38, 109, 146–47, 208–9
    associated with *Cecropia* trees, 116
    biting, 75
    conga (*Paraponera*), 109–10, 233
    leaf-cutter, 24, 38–39, 62, 109, 135, 261
arachnids
    Batman spider, *gallery*, 206
    scorpion, 133

spiders, as ecological replacement for
    frogs, 42
tailless whip scorpion, 96
tarantula, 51, 233, 250–51, 250
Arcoiris, conservation organization
    (Ecuador), 217
Argentina
    Bariloche, 186, 189
    Cholita, 186
    ethnic diversity, 166
    geographic diversity, 186, 189
    history, 166, 168–69
    Peninsula Valdés, 186–87, 189
    Salta (province; Ignacia's ranch), 170,
        184
    San Juan (province), 187
    Santiago del Estero (province), 175
    Tucumán (San Miguel de Tucumán),
        167, 169
asthmatic monster, 78–79, 93
ayahuasca (*Banisteriopsis*), 231–33

Benalcázar, Sebastián de, 85
beverages
    aguardiente (sugarcane alcohol), 211–12

beverages (*continued*)
  banana wine, 89–90
  cafezinho, 33, 46
  chicha (fermented *yuca*), 92
  maté, 170
biodiversity, species richness, 1, 27, 43,
    53–54, 73–74, 95–96, 117, 121, 200,
    209, 217, 269
birds
  ant-following birds, 38
  bare-necked umbrellabird, 162
  black guan, 162
  blue-crowned motmot, *gallery,* 37
  chucao, chucao tapaculo, 244, 256–57,
    259, 262
  flamingo, 187
  fork-tailed woodnymph, 37
  hoatzin, 106–7
  hummingbird, 16, 22, 67–68, 215, 246
  kiskadee, 173–74
  macaw, 106, 209
  Magellanic penguin, 187
  opal-crowned manakin, 37
  parrot, 54–55, *54,* 106, 209
  partial list, Río Yasuní survey, 116
  quetzal, resplendent quetzal, 161–63
  red-headed manakin, 38
  rhea, 187
  royal flycatcher, 38
  rufous-breasted hermit, 67
  rufous-tailed hummingbird, 67
  squirrel cuckoo, 35
  swallow-tailed kite, 161
  three-wattled bellbird, 161–62
  white-tailed emerald, 67
  yellow-billed jacamar, 37–38
bladderworts, 111–12
blowgun, 12, 21
Bonaparte, Napoléon, 239
border dispute, Ecuador and Peru, 105–6,
    118
boto (Amazon River dolphin), myth, 36
Brazil
  Amazonia, Amazon Basin, 10, 33–34,
    43–44, 47–50, 231, 269
  Belém, 29–30, 46–47, 52, 108
  geography, 30
  history, 30
  Manaus, 46–50

  Óbidos, 50–51
  Santarém, 51–52
brujo (witch doctor), 228, 231–32
Bucaram, Assad, 91

Cabral, Pedro Alvares, 30
caecilians, 11–12
caiman, 21, 51, 82, 99, *113,* 116, 209
Chile
  Aguas Calientes, 241
  Angol, 244
  Archipelago, 239, 247–49, 254–55
  Atacama Desert, 238, 252
  Central Valley, 238–39, 252
  Chiloé, 238–39, 247, 254
  Contulmo, 244
  geography, 238–39
  Gulf of Corcovado, 248
  history, 239–40, 252–53
  La Picada, 243
  Lake Country, 238
  Mehuín, 243
  Melimoyu, 248, *249,* 252, 254–55, *255,*
    259–60
  Melinka, 248, 257–58
  Osorno, 252
  Puerto Montt, 238, 247, 257–58
  Quellón, 247–48, 254, 257
  Santiago, 236, 239–40, 254–55
  Trafunco los Bados, 252–53
  Valdivia, 247, 258
chucao superstition, antidote, 244–46, 262
coloration
  cryptic, 98, 257
  warning, 12–13, 99, 132, 257
Columbus, Christopher, 57
coping with dry environments, Argentine
    frogs, 180, 189
  cocoon formation, 177
  foam nest, 178
  mud nest, 178–80
  waterproofing secretions, 177–78
Costa Rica
  Finca las Cruces, 66–68
  Finca Taboga, 58–60, 70
  geography, 57
  Guanacaste, 58–62, 68–70
  Hacienda La Pacifica, 58, 62
  history, 57–58

Monteverde, 119–21, 129, 133, 137, 139, 145, 148, 161–63, 282–83
Osa Peninsula, 62–66
Puerto Limón, 57
San José, 57–58, 70, 121, 127, 147
San Vito, 66–68
Santa Elena, 139
courtship behavior, granular poison dart frog, 64–66

Darwin, Charles, 104, 186–87, 237
Darwin's frog
   appearance, description, *gallery*, 237–38, 238, 248, 250
   parental care, 237–38, 248–49, 256, 259, 262
   population status, 239, 259
   search for, 241, 243–44, 246, 248–51, 254
deadfall trap, 229
declining amphibian populations, 172–73, 186, 214, 217–18, 234, 261, 264–69, 282–86
Declining Amphibian Populations Task Force (DAPTF), 286
declining amphibians, causes
   acidified rain, 266
   climate change, 266, 282–83
   environmental contamination, 284–85
   habitat destruction, 265
   herpetologists, 186
   introduced organisms, 286
   pathogenic fungus (chytrid), 266–68, 284
   red-leg bacteria, 266
   space aliens, 285–86
   trematodes (parasitic flatworms), 285
   ultraviolet (UV-B) radiation, 266, 283–84
declining amphibians, species
   Darwin's frogs, 248, 259, 265
   dink frogs, 163, 199
   glass frogs, 163
   golden toads, 157–58, 160–61, 163–65, 191, 246, 264, 266, 282–83
   harlequin frogs, 160–61, 163, 264, 266, 283
   stubfoot frogs, 211–12
   treefrogs, 199

defensive behavior, 98–99
   birds, 37
   caiman, 99
   caterpillar, 40–41
   coral snake, 99
   egg-brooding horned treefrog, 20, 98, 113, 200, 262
   electric eel, 26–27, 262
   fer-de-lance, 23
   giant swallowtail caterpillar, 66
   howler monkey, 60, 70, 163
   leaf frogs, 98–99
   lizards, 98–99
   poison dart frogs, 12–13, 99, 257
   royal flycatcher, 38
   South American bullfrog, 27, 49
   toad, 99, 130
   walkingstick, 215
deforestation, destruction of rain forest
   colonization, 83, 117, 119, 196, 208, 261, 263–64
   oil exploration, 83, 84, 201, 203–4, 204, 207–9, 207, 218, 261, 263–64
Díaz de Solís, Juan, 166
Dirty War (Argentina), 168–69
Dr. Seuss, 222, 228

earthworms, giant, 214
EcoCiencia, 195–96, 202–3, 209, 211, 213–14, 216–17, 219–21, 227, 235
Ecuador
   Amazon Basin, 10, 73–74, 92, 102, 197, 231, 262, 269
   Añangu, 103
   Baeza, 103, 212
   Bermejo, 198
   Borbón, 220, 226–28, 233
   Campana Cocha, 24–25, 107
   Coca, 102, 104–5, 116, 202–3, 208, 210, 241–42, 263
   Dureno, 21
   Esmeraldas, 220, 226
   geography, 1–2
   Guayaquil, 211, 228
   history, 1, 84–85
   La Troncal, 211
   Lago Agrio (Nueva Loja), 72–73, 86–87, 102–4, 103, 116, 196, 199, 263
   Loja, 216–17

Ecuador (continued)
  Loma Linda, 220, 222–27, 229
  Manta Real, 211–12
  Minga, 202
  Muñozlandia, 5, 71–74, 72, 79, 81, 87,
    95, 197, 231, 263
  Nuevo Rocafuerte, 105, 108, 112,
    115–18
  Oriente, 2, 101, 105, 108, 231, 261,
    263–64
  Otavalo, 116, 258
  Pastaza, 4
  Pindo, 209
  Piraña camp, 204–6, 205, 206, 210
  Pompeya, 202
  Puerto Libre, 22–23
  Quito, 2–4, 27–28, 49, 84–85, 90, 102,
    116, 210–12, 217, 227, 263
  San Miguel, 220–28, 225, 235
  Santa Cecilia, 5–6, 10, 13, 16, 18, 23,
    27, 42, 71–73, 99, 104, 108–10, 121,
    139, 196–97, 199–200, 209, 231, 261,
    263–65
  Sierra Azul, 212–14
  Tiputini camp, 203–4, 206, 208–9
El Dorado, myth, 44
El Niño, effect of, 148–49, 153, 254, 257,
  282–83
epiphytes, 103, 112, 121

feeding, methods of
  active forager, 83
  adhesive slime, onychophoran, 9
  army ants, 32
  bats, 42, 59–60
  bot fly larva, 69
  chiggers, 51
  egg-eating, snake, 16–17
  escuerzo tadpoles, 176–77, 181–82, 190
  fangs and venom glands, fer-de-lance,
    23
  following army ants, birds, 38
  llanos frog tadpoles, 176–77, 177,
    181–82, 190
  matamata turtle, 83
  sit-and-wait predator, 83, 251
  snail-eating, snake, 8
  tailless whip scorpion, 96
  tarantula, 251

termite-eating, anteater, 39
toe-twitching, frogs, 269
traplines, hummingbirds, 67
"typical" tadpoles, 176
field biology, tradition in Latin America,
  118
field methods and sampling techniques
  behavioral manipulations, 124, 141
  bird-banding, 32, 37
  boardwalk, 31
  canopy observation tower, 41–42
  framing questions, 215–16, 223
  "frog walk," 215
  grid system, 35
  mist nets, 31–32, 37, 230
  monitoring study, 197–98
  quadrat, 197–98
  survey/inventory, 1, 5–7, 101, 117, 121,
    197–98, 201, 206, 213–14, 217, 251
  time blocks, 74
  transect, 197–98
  unmanipulated behavioral observa-
    tions, 127–28, 140–41, 152, 178–80,
    251–52, 255–56
First World Congress of Herpetology,
  172–73, 264
fish
  candiru, 34
  electric eel, 26–27, 110, 262
  four-eyed fish, 41
  lungfish, 41
  piranha, 110
  pufferfish, 131
FitzRoy, Robert, 187
flowers
  fly-pollinated, 39
  ginger, 67
  Heliconia (wild plantain), 67, 74–75, 75
  hot lips, gallery, 163
  hummingbird-pollinated, gallery, 67–68,
    74
  lobelia, 67
  morning glories, 106
  passion flower, gallery, 39, 67, 106
  "rattlesnake plant," 67
  trumpet vine, 106
focus on babies, Costa Rica, 121–22
folk medicines and potions, 36, 54–55,
  130–31

food
  armadillo, 14
  arroz con pollo, 147
  beans, 14, 97
  bocas, bocaditos, 147
  calamares, 236–37
  caldeirada, 47
  caldo de gallina, chicken foot soup, 14, 97, 199
  cebiche, 147
  chifles, 13
  chinchulín, 175
  choclo, 86
  chorizo, 175
  congrio, caldillo de congrio, 236, 259
  crayfish freshwater, 220
  cuy, 212
  dulce de leche, 132
  empanadas, 255
  farinha, 33–34, 47
  feijoada completa, 33
  goat cheese, 184, 189
  guayaba jelly, 115
  higado, 175
  jambu, 35–36, 53
  llapingachos, 14
  mollejas, 175
  monkey, 14
  morcilla, 175
  papaya, 14
  parillada mixta, 175
  parrot, 14
  patacones, 13–14
  pato no tucupi, 53
  plátano, 13–14, 21, 73, 86, 105, 196, 233
  rice, 96–97
  riñones, 175
  salchicha, 175
  seaweed, *256*
  snake, 14
  tacacá, 35–36
  tamales, 132
  tucupi sauce, 35
  ubre, 175
  ulte, 243
  water buffalo steak, 46
  white-lipped peccary, 112
  wild rat, 222, 229–30, *230*
  yuca, 14, 21, 73, 86, 92, 105, 107, 196

frogs and toads
  Agua Buena dink frog, 68
  Amazon Basin white-lipped frog, *201*
  Argentine common toad, *183*
  black-legged poison dart frog, 12
  bleating narrowmouth toad, 200
  blue-sided leaf frog, *gallery*
  brilliant-thighed poison dart frog, 200
  brownbelly leaf frog, 76–77
  Cascades frog, 283–84
  crested toad, 34, 108–9, *109*
  dink frog, 18–19, 77–78, 81, 103, 163, 199, 213–15, 217
  egg-brooding horned treefrog, *gallery*, 20–21, 71, 93, 98, 113, 200, 262
  escuerzo, 176–77, 181–85, *183*, 189–90
  evergreen toad, 154–57
  giant monkey frog, 52–53, *53*, 177
  gladiator frog, 16–17, *17*, 49
  glass frog, 63, 116, 163, 215–16
  golden poison dart frog, 12–13
  granular poison dart frog, 63–66
  harlequin poison dart frog, *gallery*
  jaguar leaf frog, 79, 200
  Kokoe poison dart frog, 12
  La Palma glass frog, 62–63
  leaf frog, 16, 49, 76, 78, 88, 93, 98–99, 111
  leopard frog, 284–85
  llanos frog, 176–77, 181–82, 185, 189–90
  marine toad, 78, 130–31, *131*, 154–57, 266
  Mexican burrowing frog, 68
  mud-nesting frog, *176*, 178–80
  Muñoz's glass frog, 110
  narrowmouth toad, 88
  natterjack toad, 266
  Pacific treefrog, 283–84
  painted-belly monkey frog, 176–78, *178*, 182, 189
  plantation glass frog, 62–63
  poison dart frog, 12–13, 17, 49, 63–64, 99, 113, 116, 128, 209, 214, 268
  red-eyed treefrog, 268
  ruby poison dart frog, 12
  slender-legged treefrog, 88
  South American bullfrog, 27, 49, 88
  stubfoot frog, 211–12, 234
  Surinam toad, 19–20, *19*, 25, 71

frogs and toads (*continued*)
tiger-striped leaf frog, *gallery*
toad, 116, 182, 190, 214, 268
treefrog, 88, 116
weeping frog, 176, 178, 182, 189–90
western toad, 283–84
white-lined leaf frog, *gallery,* 110–11
white-lipped frog, 18
See also Darwin's frog; golden frog;
golden toad; harlequin frog; meadow
treefrog
fungus
attack on insects, 95
nightmare, 93
on shoes, clothes, sheets, 81, 92
pathogenic (chytrid), on frogs, 266–68,
284

golden frog, legend, xi–xii, 149, 270
golden toad
appearance, description, *gallery,* xi,
149–51, *151*
breeding, 150–57
decline of, 157–58, 160–61, 163–65, 191,
246, 264, 266, 282–83
experiment, nonfeeding tadpoles, 154–57
large eggs, *154*
restricted distribution, 150

habitat
altiplano, 171
chaco, 170, 176, 185, 191
cloud forest, xi, 121, 163, 217
elfin forest, xi, 149–50, 191, 217
igapó forest, 34, 54
montane rain forest, 215
páramo, 217
terra firme forest, 34, 42, 54
tropical lowlands, 219
varzea forest, 31, 40, 54
harlequin frog
aggressive behavior, 124, 127–29, 140–41
appearance of, *gallery,* 123–24, 128,
135–36, *136*
homing, 135–37, 141–42
parasitism, 129–32, 143, 148–49
population density, 123–24, 129, 142,
148–49, 160–61

prolonged breeders, 151–52
skewed sex ratio, 141
hunting magic, 52

Ibarra, Velasco ("El Viejo"), 90–91
Incas, Inca Empire, 1, 84–85, 239, 252
indigenous peoples, culture
Chachi, 220, 222–27, *224, 225, 229,* 231
Cofán, 5–6, 21–22, 264
Huaorani (and Tagaeri), 101–2, 108,
110, 114, 117–18, 206–10, 218,
263–64
Mapuche (Araucanian), 252–54
Mayoruna, 52
Quechua, 5–6, *6,* 11, 25, 73, 82, 91–92,
107, 204–6, 208–10, 231–33
Shuar, 208
inflation, 168, 188–89, 240
insects
crickets, 232
dragonfly, dragonfly nymphs, 83,
125–27, 190
dung beetles, 61–62
giant swallowtail caterpillar, 66
grasshoppers, 23, 90
Hercules beetle, 24, *138,* 261
katydid, 24, 163, 215
morpho butterfly, 66
walkingstick, 23–24, 215
weevil, 95
See also ants; parasites, on humans

La Difunta Correa, shrine, legend, 186–88
La Violencia (Colombia), 6
Lara, General Guillermo Rodríguez, 90
lizards
ameiva, 83
anole, 11, 22, 83, *108,* 134–35, 163, 283
black tegu, 11
copper anole, 62
dwarf iguana, *gallery,* 82, 110
gecko, 111
helmeted iguana, 65–66, *65*
Jesus Christ lizard, 68–69
many-colored bush anole, *200*
roughskin anole, 200
tegu, 170–71
lost in forest, 15, 39–40, 90

machismo, 111
macumba, 36–37
malaria, 219, 222–23, 263
mammals
Amazon River dolphin (*boto*), 36
anteater (*tamandua*), 39
bat, 42, 58–61, *61*, 215, 222, 230, 233
capybara, 113
dolphin, 247
elephant seal, 187
guanaco, 187
howler monkey, 59–60, 70, 161, 163–64, 233
jaguar, 209
llama, 171–72
monkey, 15, 79–80, *80*, 205, 209
mountain tapir, 213
otter, 129
parasites on, 69–70, 139–40
partial list, Río Yasuní survey, 115–16
pig, feral, 124
puma, 213
sea lion, 187
sloth (*perezoso*), 10
spectacled bear, 213
spiny rat, 93–95
water buffalo, 46
white-lipped peccary, peccary, 112, 209
wild rodents, small, 222, 230
maps
Argentina, 277
Brazil, 276
Central America, 271
Chile, 278
Costa Rica, 273
Ecuador, 274, 275
South America, 272
market
duty free, Manaus, 46–47
floating market, Manaus, 47
Quito, 4
Valdivia, 258–59
Ver-O-Peso, Belém, 35–38, *36*, 54–55
meadow treefrog
appearance, *126*
cannibalistic tadpoles, 144
experiment, egg-laying sites, 158–60, *159*

experiment, flexibility in developmental time, 146, 148
experiment, vulnerability of tadpoles to predation, 125–27
Menem, Carlos, 189
military coup
Argentina, 168
Chile, 239–40
Ecuador, 90–91
Minnesota Pollution Control Agency, 284–85
mode of reproduction, frogs and toads, 16–21, 49, 71, 74, 93, 95–96, 99, 110
direct development, 18–19, 77–78
eggs above water, 16, 49, 76–77, *77*, 93–95, *94*
eggs and tadpoles in water, 16, 49, 93, 95
foam nest, *18*, 178, 201
mud nest, 178–80, *179*
parental care, 16–21, 49, 63, 113, 128, 178–80, 214–16, 237–39, 248–49, 256, 259, 261–62, 269
and resource partitioning, 99
moon landing, 42
Museu Goeldi, 33
music, dance
cumbia, 3, 26
marimba, 226
pasillos, 3
Quechua wedding, 91–92
traditional Andean, 3

National Geographic Society, 157, 165, 237, 239, 251, 259
National Institute of Amazonian Research (INPA), 46
National Parks
Los Alerces (Argentina), 187
Nahuelbuta (Chile), 244–46, 249, 252
Podocarpus (Ecuador), 217
Puyehue (Chile), 241
Yasuní (Ecuador), 101, 117, 196, 201, 203, 207, 210, 214, 218, 263
National Science Foundation, 71

O'Higgins, Bernardo, 239
oil companies
Maxus Energy, 201–2, 204, 207–10, 214, 216–18

INDEX

oil companies (*continued*)
Texaco, 5, 72–73, 104, 263–64
onychophoran, 8–9, *9*
Orellana, Francisco de, 44–45, 105
Organization for Tropical Studies (OTS),
56–57

parasites, on humans
bot fly, 69–70, 129
chiggers, 51, 105, 219
chigoe fleas (jiggers), 139–40
Giardia (giardiasis), 142
head lice, nits, 188
ticks, 105
paro (work standstill), 204–6, 208–9
Perón, Eva, Evita, 168, 189–90
Perón, Isabel, 168
Perón, Juan, 168
Pinochet, Augusto, 240, 254
Pizarro, Francisco, 84–85
Pizarro, Gonzalo, 44

rampira (Panama hat plant), 223, 226–27,
229
rats, as pests, 79, 87, 92–93, 232
reserves, ecological research areas
Chinchilla National Reserve (Chile), 236
Cotacachi-Cayapas Ecological Reserve
(Ecuador), 219
Ducke Reserve (Brazil), 46, 49
Guamá Ecological Research Area
(Brazil), 29, 35, 46
La Planada (Colombia), 215–16
Monteverde Cloud Forest Reserve
(Costa Rica), 121, 123, 149, 162
Sierra Azul (Ecuador), 212–13
reserves, indigenous
Huaorani, 203–4, 206–8, 210
Mapuche, 252–53
rivers
Aguarico (Ecuador), 5–6, 21, 24–25, 73,
95, 104, 197, 261, 263
Amazon (Brazil), 5, 30, 44–46, 50–53, 246
Aragón (Ecuador), 213
Cayapas (Ecuador), 220, 222
Coca (Ecuador), 104, 242
Curaray (Ecuador), 102
Guacimal (Costa Rica), 163
Guamá (Brazil), 30–31

Lagarto (Costa Rica), *gallery*, 123–25,
127, 129–30, 133, 138, 148, 151, 160
Napo (Ecuador), 5, 102, 104–5, 107, 115,
242
Tapajós (Brazil), 52
Tiputini (Ecuador), 203–4, 210
Yasuní (Ecuador), 105–7, *107*, 116–18
rubber boom, Amazonia, 47–49, 101

Saint, Rachel, 102
salamanders, 7, 22–23, 43–44, *43*, 49–53,
116, 246
San Martín, José de, 166, 239
snakes
blunthead tree snake, 113–14, *114*
boa constrictor, 16, 50–51
bushmaster, 88–89
calico false coral snake, 110
cat-eyed snake, 11, 16–17, 79–80, 93, 200
coral snake, coral snake mimic, 82, 99
emerald tree boa, 82
fer-de-lance, 22–23, 93, 185–86, 200, 262
rainbow boa, *gallery,* 200
snail-eating snake, 7–8, *8*
two-striped forest pit viper, 111
vine snake, 11, 133

tadpoles
cannibalism in, 68, 144, 190
descriptions, 10, 68, 181
experiments, 125–27, 146, 148, 154–57,
173–74, 182
feeding in, 68, 176–77, 181–82, 190
flexible development, 146, 148
magic of metamorphosis, 148
nonfeeding, 18, 154–57
plastic containers for, 145–46, *155*, 159
predators on, 83, 125
raising for identification, 10
raising for size measurements, 76
vulnerability to predators, 125–27,
173–74
teaching, courses and workshops, 190–91,
196–200, 215–17, 220–23, 226
tourism, ecotourism, effect on
Huaorani, 118, 264
Monteverde, 162–63
San Miguel, 235
Trafunco los Bados, 253

toxins, amphibian
  batrachotoxin, 12–13
  parotoid secretions, 130–31
  tetrodotoxin, 131–32
transportation
  chivo, 226–27, 233
  dugout canoe, 5, 21, 25, 105–6, 108,
    115, 204, 209–10, 220, 222, 226–28,
    233, 261
  ferry, *La Pincoya*, 247–48, 254, 257–58
  gaiola, 50
  helicopter, 22–23
  horseback, 212–14, 253
  on foot, 203–4
  piragua, 5, 21, 25, 73
  tractor, 203
trees
  alerce, *Fitzroya*, 187
  araucaria, monkey puzzle tree, 246
  arrayán, 187
  Cecropia, 116
  chontaduro, 226

rubber, *48*
southern beech (*Nothofagus*), 246
spiny palm, 41, 76
turtle, tortoise
  matamata, 82–83, *82*
  river turtle, 113, 220
  South American yellowfoot tortoise, 82

Valdivia, Pedro de, 252
Videla, Jorge, 168
vocalization, frogs and toads, 68, 81, 88,
    95, 175, *183*
volcanoes
  Arenal (Costa Rica), 160
  Chimborazo (Ecuador), 2, 97
  Cotopaxi (Ecuador), 2
  Irazú (Costa Rica), 132
  Pichincha (Ecuador), 2
  Reventador (Ecuador), 98

wedding, Quechua, 91–92

DATE DUE

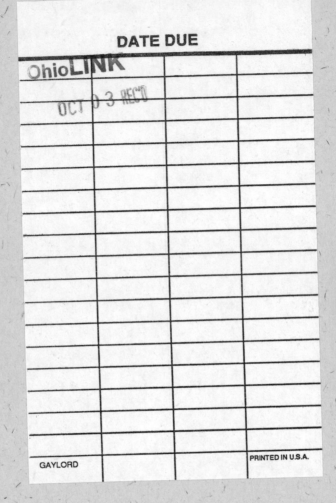

OhioLINK

OCT 0 3 REC'D

GAYLORD   PRINTED IN U.S.A.

SCI QL 656 .C35 C78 2000

Crump, Martha L.

In search of the golden frog